RIG-VEDA SAMHITA

TEXT WITH SAYANA,S COMMENTARY

EDITED BY

MANMATHA NATH DUTT

GYAN

Published by

Gyan Publishing House
5, Ansari Road
Daryaganj, New Delhi-110002
Phone: 011-47034999, 9811692060
E-mail: books@gyanbooks.com

Distribution Network
gyanbooks.com
India, USA, Canada, UK, Australia

ISBN: 978-93-7225-292-7 (PB)

First Published, 1908

2nd Impression 2025

Printed at: Gyan Press, Delhi.

RIG-VEDA SAMHITA
Author: MANMATHA NATH DUTT

RIG-VEDA SAMHITA

RIG-VEDA SAMHITA.

FIRST ASHTAKA.

EDITED AND PUBLISHED BY

MANMATHA NATH DUTT (Shastri), M.A., M.R.A.S.

Rector, Keshub Academy,
Author of the English Translations of The Râmâyana, Mahâ-Bhârata, S'rimadbhâgavatam, Mahânirvâna-Tantram, Harivaṁs'a, Agni Purânam, Mârkandéya Purânam, &c., &c.

CALCUTTA

SOCIETY FOR THE RESUSCITATION OF
INDIAN LITERATURE.

40, NAYAN CHAND DUTT'S STREET.

1906.

INTRODUCTION.

It is almost superfluous to inform the reader that the earliest, and the most important, record of the religion and the institutions of the Aryans, is the *Véda*. *Véda*, derived from the Saṁskrit root *Vid* to know, means the sum of knowledge. It, also, means the knowledge which contains, within itself, evidence for its truth,—that is, Revelation. In some cases the word means the entire learning, the eighteen *Vidyâs* or sciences of the Hindus. But it generally refers to the four sacred works of the Hindus, *viz*., the Rich, or Rig-*véda*; the *Yajush*, or *Yajur-véda*; the *Sâman*, or *Sâma-véda*; and the *Atharvâṇ*, or *Atharva-véda*. Many passages,—found in the scriptural writings of the Hindus, and some, in the *Védâs* themselves,—limit the number to three. The fourth or *Atharva-véda*, which borrows freely from the R*ich*, is considered as a supplement to the other three.

The R*ig-véda*, derived from the root *ṛich* to laud, is intended to be read on occasions when encomiastic pravers and hymns to the Elemental Deities are prescribed by the Law; the *Yajush* (*Yaj* to sacrifice) deals principally with oblations and sacrifices, and consists of prayers adapted for certain rites to be performed at the Full, and change of, the Moon, and hymns and directions regarding oblations to the Manes. The *Sâma-véda* is nothing but a recast of the R*ich*, composed, with very few exceptions, of the same hymns, broken into parts and arranged newly for being chanted on ceremonial occasions. The *Atharva-véda*, which is decidedly of a later origin, consists of hymns and incantations, the greater part of which is intended for the destruction and perdition of enemies.

According to tradition, the *Védâs* were cœval with creation which had itself taken place according to the laws of the pre-existing *Vêda*. They, however, lay in a scattered form. According to some legends, they were entirely lost, and it was after many a long year that a *Rishi* or Sage arranged them and gave them the form in which they are now known. This arrangement procured to the Editor the name of *Vyása*, or 'Arranger.' He is said to have flourished in the Second *Yuga*, and hence is his surname *Dwaipáyana*, that is, he who belongs to the Second Age, or *Yuga*, of the World. A number of learned Sages helped him in his labour. After he had divided the whole of the fragments of the *Védás* into four parts, he taught them severally to four different pupils. Paila learnt the *Rig-véda*; Vais'ampâyana, the *Yajur-véda*, whilst the *Sáman* was taught to Jaimini, and the *Atharvâṇ* to Sumantu. In time, however, the pupils of those four Sages made some alterations in the original arrangement of the several *Védâs* which had been handed down to them, and they thereby became Founders of the different schools which are called the *S'âkhâs*.

Each of these *Védás*, is divided into two parts, *viz.*, *Saṁhitás*, or the aggregate assemblage of the prayers, hymns and the liturgic formulæ of which they are composed, and the *Bráhmaṇás* containing precepts which inculcate religious duties and maxims which explain these precepts and arguments relating to theology. According to the Brahmanical writers, the *Véda* consists of two component parts called the *Mantra* and the *Bráhmaṇa*: the first being the hymns and formulæ collected in the *Samhitá*, and the second contains rules for the application of the *Mantrás*, directions for the performance of Vedic rites and citations of hymns to be repeated on such occasions. The *Upanishadas*, or the gnostic portions of the *Védás*, are also comprehended under the *Bráhmaṇás*. Connected with the *Védás* are the treatises on Grammar, Astronomy, Intonation, Prosody, Ritual, and the meaning of obsolete words, designated as the *Vedângas*, or the Auxiliaries of the *Védás*. They do not constitute portions of the *Véda* itself, but are supplementary to it. Besides these, there are *Prátis'akhyás* or treatises on the Grammar of the *Véda*, and the *Sûtras* or Aphorisms inculcating and describing its practices.

There are various accounts to be found in the scriptural writings of the Hindus, regarding the origin of the *Védás*. In the ninth verse of the *Purusha-Sûkta* in the R*ig-véda* the three *Védás* are said to have been produced from the mystical victim *Purusha*. In *Atharva-véda* Texts X. 7, 14 refer to that subject. We here simply give the translation. "Declare, who is that Skambha, from whom they cut off the R*ich*-Verses, from whom they scraped off the *Yajush*, of whom the *Sáman*-Verses are the hairs, and the Verses of the *Atharváṇ* and *Angiras* the mouth." The following account occurs in the *S'atapatha Bráhmaṇa* :—"From them so heated the three *Védás* were produced,—the R*ig-véda* from Agni (Fire); the *Yajur-véda*, from Váyu (Wind); and the *Sáma-véda*, from S'úryya (the Sun)." A similar account is also found in the *Chhándogya-Upanishad*. The same origin is, also, assigned to the *Védás* by the great Hindu Lawgiver Manu. Médhâtithi, a Commentator on Manu, however, explains this passage in a more rationalistic way by remarking that "the Rig-*véda* opens with a hymn to Fire, and the *Yujur-véda* with one in which air is mentioned." In the *S'atapatha-Bráhmaṇa* it is said:—"The three *Védâs* are identifiable with Speech, Mind and Breath."

The Rig-*véda*, as it is admitted on all hands, is the earliest of all the *Védâs*, and the mode of worship, which the *Sûktas* of this *Véda* inculcate, we doubt not, will be highly interesting to the reader. It comprises offerings, prayer and praise; the former are mainly oblations and libations—clarified butter poured on fire, and the fermented juice of the *Soma*-Plant presented in ladles to the Deities invoked. The ceremony of Vedic worship takes place in the house of the worshipper, in a room appropriated for the purpose and in which a sacred fire is perpetually maintained. The worship is purely domestic, for there is no mention, in the Rig-*veda*, of any temple or any reference to a public place of worship. The worshipper, or *Yajamâna*, does not necessarily take any personal part in the ceremony, and a number of officiating priests, sometimes seven and sometimes sixteen, are engaged in performing different ceremonial rites and in reciting prayers or hymns. It appears also from some hymns that animal victims were offered on particular occasions.

Each *Sûkta* consists of prayer and praise, and describes the power, the vastness, the generosity, the goodness, and even the personal beauty, of the Deity invoked. The priest also implores him to confer blessings on the person who has undertaken the celebration of the ceremony. These blessings generally partake of the nature of a temporal and personal nature, such as wealth, food, life, children, cattle, cows, horses and protection against enemies. There are occasional references to a hope of immortality and future happiness. But the immortality of the Deities is always recognized as well as the possibility of its attainment by human beings. In some cases they seek moral benefits, such as hatred of untruth and abhorrence of sin, but the main objects of the prayers being temporal and physical benefits.

The Deities, to whom prayers and praises are addressed in the *Rig-véda*, are generally different from those of the heroic poems and the *Puráṇás*. The names of S'iva, of Mahâdéva, of Durgâ, of Kâli, or of Râma, never occur in the *Rig-véda*. The chief Deities are Agni and Indra. The former describes the three aspects of the Element of Fire: 1st., as it exists on earth, not for cooking and sacred purposes, but as the heat of digestion and of life, and the vivifying principle of vegetation; 2nd., as it exists in the atmosphere in the shape of lightning; and 3rd., as it appears in the heavens, as light, the sun, the dawn and the planetary bodies. Although the Sun is acknowledged and lauded as a Divinity, the soul of all movable and immovable beings, still he does not occupy that prominent position in the *Vaidik* liturgy as he does in that of the ancient Persians. He is principally regarded as the celestial representative of Fire and his manifestations are known as the *A'dityas*.

To Agni is attributed various functions and offices by the Vedic Rishis. As the Fire of Sacrifice he conveys the offerings and invocations of men to the celestials; he is the *Hotri*, or priest, who invites the Deities to the ceremony; he is the *Purohita*, or the family priest, who performs the rite on behalf of the *Yajamána*. As a Divinity he is immortal, gifted with infinite power and splendour, and enjoying perpetual youth. He has the power of granting riches, food, cattle, health and life. He is, sometimes, mentioned under various appellations, being identified with Yama, Varuṇa, Mitra, and the Sun. He is, again, mentioned as the first Aṅgirás, who, in the *Védas*, as well as in the *Puráṇás*, is a patriarch and R*ishi*. The Vedic myth of Aṅgirás has, however, a special significance. It appears that this priestly family or school either introduced Fire-Worship or organized it in various forms.

Indra is regarded in the *Védás* as a personification of the phenomenon of the Firmament capable of sending down rain. Rain was particularly necessary to an agricultural people like the Vedic Hindus, and, therefore, Indra was deified. The Clouds are described as being unwilling to part with their watery stores and Indra attacks them with his thunderbolt. The Cloud is personified as Ahi or Vṛitra, and is described as fighting with Indra. This is merely an allegory describing the power of Indra in sending down rain for the behoof of humanity. The allegorical character of this Vedic myth is lost sight of in the *Puráṇás*, and Vṛitra becomes a real personage, the King of the *Asuras*, who combats with the King of the Celestials. For his combating with the Clouds, Indra is specially described, in the *Súktas*, as the Martial Deity, the giver of victory to his votaries and the destroyer of the enemies of religious rites. Like Agni he also confers riches and other temporal blessings on his worshippers.

The Sun, Súryya, or Savitrí, occupies a much less prominent place in the *Vaidik* liturgy. In the first book of the R*ig-véda* we have only three *Súktas* addressed to him individually, but they do not describe more strikingly his supremacy. Like Agni and Indra he, too, bestows temporal blessings on his worshippers. He is described as the source of light coursing quickly between heaven and earth, in a car drawn by the seven days of the week.

A number of lesser Divinities is, also, mentioned as subordinate to Indra and Agni. The Maruts or Winds are associated with the Firmament. Vâyu or Wind is, also, mentioned as a Divinity but always in association with Indra. The Maruts are frequently addressed as the attendants of Indra. They are called the sons of Pṛis'ni or the Earth, and also Rudrás, or sons of Rudra. This is a pure and simple metaphor expressing, as Professor Wilson holds, the action of wind upon fire. It is, furthermore, described in the *Rig-véda* that they were originally mortal, but became immortal by worshipping Agni.

The *A'dityas*, or the lesser Suns, are described as the sons of Aditi, who is known as the Mother of the Celestials and identified with the Earth. There is no separate hymn to Vishṇu, but he is mentioned as Tṛivikrama, taking three steps or paces. Mitra is never addressed alone; he appears amongst the Vis'wadévás, or is associated with Varuṇa and Aryyamán. He presides over the day, and in combination with Varuṇa, dispenses water. Varuṇa presides over the night, and is very commonly called *Rájá*, or King. Pushán is another name of the A'ditya or the Sun, presiding over the earth. His protection is solicited on a journey, particularly against robbers.

The two A'swins are described as demigods. They are mentioned in the later mythology as the sons of the Sun, but no such legend occurs in the *Rig-véda*. They are, however, described, in one place, as having the sea (*Sindhu*) for their Mother. This merely shows their identity with the Sun and Moon which apparently rise out of the ocean. They are described as the destroyers of enemies and diseases. They are known as the physicians of the celestials.

We thus find that the hymns of the *Rig-véda* are addressed to the three Deities,—Agni or Fire, Indra or the Firmament, and the Sun. Or it may be said that there are only two Deities, for the Sun is only a manifestation of Fire. Yáksha, in the *Daivata-Kâṇḍam* of his *Nirukta*, asserts that there are in the *Véda* "three divinities: Agni on the earth; Vâyu, or Indra in the sky, and Suryya in heaven; of each of whom there are many appellations expressive of his greatness and of the variety of his functions." Yáksha further asserts that "all the Deities are but parts of one *átman*, or soul, subservient to the diversification of his praises through the immensity and variety of his attributes." The *Anukramaṇiká* goes further, and affirms that there is but *One Deity*, the *Great Soul*, quoting in support of this doctrine, a passage which applies only to the Sun, who is there called "the Soul of all that moves or is immovable."

Thus we see that in invoking the different phenomena of nature, the Vedic Aryans had evidently in view the Supreme Energy underlying them all. It is not the rain or the lightning that is worshipped, but the Deity or the Divine Power that rules them; and this Divine Power is designated by the Vedic Rishis as Parjanya.

The fire, that we see before us and which is so useful to the people, is not the Deity who is invoked by the Rishis—but the Divine Power which is designated by them as Agni, "who bursts forth from the wood when the fire is churned with a stick." It is thus clear that the Vedic Aryans did not merely worship the natural phenomena, but the Energy underlying them all, which they denominated by various names, such as, Suryya, Agni, Indra, etc. To them either Indra only, or Agni, or Suryya, or all of them, together with the other Powers of Nature, did not complete the conception of God. Nor was any of them regarded by them as the Supreme Ruler of the Universe, Omniscient and Omnipotent. They represented merely the various Energies of the All-Powerful Providence manifested to humanity through diverse natural phenomena.

The *Rig-véda* throws a considerable light upon the social and political condition of the then Hindus. The following observations, made by that eminent and erudite scholar Professor H. H. Wilson, will give a sufficient idea to the reader.

"It has been a favourite notion with some eminent scholars, that the Hindus, at the period of the composition of the hymns, were a nomadic and pastoral people. This opinion seems to rest solely upon the frequent solicitations for food, and for horses and cattle which are found in the hymns, and is unsupported by any more positive statements. That the Hindus were not Nomads, is evident from the repeated allusions to fixed dwellings, and villages, and towns; and we can scarcely suppose them to have been in this respect behind their barbarian enemies, the overthrow of whose numerous cities is so often spoken of. A pastoral people they might have been to some extent; but they were, also, and, perhaps, in a still greater degree, an agricultural people, as is evidenced by their supplications for abundant rain and for the fertility of the earth, and by the mention of agricultural products, particularly barley. They were a manufacturing people; for the art of weaving, the labours of the carpenter, and the fabrication of golden and of iron mail, are alluded to; and, what is more remarkable, they were a maritime and mercantile people.

"Not only are the *Sûktas* familar with the ocean and its phenomena, but we have merchants described as pressing earnestly on board ship, for the sake of gain; and we have a naval expedition against a foreign island, or continent *(dwipa)*, frustrated by a shipwreck. They must, also, have made some advance in astronomical computation, as the adoption of an intercalary month, for the purpose of adjusting the solar and lunar years to each other, is made mention of. Civilization must have therefore made considerable progress; and the Hindus must have spread to the seacoast, possibly along the Sindhu or Indus, into Cutch and Guzerat, before they could have engaged in navigation and commerce. That they had extended themselves from a more northern site, or that they were a northern race, is rendered probable from the peculiar expression used, on more than one occasion, in soliciting long life—when the worshipper asks for a hundred *winters* (*himas*), a boon not likely to have been desired by the natives of a warm climate. They appear, also, to have been a fair-complexioned people, at least comparatively, and foreign invaders of India, as it is said that Indra divided the fields among his *white*-complexioned friends, after destroying the indigenous barbarian races, for such there can be little doubt we are to understand by the expression *Dasyu*, which so often recurs, and which is often defined to signify one who not only does not perform religious rites, but attempts to disturb them, and harass their performers: the latter are the *A'ryyas*, the *A'ryya*, or respectable, or Hindu, or *Arian* race. *Dasyu*, in later language, signifies a thief, a robber, and *A'ryya* a wealthy or respectable man; but the two terms are constantly used in the Text of the *Véda* as contrasted with each other, and as expressions of religious and political antagonists, requiring, therefore, no violence of conjecture to identify the *Dasyus* with the indigenous tribes of India refusing to adopt the ceremonial of the *A'ryyas*, a more civilized, but intrusive, race, and availing themselves of every opportunity to assail them, to carry off their cattle, disturb their rites and impede their progress; to little purpose, it should seem, as the *A'ryyas* commanded the aid of Indra, before whose thunderbolt the numerous cities, or hamlets of the *Dasyus* were swept away.

"We have no particular intimation of the political condition of the Hindus, except the specification of a number of names of princes, many of which are peculiar to the *Véda*, and differ from those of the heroic poems and *Puráṇás*: a few are identical, but the nomenclature, evidently, belongs to a period anterior to the construction of the dynasties of the Sun and Moon, no allusion to which thus far occurs. The princes named are sometimes described as in hostility with each other, and the condition of the provinces of India occupied by the Hindus was, no doubt, the same, which it continued to be until the Mahommedan conquest,—parcelled out amongst insignificient principalities, under petty and contending princes.

"Upon a subject of primary importance in the history of Hindu society,—the distinctions of caste,—

the language of the *Sûktâs*, of the first *Ashtaka* at least, is by no means explicit. Whenever collectively alluded to, mankind are said to be distinguished into five sorts, or classes, or, literally, five men, or beings *(pancha kshitayah)*. The Commentator explains this term to denote the four castes, *Brâhmaṇ*, *Kshatriya*, *Vais'ya* and *Sûdra*, and the barbarian, or *Nishada*; but Sáyana, of course, expresses the received impressions of his own age. We do not meet with the denomination *Kshatriya* or *Sûdra* in any Text of the First Book, nor with that of *Vais'ya*; for *Vis'*, which does occur, is there a synonym of man in general. *Brâhmaṇ* is met with, but in what sense is questionable. In the neuter form *Brahma*, it usually implies prayer or praise, or sacrificial food, or, in one place, preservation; in its masculine form *Brahmá*, it occurs as the praiser or reciter of the hymn, or, as the particular priest, so denominated, who presides over the ceremonial of a sacrifice; and in neither case does it necessarily imply a *Brâhmaṇa* by caste; for that the officiating priests might not be *Brâhmaṇâs* appears from the part taken by Vis'wâmitra at the sacrifice of S'unahs'epas, who, although, according to tradition, by birth a *Kshatriya*, exercises the functions of the priesthood. There is one phrase which is in favour of considering the *Brâhmaṇa* as the member of a caste, as distinguished from that of the military caste: 'If you Indra and Agni, have ever delighted in a *Brâhmaṇ* or a *Rájá*, then come hither;' but even this can scarcely be regarded as decisive. A hymn that occurs in a subsequent part of the *Véda* has, however, been translated by Mr. Colebrooke, in which the four castes are specified by name, and the usual fable of their origin from *Brahmâ* alluded to."

Even from a careful perusal of this hymn and the observation of the practices of the Vedic people as recorded in the hymns we find that they were divided into four classes after their respective callings. The promulgator of the system had, evidently, in view the organization of the various classes of people with reference to their trades and professions. But we have no such proof, in the whole range of the Vedic literature, as prohibits one class from taking food with another. Besides we have no proof against inter-marriages—but, on the other hand, we have overwhelming evidence of R*ishis* marrying the daughters of the kings. The classification, of the people, however, did not at all depend on their birth but upon their character and attainments. We have allusions of *Kshatriyâs* attaining to the dignity of a *Brâhmaṇaḥ* on account of their spiritual attainments and many of them were authors of several *Upanishadâs*. The system, as it appears, was evidently instituted to divide the functions of the respective classes so that the great work, of conquering the country and establishing a good and just government which the Aryans took up, might go on without any interruption.

The condition of women in India, during the Vedic Age, was immensely superior to what we find now. They were not required to remain behind a curtain, a loathsome practice, which is evidently an outcome of the Mahommedan Rule, for it finds only in Bengal, North-Western Provinces and the Punjâb where the Mahomedan rule was most dominant, whereas their sisters of Madras and Bombay enjoy, even now, the sweet air of freedom. Vedic Hymns clearly prove that women, in that Age, used to come out before the public. The daughter and her mother were present at the public sacrifice made by the "Opulent Rathávati." The presence of women in public was recognised in the Vedic Age.

There was no early marriage in the Vedic Age and maidens, when of proper age and education, used to take husbands after their hearts. It is to the accomplishments and character of a husband that they, always, looked, and the son of a *Rishi* was, always, considered the desirable match for the daughter of a *Râjâ*. Monogamy was practised in the Vedic Period and women had a recognized position of their own. Husbands and wives, as a married pair, used to perform sacrifices conjointly. The wife was a necessary fáctor, in a household, in carrying on sacrifices, preserving sacred fire and performing other duties of life. Women used to receive education and such was the extent of this education that some of them were the authors of Hymns. One of them is Viswavará ; she was the authoress of the 2nd Song of the Fifth Chapter of the *Rig-vêda* which contains twenty-eight most beautiful stànzas.

Another is Vak, the authoress of the 125th Song in the Tenth Chapter of the *Rig-vêda*. The hymn contains the highest ideal of the conception of God. The great Commentators on these Songs have said that they are the root of the *Védânta* Philosophy. She lived the life of an ascetic and passed her days in prayers and meditation.

Another is Lopámudrá ; she was the authoress of the 79th Song of the *Rig-véda*, containing two most excellent stanzas. She was the daughter of a king and the wife of the great *Rishi* Agastya ; though she was a princess, born and bred in luxury, she lived, with her husband, as an ascetic and followed him like a shadow.

We need not mention more,—these three will give

our reader an idea of some of the ideal Vedic women and of the extent of their education.

It is not easy to determine accurately the Age of Vedic Composition. Many European Scholars have exhausted, with no useful result, their ingenuity on this question. Professor Max-Müller maintains that Saṁskrit-speaking Aryans lived in India about at least 3,000 B.C. This he proves from the mention of *Sindhu*, a vegetable fibre, in the list of the vegatable-clothing made for the library of Assur-bam-pal in Babylonia. This vegetable fibre, which is cotton, is not mentioned in the Vedic Hymns, or the *Brâhmaṇâs*, but in the *Sûtrâs*.

According to him, however, there are three literary periods of the Vedic Age, *viz*., that of the Hymns, that of the *Brâhmaṇâs*, and that of the *Sûtrâs*. He then attempts to fix dates for these Periods. The only historical date, on which we can rely is that of the rise of Buddhism. This, according to the information contained in the Buddhist Cannon, is about 500 B.C. Buddhism is really the Protestantism of India, and is, decidedly, a movement against the rise of the *Brâhmaṇâs*. The word *Upanishad* is, also, mentioned in the Cannon of the Southern Buddhists. This fact goes to prove that Buddhism pre-supposes the Period of the *Brâhmaṇâs*. Thus the learned Professor attempts to build up the Vedic Age beginning with the rise of Buddhism. His conclusion is, in his own words, thus summed up :—"If, then, we place the rise of Buddhism between 500 and 600 B.C., and assign, provisionally, 200 years to the *Sûtra*-Period, another 200 years to the *Brâhmaṇa*-Period, we should arrrive at about 1,000 B.C., as the date when the collection of the ten books of the ancient hymns must have taken place." But he gives no reason which justifies him to give 200 years to each Period. If this duration of several Periods be a child of imagination, we may, as well, extend it to 500 or 1,000 years.

The views, of other Western Scholars, tally more or less with that of Professor MaxMüller. We can, very well understand the difficulties under which they labour in ascertaining the date of the composition of the Vedic Hymns.

Attempts have also been made to ascertain the date of Vedic Hymns from Astronomical Calculations. Professor Tilak, of Bombay, has written a learned treatise on the Antiquity of the *Védás* in which he has made use of astronomical observations for ascertaining the Vedic Age. According to him, the marking of the changes, in the position of heavenly bodies, "is the best measurement of time for determining the periods of antiquity, only if we have reliable records about the position of heavenly bodies in early days; fortunately, such records of the time, when the Hellenic, the Iranian, and the Indian, Aryans lived together, have been preserved for us in the *Rig-véda*, and, with the help of Greek and Parsi traditions, we can now decipher these records."

By various internal evidence and other researches he has proved that "the oldest Vedic Calendar, like the oldest Hymn, was sacrificial; and that the sacrifice or the year commenced with *Aditi* at the vernal equinox in or near *Puṇarvasu*. The phase of the Moon, the seasons and the *Ayanás* further guided the ancient *A'ryyas* in measuring time for sacrificial purposes. The asterism of *Abhijit* marked the approach of *Vishuvau* or the central day, while *Puṇarvasu*, which soon after came to be called *Jamakau*, indicated the beginning of the year. Sometime after this and before the vernal equinox had receded to Orio the lunar months, and *tithis* or days appear to have come in use; and, in fact, the whole Calendar seems to have been re-arranged, the year being made to commence from the winter solistice in the *Chitrâ* Full-Moon. But this did not alter the sacrificial system, which, so far as the procedure is concerned, still continues to be what it was in the oldest day."

The oldest Period, therefore, according to him, in the Aryan Civilization, "may be called the *Aditi*, or the pre-Orion-Period, and we may, roughly, assign 6,000-4,000 B.C., as its limits. It was a period when the finished hymns do not seem to have been known, and half-prose and half-poetical *Nivids*, or sacrificial formulæ, were probably in use."

The next is the Orion-Period, "which, roughly speaking, extended from 4,000 to 5,000 B.C., from the time when the vernal equinox was in the asterism of *A'drâ* to the time when it receded to the asterism of *Krittikâs*. This is the most important period in the history of the Aryan Civilization. A good many *Suktas*, in the Rig-*vêda*, were sung at the time, and several legends were either formed anew or developed from the older ones. This was pre-eminently the Period of Hymns."

"The Third, or the *Krittikâ*-Period commences with the vernal equinox in the asterism of the *Krittikâs* and extends up to the period recorded in the *Védânga Jyotisha*, that is, from 2500 B.C., to 1400 B.C. It was the Period of *Taittiriya Samhitâ* and several of the *Brâhmaṇâs*. The hymns of the Rig-*vêda* had, already, become antique and unintelligible by this time, and the *Brahmavâdins* indulged in speculations, often too free, about the real meaning of those hymns and legends. It was at this time that the *Samhitâs* were probably compiled into systematic books and attempts made to ascertain the meanings of the oldest hymns and formulæ."

"The Fourth, and the Last, Period, of the old Saṁskrit literature, extends from 1400 B.C., to 500 B.C., or the birth and rise of Buddhism. It was the Period of *Sútrás* and philosophical systems."

Thus we see that the terminus of the Vedic Age is placed about 500 B.C., the birth and rise of Buddhism. From the above results it is evident that the Vedic Hymns were composed in the Period extending from 4000 to 2500 B.C. From internal evidence, in the R*ig-véda*, it is seen that the ancient Hindu Civilization reached its zenith during this Period. It must have taken a considerable time, not less than one thousand, or two thousand, years, for a civilization to attain to such a maturity as is seen in the R*ig-véda*. Besides, a literature cannot grow so very antique as to require attempts of the learned writers to explain it within a short period of two hundred years. The *Bráhmaṇás* and the *Upanishadás* are, undoubtedly, attempts to decipher the rituals and the theosophy of the *Védás*.

Although, therefore, the Vedic Age is more a matter of speculation, yet the birth, of the Hymns of the R*ig-véda* must have been very early, decidedly earlier than 10,000 B.C. And it is not improbable, as proved by Professor Tilak, that they must have been composed about 4,000 B.C. Two hundred years is too short a period for a literature to pass through such stages.

The *Saṁhitá*, of the First *Véda*, contains *Mantrás* or prayers, which for the most part are encomiastic, as the name of the R*ig-véda* implies. This collection is divided into eight parts (*Ashtaka*), each of which is sub-divided into as many lectures (*Adhyáya*). Another mode of division, also, runs through the volume, distinguishing ten books (*Maṇḍala*) which are, again, sub-divided into more than a hundred chapters (*Anuváka*) and comprise a thousand hymns or invocations (*Súkta*.) A further sub-division, of more than two thousand sections (*Varga*), is common to both methods: and the whole contains above ten thousand verses, or rather stanzas, of various measures.

On examining this voluminous compilation, a systematic arrangement is readily perceived. Successive chapters, even entire books, comprise hymns of a single author; invocations, too, addressed to the same Deities, hymns relating to like subjects, and prayers intended for similar occasions, are, frequently, classed together.

The *Rishi*, or saint of a *Mantra*, is defined both in the Index of the R*ig-véda* and by the Commentators, as, "he by whom it is spoken;" as, the *Dévatá*, or Deity, is "that which is therein mentioned." In the Index to the *Vájasanéyi Yajur-véda*, the *Rishi* is interpreted as "the Seer, or the Rememberer," of the Text and the *Dévatá* is said to be "contained in the prayer."

The names, of the respective Authors of each passage, are preserved in the *Aṇukramaṇí*, or Explanatory Table of Contents, which has been handed down with the *Véda* itself, and of which the authority is unquestioned. According to this Index, Vis'wámitra is the Author of all the Hymns contained in the Third Book of the R*ig-véda*; as Bharadwája is, with rare exceptions, the Composer of those collected in the Sixth Book; Vasishtha in the Seventh; Gritsamada in the Second; Vámadéva in the Fourth; and Buddha and other descendants of Atri, in the Fifth. But in the remaining Books of this

Véda, the Authors are more various; among these, besides Agastya, Kas'yapa son of Marichi, Aṅgiras, Jamadagni son of Bhrigu, Parásara father of Vyása, Gotama and his son Nodhas, Vṛihaspati, Nárada and other celebrated Indian Saints, the most conspicuous of whom are Kaṇwa and his numerous descendants,—Medhátithi, etc.; Madhuchhandas and others among the posterity of Vishwámitra; Sunahsepha son of Ajigarta; Kutsa, Hiraṇyastup, Savya and other descendants of Aṅgiras, besides many other saints among the posterity of the personages above-mentioned.

Several persons of royal birth are mentioned among the Authors of the Hymns which constitute this *Véda.*

The Deities, invoked, appear, on a cursory inspection of the *Véda*, to be as various as the Authors of prayers addressed to them; but according to most ancient annotations on the Indian Scriptures, those numerous names, of persons and things, are all resolvable into different titles of three Deities, and, ultimately, of One God.

The places of these three Deities are the earth, the intermediate region and heaven—they are the Fire, Air and the Sun. They are pronounced to be the Deities of the mysterious names severally; and (*Prajápati*) the lord of creatures is the Deity of them collectively. The syllable OM intends every Deity; it belongs to (*Paraméshthi*) Him, who dwells in the supreme abode; it appertains to (*Brahma*) the vast one; to (*Déva*) God; to (*Adhyátmá*) the superintending soul. Other Deities, belonging to those several regions, are portions of the three Divinities; for they are, variously, named and described, on account of their different operations: but, in fact, there is only One Deity, the Great Soul. He is called the Sun, for He is the Soul of all beings; (and) that is declared by the Sage, "the Sun is the Soul of (*Jagat*) what moves and of that which is fixed." Other Deities are portions of Him; and that is expressly declared by the Text,—"the wise call Fire, Indra, Mitra, and Varuṇa."

The subject and uses of the prayers contained in the *Véda* differ more than the Deities by which they are addressed. Every line is replete with allusions to mythology and to the Indian notion of the Divine Nature and of Celestial Spirits. For the innumerable ceremonies to be performed by a householder, and, still more, for those endless rites enjoined for hermits and ascetics, a choice of prayer is offered in every stage of the celebration. It may be sufficient here to observe that Indra or the Firmament, Fire, the Sun, the Moon, Water, Air, the Spirits, the Atmosphere, and the Earth, are the objects, most frequently, addressed; and the various and repeated sacrifices with Fire and the drinking of the milky-juice of the Moon-Plant, furnish an abundant occasion for numerous prayers adapted to the many stages of those religious rites.

RIG-VEDA SAMHITA.

FIRST ASHTAKA.

FIRST MAṆDALA.

FIRST ADHYA'YA.

ANUVAKA I.

SUKTA I.

THE first *Sukta* or hymn, is addressed to Agni. The *Rishi* or the saintly author, is Madhuchhandas, the son of Viswámitra. The metre is *Gáyatrí*.

I WORSHIP by hymns Agni,[1] the high-priest of the sacrifice,[2] the deity,[3] the sacrificial priest who presents oblations (to the deities) and is the possessor of great riches.[4]

2. May Agni, lauded by the ancient[5] and modern *Rishis*, conduct the deities hither, (*i.e.*, in this sacrifice).

3. Through Agni, (the worshipper) comes by riches which multiplies daily, which is the source of fame[6] (and) which secures heroes.[7]

---

1 Agni or Fire was an object of worship with the ancient Aryáns.

2 Agni is called the *Purohita*. As a priest performs religious rites for a king for accomplishing all his desired-for objects, so *Agni* performs *Homa* for the sacrifice.

3 *Devam* here means endued with feelings of charity and other accomplishments.

4 The word in the Text is *ratnadhátama*, *i.e.*, holder of jewels. Figuratively it means here "the multiplier of jewels" in the shape of sacrificial fruits.

5 The ancient *Rishis* were Bhrigu, Angiras, etc.

6 *Yas'asam*, *i.e.*, endued with fame for charity, etc.

7 *Veeravattamam*, *i.e.*, having heroic servants and sons.

4. O Agni, the sacrifice, around[1] which thou residest, is unimpeded[2] and reaches the celestials in heaven.

5. May Agni, the presenter of oblations, the attainer of success in works,[3] ever truthful, highly illustrious for many noble deeds, divine, come hither with the celestials.

6. Whatever good, O Agni, thou mayst confer upon the giver of oblations that, indeed, O Aṅgiras, belongs to thee.[4]

7. Bowing unto thee mentally, O Agni, we approach thee daily, both morning and evening.

8. Thee, the radiant, the protector of sacrifices

---

1 It means that at a sacrifice fire should be lighted at the four cardinal points, east, west, south and north, termed severally *A'havaníya*, *Mánjáliya*, *Gárhapatya* and *Agnidhriya*.

2 *Adhvaram*, *i.e.*, free from injury offered by *Rákshasás*.

3 *Kavikratu.*—Sáyana has explained it as *krántaprajña* (attainer of knowledge) and *krántakarma* (attainer of success in works). Wilson has adopted the former meaning. But we prefer the latter, as Agni is better known as the successful performer of religious rites for the celestials.

4 That is the riches, etc., which Agni will confer upon the performer of sacrifices, will enable him to multiply his oblations, the fruits of which Agni will ultimately reap. Here Aṅgiras is a synonym for Agni. The Commentator quotes Yáksha for the identity of Aṅgiras with *Aṅgára*, live coal; and a passage from the *Aitaréya Bráhmana* is cited in which it is said, "the coals became the Aṅgirás." The identification of Aṅgiras with Agni in function, though not in person, is the subject of a legend told in the *Mahábhárata*, *Vanaparvan*. There Márkandéya relates that Agni, having engaged in penance and relinquished his duties, the Muni Aṅgiras took upon him his office, and when he prevailed upon Agni to resume it, became his son; his descendants, the Aṅgirás, are, therefore, also the descendants of Agni, or so many Agnis or Fires.

(unobstructed by Râkshasâs), the perpetual illuminator of truth[1] and increasing in thine own room.[2]

9. Like unto a father to his son, O Agni, be easily accessible unto us; be ever present with us for our well-being.

SUKTA II.

THE *Rishi* is Madhuchhandas; the metre *Gáyatrí*. This hymn consists of nine *Riks* or stanzas. Of these three are addressed to Váyu; three, to Indra and Váyu conjointly; and three, to Mitra and Varuna.

VA'YU, worthy of being seen, (libations of) Soma[3] have been dressed, come, drink of them; (and) hear our invocation.

2. Váyu, the eulogists who have prepared the Soma-Juice, who know the sacrifice,[4] praise thee with encomiastic verses.

3. Váyu, thy speech[5] describing the qualities of Soma, comes to the giver (of the libation) and to many others (who invite thee) to drink of the Soma-Juice.

---

1 The word in the Text is *Ritam* which means truth or future fruits of religious rites.

2 *Swedame.*—The chamber in which Fire-Worship is performed.

3 *Arangkrita* or *alangkrita*, literally dressed or prepared. The Soma-Plant, being pressed, yields a profuse milky juice of a mild nature. It is used in sacrifice when it goes through a process of fermentation. This view of Mr. Stevenson is warranted by various expressions in the succeeding hymns.

4 *Aharvidah.* Sáyana translates it as *kratvabhijña, i.e.*, knowing all the sacrificial rituals. Wilson has translated it as "knowing the fit season."

5 Váyu is supposed to say,—"O performer of sacrifice, I will drink the libation of Soma."

4. Indra and Váyu, these libations are prepared (for you), come hither with food (for us); indeed, the drops of (Soma-Juice) await you both.

5. Indra and Váyu, living in oblations containing boiled rice,[1] you are aware of these libations; come near quickly.

6. Indra and Váyu, come near the prepared libation of the sacrificer who presses or extracts out the Soma-Juice for these men;[2] the ceremony will be speedily completed.

7. I invoke Mitra of pure strength and Varuṇa—the destroyer of enemies, (the joint) performers of the act of water-shedding.[3]

8. Mitra and Varuṇa, augmenters of water,[4] dispensers of water, you exist in this great sacrifice for bestowing reward (of sacrifice).

9. May Indra and Varuṇa, endued with mental powers, born for doing good to many and the refuge of multitudes, multiply our strength and sacrifice.

---

1 *Vájeenivasu.*—Sáyana explains *Vajeeni* as *Havi* (oblation) in which there is *anna* (boiled rice). The meaning is, therefore, *residing in such Havi.* Wilson translates the word as *abiding in the sacrificial rite.*

2 *Nará,* dual of *nara,* a man. Sáyana explains the word as "gifted with manly vigour," and it applies to Váyu and Indra.

3 The word in the Text is *Ghritáchi.* Sáyana explains it as water-shedding. Mitra and Varuna are said to cause rain indirectly by evaporation. Ramánáth Saraswatí explains it as *ghritáhuti,* oblation of clarified butter. But Sáyana's explanation is particularly applicable here.

4 *Ritavridhau:* Sáyana has explained the word *Ritu* as water and truth. It may also import sacrifice. Ramánáth Saraswatí has explained it as sacrifice and so has Langlois.

SUKTA III.

THE *Rishi* and metre are the same; of twelve stanzas; three are addressed to the As'wins; three to Indra; three, to the Vis'wadévás; and three' to Saraswatí.

AS'WINS,[1] cherishers of pious deeds, having outstretched hands[2] (for accepting the oblation), long-armed,[3] desire for sacrificial viands.

2. As'wins, of many acts, guides (of devotion), endowed with intellect, accept our eulogistic words with unaverted minds.[4]

3. As'wins, destroyers of diseases,[5] shorn of falsehood, leaders in the van of heroes,[6] come to the mixed libations of Soma, extracted and placed on lopped Kus'a-grass.[7]

---

1 As'wins are the two sons of the Sun, begotten during his metamorphosis as a horse endowed with perpetual youth and beauty. They are known as the celestial physicians and are the heroes of the many Védic and Pauránic legends.

2 *Dravatpâni.*—Having arms outstretched for receiving oblations offered in a sacrifice.

3 *Purubhuta.*—It may be translated as both long-armed and "great eaters."

4 *Shaviraya.*—Moving or unobstructed. *Dhiya.*—Loving mind, *i.e.*, accept our praises with a loving mind unobstructed.

5 *Dasra.*—Destroyers of enemies or diseases. The latter is preferable, for As'wins are known as the celestial physicians.

6 *Rudra-Varttani.*—Sáyana translates *Rudra* as heroes from the root *rúd*,—to weep, *i.e.*, those who make the enemies weep. *Varttani* means road: hence the compound means,—"they who are in the van of warriors." Wilson has followed Sáyana. K. M. Bannerjee renders it as "Ye of terrific paths."

7 *Vriktavarhisha.*—The sacred Kus'a-grass, having the roots cut off, is spread on the altar and upon it the libation of Soma-Juice is poured out. According to Mr. Stevenson, it is also strewn over the floor of the chamber in which the worship is performed.—*Wilson.*

4. Indra of variegated splendour, come hither; these libations, ever pure and extracted by fingers, are seeking thee.

5. Indra, drawn by the devotion (of the sacrificer) (and) invoked by the intelligent (priest), come hither and accept the prayers of the priest as he offers the libation.

6. Indra, having twany horses, come hither speedily, to accept the prayers (of the priest); in this sacrifice (of extrated Soma-Juice), accept our (proferred) food.

7. Vis'wadévâs,[1] protectors, supporters of men,[2] granters of (sacrificial) rewards, come to the extracted Soma-Juice of the worshipper.

8. May Vis'wadévâs, the bestowers of rain, come speedily to the libation, as the rays of the sun come diligently to the days.[3]

9. May Vis'wadévás, who are exempt from deterioration, omniscient,[4] shorn of malice, givers of wealth, partake of this sacrifice.

10. May Saraswatí,[5] the purifier, the giver of

---

1 The Vis'wadévás are sometimes vaguely applied to the divinities in general, but they also form a class. Some of their attributes are particularized, connecting them with the elements.—*Wilson.*

"To comprehend all the gods by one common name, to call them Vis'wadévás, the All-gods and to address prayers and sacrifices to them in their collective capacity."—Max Müller's *Origin and Growth of Religion.*

2 *Charshani-dritah.*—The root-meaning, according to Sáyana, would be,—*supporters of the cultivators.*

3 *Usra iva svasarani.* We have followed Sáyana. Ramánáth Saraswatí has rendered it as "the kine come to their own fold." This meaning does not appear to be unreasonable, for in many places the word *Usra* means cow.

4 *Ehimayasha.*—Sáyana explains it as "those who have obtained knowledge universally."

5 *Saraswatí* is here mentioned as "The Divinity of Speech."

food, the bestower of wealth in the shape of sacrificial fruits, seek viands in our sacrificial rite.

11. Saraswatí, the inspirer of truthful words, the instructress of the right-minded, has accepted our sacrifice.

12. Saraswatí[1] makes manifest by her deeds a huge river, and (in her own form) enlightens all her undertakings.

ANUVAKA II.

SUKTA I. (IV.)

The *Rishi* and metre the same: the hymn is addressed to Indra.

DAY by day we invoke (Indra) the performer of good deeds for our protection, as a milker (does) a good milch-cow for (the purpose of) milking.

2. (Indra) drinker of the Soma-Juice, come to our (daily) rites and drink of the libation; rich as you are, your delight gives kine.[2]

3. May we recognise thee in the midst of the right-minded who are nearest to thee: come to us; pass us not by to reveal (thyself to others).[3]

4. Go, worshipper to the intelligent and uninjuired Indra who confers the best riches (sons, etc.,) on thy

---

1 Saraswatí (from *Saras*, water) a river. The Hindus at that time used to worship a river of that name.

2 *I.e.*, You are endued with riches; when you are pleased, we get kine from you.

3 The Text *ma no ati khyah* is perfectly elliptical. But the Commentator has supplied the complete sense by rendering "neglecting us, do not reveal yourself to others."

friends[1] and ask him about the learned (priest, *i.e.*, myself).[2]

5. Let our sacrificial priests, serving Indra, sing his praises; O revilers, depart from hence and every other place.

6. Destroyer of enemies, let our enemies say that we are prosperous; men[3] (friends) (must say so); may we live in the felicity (derived from the favour) of Indra.

7. Offer to Indra, the pervader (of every rite of libation), the Soma-Juice that is present (at the three ceremonies), the wealth of the sacrifice, the source of joy to mankind,[4] which brings about the accomplishment of an act,[5] the favourite of (that Indra) who confers happiness (on the worshipper).

8. Having drunk, S'atakratu[6] of this (Soma-Juice) thou hadst killed Vitras;[7] thou defendest (thine devoted) warrior in battle.

9. O S'atakratu,[8] we offer to thee, powerful in

---

1 *Sakhibhya*: Sáyana explains it as *Ritwik* or sacrificial priest who is supposed to be the best friend of the worshipper.

2 The Text is elliptical. The sense is :—"Go to Indra and ask him about the fitness of myself who am the learned priest."

3 *Kristaya*.—Sáyana explains it as "men who are friends." The root-meaning is *cultivators*. Perhaps the word is used for *men in general*, because the Aryáns were cultivators.

4 *Nri*.—Sáyana explains it as "the worshipper and priest."

5 *I.e.*, Religious rite.

6 S'atakratu.—A name of Indra, the performer of a hundred sacrificial rites. Sáyana explains it as *vahukarmayukta*, either as their performer or their object.

7 The leading Asurás headed by Vitra.

8 Sáyana also explains *Kratu* as *prajña*—knowledge, *i.e.*, "endowed with great wisdom."

battle, sacrificial viands, O Indra, for the acquirement of wealth.

10. Sing unto that Indra, who is the protector of riches, who is endued with many great accomplishments, the perfecter of good deeds, the friend of the worshipper.

SUKTA II. (V.)

The Deity, *Rishi* and metre the same.

COME here, (priestly) friends, offering praises;[1] sit down and sing, again and again, the praises of Indra.

2. When Soma is extracted and poured, sing in a body unto Indra, the subduer of many enemies, the lord of many adorable deities.

3. May he[2] secure for us manliness (energy), may he secure for us riches, may he confer on us women,[3] may he come to us with food.

4. Sing to that Indra, before whose pair of steeds, carrying car in battle, enemies cannot stand.

5. These pure, extracted Soma-Juices, mixed with curds, are poured out for being drunk by the drinker of extracted libations.

6. Indra, performer of good sacrificial rites, for drinking extracted Soma-Juice, for acquiring seniority

---

1 "*Stoma váhasa*, literally, bearing praises. Sáyana explains the expression presenting in this rite *Trivit*, *Pañchadas'í*, and others, *i.e.*, collections of laudatory stanzas in the *Rig-Véda* so denominated."—*Wilson*.

2 Indra, endued with accomplishments, described in the previous *Mantram*.

3 *Purandhyam*.—Sáyana has explained it as, both "women" and "knowledge." Wilson has rendered it as, "knowledge."

amongst the celestials,[1] thou hast suddenly become endued with great energy.

7. Indra, adored by encomiastic hymns, may these pervading (quickly intoxicating) Soma-Juices enter into thee; may they be of good unto thee for the acquirement of superior knowledge.

8. The chants (of the *Sáma*)[2] have magnified thee, S'atakratu; the hymns (of the *Rich*) have magnified thee: may our eulogies magnify thee.

9. May Indra, the unobstructed protector,[3] accept these thousand (sacrificial) viands in which exist all manly properties.

10. Indra, the object of eulogistic verses, let not (inimical) men do injury to our persons. Thou art powerful, ward off our destruction (by enemies).

SUKTA III.' (VI.)

The *Rishi* and metre the same. The first three stanzas and the last are addressed to Indra, the rest to the *Maruts* or Winds.

THE circumstationed (inhabitants of the three worlds),[4] associate with (Indra), the mighty (Sun), the indestructive

---

1 *Jyaisthyam.*—Seniority amongst the celestials or the highest place.

2 The terms in the Text are *stomah* and *ukthah*: the former means the hymns of the *Sáma*-, and the latter the verses of the Rig-, *Véda.*

3 *I.e.*, who never renounces the work of protection.

4 "The Text has only *Paritasthushah*, those who are standing around; *lokatraya varttinah práninâh*, the living beings of the three worlds, is the explanation of the Scholiast."—*Wilson.*

(Fire), the moving (Wind), and the Lights that shine in the sky.[1]

2. They (the charioteers) harness to his chariot two beautiful steeds,[2] placed in different sides, bay-colored, high-spirited and chief-bearing.[3]

3. Mortals, (Indra as the Sun): rises with burning rays, giving sense to the senseless (in the night) and form to the formless (in darkness).[4]

4. Thereafter, verily those who bear names invoked in holy rites, (the Maruts,)[5] having seen the rain (about to be engendered), instigated him to resume his embryo condition (in the clouds).

5. In company with the carrying Maruts, the

---

1 "Of the three first objects, the Text gives only the epithets *Vradhna*, the mighty, to which Sáyana adds *A'ditya*, the Sun, *Arusha*, the non-injuring, to which Fire is supplied and *Charan*, the moving, an epithet of Wind. The last phrase is complete,—*rochante rochaná dévi*. Sáyana's additions are supported by a *Bráhmana* which explains the epithets as equivalent severally to A'ditya, Agni, and Váyu. The identification of Indra with the three, implies, the Scholiast says, his supremacy—he is *paramais'waryyayukta*."—*Wilson*.

The meaning of the Rich is really very obscure, and the sense can only be made out by following the explanation given by Sáyana in his Commentary.

2 The horses of Indra are called *Hari*, green or yellow-coloured.

3 *Nrivahasa*, literally, men-bearing.

4 "Indra is here, again, identified with the Sun, whose morning rays may be said to re-animate those who have been dead in sleep through the night. There is some difficulty in the construction, for *Maryáh*, mortals, is plural while *Ajayathah* is the second person singular of the first preterite. Sáyana is of opinion that the want of concord is a *Vaidik* license."—*Wilson*.

5 Maruts are not named in the Text, but the allusions justify the specification.

traversors of strong places, thou, Indra, hast discovered the cows hidden in the cave.[1]

6. The reciters of laudatory verses, desirous of seeking the celestials (the Maruts), laud the powerful (Maruts), illustrious, and conscious of the powers of bestowing riches as they glorify the good counsellor (Indra).

7. May you be seen, ye Maruts, in the company of the fearless Indra, always full of joy and equally brilliant.

8. This sacrifice adores the powerful Indra along with bands (of the Maruts), shorn of all shortcomings, proceeding towards the celestial region and desired (for granting fruits).

9. Therefore, (ye Maruts,) abiding on all sides, come hither, whether from the sky or from the radiant solar sphere ;[2] in this sacrifice (the priest) sings your praises.

10. We invoke Indra, for giving us riches, whether he comes from this earth, the sky, or from the vast firmament.

SUKTA IV. (VII).

The Deity, *Rishi* and metre the same.

THE chanters (of the *Sâma*) laud Indra with songs; the reciters of the *Rich*, with prayers; (the priests of the *Yajush*), with Texts.[3]

---

1 The allusion is to a legend. The Asurâs named Pânis stole the cows of the celestials and hid them in a cave which Indra found out with the help of a bitch named Saramá.

2 The region of the Winds is *dyu-loka*, the celestial region, or *antariksha*, the region above the sky, or the solar region.

3 The first term *Gâthina* merely means singers with the *Virhat-Sáma*. Sáyana explains *arka* as, *Mantramás* of the *Rig-Véda*; and *varich* as, the Texts of the *Yajush*.

2. Indra, bedecked with all ornaments,[1] the wielder of the thunderbolt, comes with his steeds harnessed at his words,[2] and mixes with all.

3. Indra, to see a long distance, elevated the Sun in the sky[3] and lighted the mountain with its rays.[4]

4. Invincible Indra, with thy invincible protection protect us in battles and in thousand battles abounding in spoils of horses and elephants.

5. We invoke Indra for great affluence, for limited wealth; (our) ally and wielder of the thunderbolt against (our) enemies.

6. Giver of rain, granter of all desires, set open this cloud. Thou art never uncompliant with our (requests).[5]

7. All the encomiastic verses which are addressed to different deities (givers of different fruits) are due to Indra, the wielder of the thunderbolt; I do not know his fitting praise.

8. As a bull defends a herd of kine, so the shedder of desired-for objects, the powerful lord who never says no to any request, fills men with strength.

---

1 *Hiranmayas*, literally means made of gold. Sáyana explains it as, "decorated with all ornaments."

2 This shows that the horses are well-trained.

3 The world being covered with darkness by Vritra, Indra, in order to dispell it, elevated the Sun in heaven.

4 Sáyana has explained it, both as, "lighted the mountain with its rays," and "charged the cloud with waters." Wilson has adopted the second interpretation.

5 The words in the Text are *Asmabhyampratishkrita*. Sáyana explains it as, "Thou hast never said (no) to what we have requested thee for."

9. Indra, who alone rules over men, over riches, and over the five (classes) of the dwellers on earth.[1]

10. For you, we invoke, Indra placed over all men; may he be exclusively our own.

ANUVAKA III.

SUKTA I. (VIII.)

The Deity, *Rishi* and metre as before.

INDRA, bring for our protection riches,—profuse, enjoyable, the source of victory, (and) the humbler of our enemies.

2. Through the constant strokes of fists[2] (soldiers engaged), by which (wealth) we shall repel enemies; or protected by thee with a horse.[3]

3. Indra, protected by thee we hold weapons made of thunderbolt; by which in battle we conquer enemies elated with pride.

4. With thee for our help, Indra, and (helped by) heroes holding strong weapons, we can defeat enemies arrayed in hosts.

---

1 "The Text has, over the five men or classes of men, *pañch kshitinám*, the latter term is explained etymologically, those who are fit for habitations (*nivásarhanám*); the phrase is of not unfrequent recurrence and is usually said to imply the four castes, *Bráhmanas*, *Kshatriyas*, *Vaishyas* and *Sudras*, and *Nishádas*, barbarians or those who have no caste, intending possibly the aboriginal races of India, all in a very low stage of civilization, like the *Gonds*, *Koles* and *Bhils*, of the present day."—*Wilson.*

2 *Mushtihatyayá.*—Literally striking with a fist.

3 The Scholiast, in this and the preceding expressions, means infantry and cavalry.

5. Mighty (in strength) is Indra, supreme (in accomplishments), may greatness[1] ever abide in the holder of the thunderbolt; this army is vast like the firmament.

6. Persons engaged in battle, those seeking children, and intelligent men seeking knowledge, (obtain them by lauding Indra.)

7. The belly (of Indra) which quaffs Soma-Juice in abundance, swells like the ocean, (and is ever) moist like the ample fluids of the palate.[2]

8. The words of Indra to his worshipper, are true, of manifold (sweet) expressions, many cow-conferring, greatly adorable, and like a branch of tree loaded with ripe fruits.

9. Indra, thy lordly powers are ever protectors of every such worshipper as I am and immediate givers of fruits.

10. Indeed, encomiastic verses,[3] (sung in his praise in the *Sâma*) and recited (in the *Rich*), are to be desired and repeated to Indra that he may drink the Soma-Juice.

---

1 This indicates Indra's superiority in physical strength and in mental and intellectual accomplishments.

2 "The Scholiast expounds the Text *urwirapo na kákudha* as rendered above, but *kakuda* may refer to *kakud*, the pinnacle of a mountain, and the phrase might then be translated, like the abundant waters or (torrents) from the mountain tops."—*Wilson.*

3 "The first is the translation of *stoma*, which the Commentary defines *Sáma-Sâdhyâm Stotram*, praise to be accomplished by the *Sâma-Véda*: the second is the rendering of *uktha*, which the same authority describes as, the *Rik-Sâdhyâm S'âstram*, the unsung praise to be accomplished by the *Rich*. *S'âstram* is explained by S'rídhara Swâmi in the Scholia on the *Bhâgvat-Purânam*, to signify a sacred hymn not sung."—*Wilson.*

SUKTA II. (IX.)

The Deity, *Rishi* and metre the same.

COME, Indra, in this sacrificial rite and be gratified with all these viands and libations; growing in strength be victorious (over thy enemies).

2. The libation being prepared, present (O priests) this exhilarating and efficacious (draught) to the gratified Indra, the accomplisher of all deeds.

3. Handsome-nosed[1] (Indra), adorable unto all,[2] be gratified with these joy-producing laudatory verses; come with the deities in these sacrifices.

4. Indra, I have composed laudatory verses; they have reached thee, the showerer of desired-for objects, the protector (of thy worshippers); thou hast accepted them.

5. Send us, Indra, best and multiform riches; thou hast enough and more than enough riches.

6. Indra, lord of profuse riches, engage us, diligent by nature and renowned for the acquirement of wealth, in this rite.

7. Give us, Indra, incalculable, inexhaustible wealth, containing many kine, profuse food, full of virtues in abundance and granting sufficient longevity.

8. Indra, confer on us great renown, wealth

---

1 *Su-s'ipra.*—"S'ipra" means either the lower jaw or nose. Wilson has translated it as, "with the handsome chin." But we think "handsome-nosed" is a better rendering.

2 The Text is *vahwa charshane.*—Literally, "Oh thou! who art all men." Sâyana has explained it as, *sarva manushyayukta*, joined with all men, or *sarva yajamânais pujya*, adorable unto all sacrificers, better unto all men.

distributed in a thousand objects of charity, and food filling up many carts.[1]

9. Chanting laudatory verses, we invoke Indra, the lord of riches, fond of *Rich* (verses), the repairer[2] to the place of sacrifice, for protecting our wealth.

10. In every sacrifice the sacrificer glorifies the great prowess of Indra, powerful and ever dwelling (in an eternal mansion).

SUKTA III. (X.)

The Deity and the R*ishi* are the same; the metre is *Anushtubh.*

THE chanters (of the *Sáma*), hymn thee, S'atakratu; the reciters of the *Richas*, praise thee, worthy of adoration; the *Bráhmanás*[3] elevate thee like a bamboo pole.

2. When (the worshipper), becoming ready to perform a great (sacrificial) rite, ascends from one summit

---

1 *Rathinis ishas.*—Literally "car having viands." The Commentator has explained it fully; as, "those articles of food which are conveyed in cars, carts, or waggons from the place of production."

2 *Gantáram.*—The Commentator explains it as "going to the chamber where sacrifice is performed."

3 The first term *Gáyatrínah*, literally "those who employ the *Gáyatrí* metre," is said by Sáyana to denote the *Udgátri*, the chanter of the hymns of the *Sáma; Arkina*, the reciters of the *Rich.* The third term *Bráhmanah* is explained, the *Brahmá* of a sacrifice, or the priest so denominated, and the other *Bráhmanás.* The concluding phrase *twa vams'am iva udyemire*, "they have raised thee like bamboo," is rather obscure. The Scholiast says, "they have elevated Indra, as tumblers raise a bamboo pole, on the summit of which they balance themselves," not an uncommon feat in India; or as *vams'a* means also a family, it may be rendered as, "ambitious persons raise their family to consequence."

to another summit,[1] Indra knows his object, and, showering desired-for objects, becomes moved to come with the troops (of Maruts.)

3. Indra, the drinker of Soma-Juice, yoke thy long-maned, powerful and plump[2] horses, and come near to hear our praises.

4. Come, Vasu,[3] (to the rite), praise our hymns, accept them, (express thy delight) by sound, and multiply the food and rite (undertaken by us).

5. The hymn, the cause of increase, is to be repeated to Indra,—the repeller of many foes, that S'akra may make great sound[4] to our sons and friends.

6. We go to him, for (the favour of) his friendship, and for the acquisition of wealth and becoming strength; for the powerful Indra, conferring riches, can protect (us).

7. Indra, the food (given by thee) is everywhere profuse, easily attainable and assuredly perfect; holder of the thunderbolt, set open the habitation of cows[5] and provide (ample) riches.

---

1 The Text is *yat sanoh sanum aruhat*, which rendered into plain English would read as, "mounting from summit to summit." Sáyana completes the sense, saying,—"who goes to the mountain to collect the Soma-Plant, or fuel, or other articles required for the ceremony."

2 *Kakshyapra.*—Literally "filling out their girths; plump or well-conditioned."

3 *Vasu*, here used as a synonym of Indra, is explained as the original donor or cause of habitations.

4 *Ráranat.*—Literally making great sound: Sáyana explains it as, "being pleased with us speaks highly of our sons and friends."

5 The Text is *Gavám Vrajam.*—Sáyana has explained *Vrajam* as, *Nivása Sthánam*, "dwelling-place." Wilson has rendered it as, "cow-pastures," meaning that "Indra, as the sender of rain, should fertilize

8. Heaven and earth are unable to sustain thee, when killing thine enemies; thou mayst command (send) the waters of the sky: send us abundant kine.

9. O thou, having ears which hear all, listen speedily to my invocation; hold in thy heart my praises; keep, near to thee this, my hymn, as it were (the words of a) friend.

10. We know thee, the showerer of desired-for objects in profusion, the hearer of our call in battles; we invoke the thousandfold wealth-giving protection of thee, the showerer (of abundant bounties)

11. Come, Indra, speedily to us; son of Kus'ika,[7] delighted, drinking the fermented Soma-juice; prolong the life highly spoken of by all the Deities; make me, who am a *Rishi*, profusely endowed (with possessions).

12. O thou the object of praises, may these eulogistic verses, engaged in all rites, reach thee from all sides. May they augment, by following thee who art long-lived; and being agreeable to thee, may they give us joy.

---

the fields, and, by providing abundant pasturage, enable the cattle to yield store of milk." The rendering is, indeed, very happy, but we have followed the Text literally.

7 In all the *Paurânik* genealogies, the son of Kus'ika is the sage Vis'wâmitra, and in order to explain its application to Indra, Sâyana quotes the legend given in the Index which states that Kus'ika, the son of Is'irathi, being desirous of a son equal to Indra, adopted a life of continence, in requital of which Indra was born as the son of Gâthi, the Gâdhi of the Purânâs.—Wilson.

SUKTA IV. (XI).

THE Deity is Indra; the *Rishi* is Jetri the son of Madhuchhandas; the metre is *Anushtubh*.

ALL our eulogistic verses magnify Indra, spreading like the ocean, the most valiant of car-warriors, the lord of food, the protector of the virtuous.

2. Supported by (the favour of) thy friendship, Indra, cherisher of strength, we have no fear (of our enemies) but glorify thee, the conqueror, the unconquered.

3. Indra's gifts of wealth are known from time immemorial; his protection will not be wanting to him (the worshipper) who presents to the reciters of the hymns, wealth of food and cattle.

4. Indra,—the ever youthful, the intelligent, of great strength, the sustainer of all deeds, the wielder of the thunderbolt, the subject of profuse laudation, was born as the destroyer of the cities (of the Asurâs).

5. Thou, O wielder of the thunderbolt, didst break open the cave of Vala,[1] where he kept the kine (of the celestials concealed); the deities oppressed (by Vala) no longer feared him, having obtained thee as their protector.

6. (Drawn) by the gifts of wealth, I, again, come, O hero, to thee, describing (everywhere the virtues of) trickling Soma-Juice;[2] the performers of the rite ap-

---

1 Vala was an *Asura*, who stole the cows of the celestials and hid them in a cave. Indrâ surrounded the cave with his army and recovered the cattle.

2 The Text is *Sindhum ahvadan*. It can be rendered as both "describing the virtues of the trickling or pouring Soma-juice," or "recounting his liberality in the Soma-Sacrifice." Wilson has adopted the latter. But the former appears to be more literal.

proach thee, worthy of being lauded, for they have known thy (liberality).

7. Indra, thou didst kill by stratagem, the wily S'ushna ;[1] the intelligent know thy (greatness) ; multiply their food.

8. The reciters of *Richas*, laud Indra,—the ruler of the universe, by virtue of his power,[2] whose gifts of wealth are thousandfold or even more.

AUVANKA IV.

SUKTA I. (XII.)

THE Deity is Agni ; the *Rishi* Medhátithi, the son of Kanwa ; the metre *Gáyatri.*

WE select Agni, the messenger of the celestials, their invoker,[3] the possesser of all riches, the perfect performer[4] (of sacrificial rites.)

2. (The sacrificers), always, invoke, with their in-

---

1 S'ushna is described as an *Asura* slain by Indra ; but this is evidently a metaphorical murder. *Sushna* means dryer up ; *Bhutánám. soshanam-hetum*, "the cause of the drying or withering of beings, heat or drought ; which Indra, as the rain, would put an end to.—Wilson.

2 The text is *Ojasá* : it may apply to the reciters, *i.e.*, with all their might or to Indra. Wilson has taken the former view. But the latter rendering appears to be better.

3 Agni is described in the *Taittriya Brahmana* as the messenger of the celestials.

4 The word in the Text is *Sukratu*.—Sáyana explains it both as *Shobhanakarmánam*, "good performer of the rite," and *Shobhanaprajnam* "endued with beneficial wisdom." Wilson has translated it as, "the protector of this rite."

vocations Agni, the lord of men,[1] the carrier of oblations, the beloved of many.

3. Agni generated[2] (by attrition), bring here the celestials to the clipped sacred grass; thou art their invoker for us, and art to be adored.

4. Since thou performest the duty of messenger, arouse them desirous of the oblation; sit down with them on the sacred grass.

5. Resplendent Agni, invoked by oblations of clarified butter, consume our enemies who have been joined by *Rákshasás.*[3]

6. Agni,—the intelligent, the young,[4] the protector[5] of the dwelling (of the sacrificer), the carrier of offerings, whose mouth is the vehicle of oblation,—is kindled by Agni.

7. (O Ye chanters) approach and praise, in the sacrifice, Agni, the intelligent, the truthful, the resplendent, the destroyer of enemies.[6]

8. O resplendent Agni, thou becomest the sure protector of that sacrificer who worships thee,—the messenger of the celestials.

---

1 *Vispati.* *Vis* means *Prajáh*, "progeny, people, or man.

2 The Text is *Jajánáh*, "being born," that is being artificially produced by the friction of two pieces of a particular species of wood, that of *Premna spinosa*, used for the purpose—*Wilson.*

3 The word in the Text is *Rakshaswinah.*—Wilson has rendered it as, "defended by evil spirits," literally, it means joined by *Rákshasás.*

4 In this name *Yavishtha*, which is never given to any other Vedic Deity, we may recognize the Hellenic Hephaistos—Cox's *Mythology of Aryan Nations.*

5 *Grihapati.*—But *pati* is most usually interpreted by Sáyana, as, *pálaka* the cherisher or protector, hence it characterises Agni as the protector "of the sacrificer's dwelling."

6 It may, also, mean "the remover of diseases."

9. Be propitious, *Pávaka*,[1] to him, who, presenting oblations for the gratification of the celestials, approaches Agni.

10. Agni, the bright, the purifier, bring, here, the celestials to this our sacrifice, to our oblations.

11. Lauded with our newest hymn, confer on us riches, food and heroic sons.

12. Agni, shining with pure radiance, and charged with all the invocations of the celestials, be pleased by this our hymn.

SUKTA II. (XIII.)[2]

The *Riski* and the metre are the same, but the hymn is addressed to a number of deified objects generally named *Apri*. The first five stanzas describe the various forms of Agni; the sixth the doors of the sacrificial chamber; the seventh morning and night; the eighth two deified priests; the ninth the goddess *Ilá*, *Saraswati* and *Bhárati*; the tenth *Twashtri*; the eleventh *Vanaspati*; and the twelfth *Swáhá*. They are all connected with Agni.

AGNI, Susamiddha,[3] the invoker, the purifier, bring, here, the celestials, to the offerers of our oblation and do thou sacrifice.

---

1 Literally "purifier;" a name of Agni.

2 This Sukta is called *Apri* Sukta. It used to be applied in the sacrifice of animals. There are ten *Apri* Suktas in all the ten *Mandalas* of the Rig-Veda. The enumeration is as follows :—

1st	Mandala—	13th, 142nd and 188th Suktas.
2nd	„	3rd Sukta.
3rd	„	4th „
5th	„	5th „
7th	„	2nd „
9th	„	5th „
10th	„	70th and 110th Suktas.

3 *Su*, well; *Sam*, completely; and *iddha*, kindled ;—" the thoroughly kindled.

2. Intelligent Tanunapat,[1] carry to-day our well-flavoured sacrifice to the celestials for their food.

3. Here, in this sacrifice, I invoke the beloved Narâsansa,[2] the sweet-tongued, the offerer of oblations.

4. O Agni, Ilita,[3] bring, hither, the celestials, in an easy-going chariot; for thou art the invoker elected by men.

5. Learned priests spread the sacred grass *Varhis*,[4] bundled together and covered with clarified butter and on which is seen ambrosia-like clarified butter.[5]

6. Let the bright doors,[6] the multiplier of sacrifice, not visited by multitudes of people, be set open, for surely to-day is the sacrifice to be made.

7. I invoke the lovely night and dawn,[7] to sit upon the sacred grass, at this our sacrifice.

8. I invoke the two beautiful-tongued[8] divine and intelligent invokers,[9] that they may celebrate this our sacrifice.

---

1 *Tanunapat.*—"The devourer of clarified butter," or, according to another Etymology "the consumer of its own substance (*tanu*), a fuel." *Napât* occurs in *Nirghanta*, as the synonym of *tanaya* son or offspring; but in this compound the second member is considered to be either *ad* who eats, or *pá* who preserves, the latter with *na* prefixed, *napát*, "who does not preserve, who destroys."—*Wilson.*

2 Lauded by men.

3 The worshipped;—from the root *ila*, "to adore."

4 *Varhis* is, also, an appellative of Agni.

5 The word *amrita* may either imply the clarified butter sprinkled on the grass, or the immortal Agni.

6 Doors of the sacrificial chamber, are considered as the personification of Agni.

7 They signify the two forms of Fire presiding over those seasons.

8 It may mean, also, *Priyavachanan*, literally "sweet-speeched, or eloquent," as Wilson has rendered it.

9 The two Agnis.

9. May the three delight-giving and undecaying Goddesses—Ilá, Saraswatí and Mahí,[1] sit down upon the sacred grass.

10. The foremost Twashtri,[2] having various forms, I invoke; may he be solely ours.

11. Present, Divine Vanaspati,[3] our oblations to the Celestials; may the giver come by true knowledge.

12. Perform the sacrifice, conveyed through Swáhá[4] to Indra, in the house of the sacrificer; therefore I invoke the Celestials here.

SUKTA III (XIV).

THE Rishi and metre the same; but the hymn is addressed to Agni and other Divinities named and to the Vis'wadévás.

AGNI, come, with all the Deities, in this sacrifice, to our service and to our praises, to drink the *Soma*-Juice and perform the sacrifice (for us).

2. Intelligent Agni, *Kanwas*[5] invoke thee and highly speak of thy works. Come, O Agni, with the Celestials.

---

1 These are personifications of Agni; they are, also, called the Three personified Flames of Fire. *Mahí* is said to be a synonym of *Bhárati*. As Goddesses, *Ilá* represents the Earth; *Saraswatí*, the consort of *Brahmá* is the presiding Deity of Eloquence and *Mahí*, Speech, the consort of *Bharata*. But these mythological personifications belong to the Post-Vedic Period.

2 *Twashtri*, in the popular system, represents the Divine Architect. He is, also, one of the twelve *A'dityas*: here he is Fire.

3 Literally, "the Lord of Woods," or "a large tree," but, here, Agni.

4 An exclamation used in pouring the oblation to Fire. Here, it is identified with Agni.

5 Literally, "descendants of *Kanwa*;" but the Scholiast explains it as "intelligent *Ritwijas*."

3. (Offer sacrificial offerings)[1] to Indra, Váyu, Vṛihaspati, Mitra, Agni, Pushan and Bhaga, the A'dityas and troops of Maruts.

4. For you, are specially prepared all these *Soma*-Juices, satisfying, exhilarating, sweet, falling in drops and placed in ladles.

5. Having lopped the sacred grass, the intelligent priests, desirous of protection, laud thee with oblations and ornaments.

6. Let the steeds, which convey thee, rendered plump with being fed with clarified butter[2] and harnessed at will, bring the Celestials to drink the *Soma*-Juice.

7. Agni, unite these (Deities), worshipful and augmenters of sacrifices, with their wives; O beautiful-tongued, make them partake of the sweet *Soma*-Juice.

---

1 The ellipsis is supplied by the Commentator. Mitra, Pushan and Bhaga are forms of the Sun or A'dityás. They are the descendants of Aditi. In the 27th *Sukta* of the Second *Mandala* of the Rig-*Véda*, Six A'dityas are mentioned, *viz*., Mitra, Aryamá, Bhaga, Varuna, Daksha, and Angs'a. In the 114th *Sukta* of the 9th *Mandala*, the number is Seven, but their names are not mentioned. In the 72nd *Sukta* of the 10th *Mandala*, Eight sons of Aditi are mentioned. In *Taittiriya Bráhmana* Eight A'dityas are mentioned, *viz*., Dhátá, Aryamá, Mitra, Varuna, Angs'a, Bhaga, Indra and Vivaswán. In the *Satapatha Bráhmana* twelve A'dityas are mentioned. They are the Suns in the Twelve Months of the Year.

"Aditi, an ancient goddess, is in reality the earliest name invented to express the Infinite; not the Infinite as the result of a long process of abstract reasoning, but the visible Infinite, visible by the naked eye, etc."—MaxMüller's, Rig-*Véda*.

Pandit Satyavrata Sámas'ramí thus describes the A'dityas:—*Aruna* rises in the morning just after dawn; Bhaga appears thereafter when the rays of the Sun become a little stronger; thereafter the Sun is called Púsha till his rays do not become the fiercest; in the fore noon the Sun is called Aryamá, and in the noon, he is called Vish*nu*."

2 This is how Sáyana explains the expression. Wilson renders it as "glossy-backed."

8. Let those Celestials, who are worthy of being offered oblations and lauded, drink, with thy tongue, of the sweet *Soma*-Juice just before the termination of the sacrifice.[1]

9. Let the intelligent invoker (of the Celestials) bring hither, from the resplendent solar region, all the Divinities awaking with the dawn.

10. Agni, with all the Celestials—with Indra, Vâyu and the effulgent forms of Mitra, drink the sweet *Soma*-Juice.

11. Agni, appointed by man as the invoker (of the Celestials), preside over his sacrifice; complete this sacrifice of ours.

12. Yoke, Divine Agni, this quick-coursing and strong mares, *Rohitaḥ*[2] to thy chariot, and, by them, bring hither the Celestials.

SUKTA IV (XV).

THE *Rishi* and metre the same, the Deity is *Ritu*[3]; but in each stanza some other familiar Deity is associated with him.

INDRA, drink with *Ritu*, the *Soma*-Juice; may these satisfying drops, ever abiding in thy stomach, enter into thee.

---

1 The Text is *Vashathkriti*: The word *Vashat* is uttered when a sacrifice is about to be completed. Sáyana explains it as *Vashathárkále* "at the time of *Vashathár*," or "a sacrifice in which the word *Vashat* is uttered."

2 The Text is *Arushí haritaḥ Rohitaḥ*:—Sáyana means by the word *Rohitas*, the horses of Agni, and uses the other two words as adjectives, meaning by *Arushi*, "quick-coursing;" and by *Haritas* "capable of carrying." MaxMüller interprets *Arushi* as the red horses of Agni and uses the other two words as adjectives.

3 Personification of season.

2. Maruts, drink with *R*itu, from the sacrificial vessel *Potri*; consecrate the rite, for you are bountiful.

3. Neshtri,[1] with thy wife, commend our sacrifice to the Celestials; drink with *R*itu; for thou art the giver of jewels.

4. Agni, bring hither the Celestials, arrange them in three places,[2] bedeck them with ornaments; drink with *R*itu.

5. Drink the *Soma*-Juice, Indra, from the valuable vessel of *Brâhmana*[3] after *R*itu, since thy friendship with him is uninterrupted.

6. Mitra and Varuna, performers of promised deeds, be present with *R*itu at our sacrifice, efficacious and undisturbed (by enemies).

7. (The priests), desirous of riches, having stones in their hands (for bringing the *Soma*-Plant), laud the Divine (Agni) Dravinodâs,[4] both in the primary and subsidiary sacrifices.[5]

8. May Dravinodâs give us riches we have heard of; we ask them, for the Celestials.

---

1 *Neshtri* is another name of *Twashtri*, from his having assumed, it is said, upon some occasion, the function of *Neshtri* or priest so denominated at a saqrifice.—*Wilson*.

2 Either at the three daily ceremonies, at dawn, mid-day and sunset, or in the three fires lighted at sacrifices.—*Wilson*.

3 The Text is obscure. *Brâhmanâd-râdhasah* is literally from Brahmanical wealth; but the latter is explained a costly vessel. The *Brâhmanachchhansi* is one of the sixteen priests employed in sacrifices; his function may be to hold some ladle or vase in which the offering is presented.—*Wilson*.

4 *Dravinodâs* is an epithet of Agni, meaning "the giver of wealth or strength."

5 In the *Adhwara* and in the *Yajñas*, the first is said to be the primary or essential ceremony, *prakriti-rupa*, such as the *Agnisthoma*; the second, the modified ceremonies, *Vikriti-rupéshu*, such as the *Ukthya*.—*Wilson*.

9. Dravinodâs wishes to drink with the Ritus from the cup of Neshtri; hasten (priests to the sacrificial chamber); present the oblation and depart.

10. Since, Dravinodâs, we worship thee for the fourth time along with the *R*itus, do thou give us wealth.

11. As'wins, performers of pious deeds, bright with sacrificial fires, accepters, with the *R*itus, of sacrifice, drink the sweet juice.

12. Agni, the giver of rewards, identical with household fire, thou art the performer of sacrifice with *R*itu; worship the Celestials, on behalf of the sacrificer seeking them.

SUKTA V (XVI).

The *Rishi* and metre the same; the Deity is Indra.

INDRA, let thy horses bring here the, showerer of riches to drink the *Soma*-Juice; may (the priests) radiant as the Sun (make thee manifest).

2. Let his horses *Hari* convey Indra in an easy-going chariot here where these grains (of parched barley), steeped in clarified butter, are strewn (upon the altar).

3. We invoke Indra at the morning rite; we invoke him at the time of the celebration of the sacrifice; we invoke him to drink the *Soma*-Juice (at the time of completion).

4. Come Indra, with thy long-maned steeds, near our pressed *Soma*-Juice; we invoke, when *Soma*-Juice is extracted and poured out.

5. Do thou come to this our praise, to this our sacrifice, for which the libation is prepared; drink like a thirsty *Goura*-deer.

6. These dripping *Soma*-Juices are effused upon the sacred grass; drink them, Indra, for gaining strength.

7. Indra, may this most excellent hymn touch thy heart and afford thee delight; thereafter drink the extracted *Soma*-Juice.

8. Indra, the destroyer of enemies, goes, forsooth, to every sacrifice where the libation is poured out, to drink the *Soma*-Juice for (his) exhilaration.

9. S'atakratu, do thou fully satisfy our desires with (the gift of) kine and horses; being filled with perfect meditation we laud thee.

SUKTA VI. (XVII).

The metre and *Rishi* the same; the Deities Indra and Varuna conjointly.

I SEEK the protection of the sovereign rulers[1] Indra and Varuṇa; when thus prayed for, they make us happy.

2. For you are ever ready, guardians of mankind, to grant protection on the appeal of a minister such as I am.

3. Satisfy us with riches, Indra and Varuṇa, according to our desires; we desire you ever near us.

4. (The libations) of our holy rites have been mixed; (the laudations) of our right-minded priests have been mixed; may we, therefore, become the foremost among the givers of food.[2]

---

1 *Samrájoh*, of the two emperors; but *Rájá* is, in general, equivocally used, meaning shining, bright, as well as royal, so that Sáyana explains the term "possessed of extensive dominion," or "shining very brilliantly."—*Wilson*.

2 The Stanza is obscurely worded. We have in the Text *Yuvaku sachinám*, *Yuváku sumatinám*; the former (*sachinám*) is explained, a mixture of butter milk, water and meat, suited for acts of religious worship; the latter, the combination of choice expressions and praises which are the suitable phraseology of the right-minded or the pious (*sumatinám*).

5. Indra is a giver among the givers of thousands; Varuṇa is to be lauded among those who are deserving of laudation.

6. Through their protection we enjoy (riches) and husband them, and may there be an abundance of wealth.

7. I invoke you both Indra and Varuṇa for manifold riches: make us perfectly victorious.

8. Indra and Varuṇa, speedily bestow happiness on us for our minds are willing to serve you properly.

9. May the excellent hymn, which I offer to Indra and Varuṇa, reach you both; that conjoint praise which you (accepting) dignify.

ANUVAKA V.

SUKTA I. (XVIII.)

THE metre and *Rishi* the same. The first five stanzas are addressed to Brâhmanaspati, associated, in the fourth, with Indra and Soma; and, in the fifth, with them and Dakshinâ: the three next are addressed to Sadasaspati; and the ninth to the same or to Narás'amsa.

BRAHMANASPATI,[1] make the offerer of libation (*i.e.*, myself) illustrious among the Celestials like Kakshivat, the son of Us'ij.[2]

Ramânâth Saraswatî translates the word *Yuvaku* as "your," and renderes the stanza thus,—"may we gain your favour in the shape of protection and wealth."

1 The Deity *Brahmanaspati* is the same as *Vrikaspati*. This will be evident when the reader goes to the 23rd *Sukta* of the Second *Mandala*. Sáyana gives no account of the station of this Deity. Dr. Roth defines him as the Deity of sacred prayer, or, perhaps, of the Text of the *Véda*. The etymology justifies this definition. Sáyana, however, understands by the word *Brahma* eulogy or prayer.

2 This story is to be found in several of the *Purânás*, especially the *Matysa* and *Vâyu*, as well as in the *Mahâbhârata*. *Kakshivat* was

2. May he, who is possessed of riches, the destroyer of diseases, the acquirer of riches, the augmenter of nourishment, the prompt giver of rewards, favour us.

3. Protect us, Brahmaṇaspati, so that caluminous censure of the malevolent may not touch us.

4. That heroic mortal, whom Indra, Brahmaṇaspati and *Soma* protect, never perishes.

5. Do thou, Brahmaṇaspati and do you, *Soma*, Indra and Dakshiṇâ[1] protect that man from sin.

6. I solicit intelligence from Sadasaspati,[2] the wonderful, the friend of Indra, the beautiful and the giver of riches.

7. Without whose help, the sacrifice, even of the wise, is not perfected; he pervades the association of our thoughts.[3]

8. He rewards the presenter of the oblation; he brings the sacrifice to a consummate close; (through him) our invocation reaches the Celestials.

9. I have seen Narâs'aṁsa,[4] the most resolute, the most celebrated and radiant as the sky.

---

the son of *Dirghatamas* by Usij, a female servant of the Queen of the *Kalinga Rájá*, whom her husband had desired to submit to the embraces of the Sage, in order that he might beget a son. The Queen substituted her bondmaid Usij; the Sage, cognizant of the deception, sanctified Usij and begot by her a son named *Kakshivat*, who through his affiliation by *Kalinga* was a Kshatriya, but as the son of *Dirghatamas* was a *Bráhmana*; he was also a *Rishi*.—*Wilson*.

1 Literally it means a present made to a Bráhmana at the termination of a religious rite. But here it is personified as a female divinity.

2 Literally, the *pati* (protector) of *sadas* (assembly); it is here a name of Agni.

3 The Text is *dhinám Yogam invati* which may mean "he pervades the association of our minds," or "the object of our pious acts."

4 It is an appellation of Agni, meaning "he who is to be praised by men." According to the *Kátthakas*, it means the personified *Yajna* or sacrifice at which men (*nara*) praise (*S'ansanti*) the Celestials.

SUKTA II. (XIX.)

The metre and Rishi the same; Agni and the Maruts are the Deities.

AGNI, thou art invoked, to this perfect sacrifice, to drink the *Soma*-Juice;[1] come, Agni, with the Maruts.

2. There is no greater Deity or man, who can oust thee of thy rite, O Agni, who art supremely powerful: come with the Maruts.

3. Come, Agni, with the Maruts, who are all[2] (*i.e.*, seven in number) radiant,[3] and devoid of malignity, and who know (how to cause the descent) of great waters.[4]

4. Come, Agni, with the Maruts, who are fierce, and pour down rain,[5] and are unequalled in strength.

5. Come, Agni, with the Maruts, who are beautiful, of terrific forms, who are possessors of profuse wealth, and are devourers of the malevolent.

6. Come, Agni, with the Maruts, who are Divinities residing in the radiant heaven above the Sun.[6]

7. Come, Agni, with the Maruts, who scatter the clouds, and agitate the sea full of water.

---

1 The Text is *gopithúya*:—Sáyana explains it as, *Somapánáya*, *i.e.*, to drink *Soma*-Juice. MaxMüller translates it as, "For a draught of milk." We prefer Sáyana's explanation, for Vedic Deities are, always, mentioned as drinking *Soma*-Juice.

2 *Visve*:—Literally, all: here it refers to the seven troops of the Maruts.

3 *Devásah*:—The Scholiast explains it as, *dyotamána*, radiant. Wilson translates it as, "Divine."

4 MaxMüller translates the expression as, "Who know of the great sky;" but we follow Sáyana's rendering; for many Texts attribute to the Maruts the power of creating rain.

5 *Arka* means water or rain: but MaxMüller translates the expression *arkam ánrichuh* as, "Who sing their song."

6 *Nákasya adhi*. Sáyana explains it as, "Above the Sun," but MaxMüller translates *Náka* as, "Firmament."

8. Come, Agni, with the Maruts, who spread (through the sky) along with the rays (of the Sun), and, with their strength, agitate the sea.

9. Come, Agni, with the Maruts, I pour out the sweet *Soma*-Juice for thy drinking (as of old).[1]

---

1 MaxMüller translates the expression as, "For the early draught."

SECOND ADHYAYA.

ANUVAKA V.—(*Continued.*)

SUKTA III. (XX.)

THE metre and *Rishi* the same: the Deities are *Ribhus.*

THIS hymn, the bestower of many beautiful jewels, has been addressed, by the sages, with their own mouths, to the Deities having birth.[1]

2. They, who created, by their mind (*i.e.*, will-power), for Indra the steeds that are harnessed at his words, have spread over this (our) sacrifice with the ceremonial utensils.[2]

---

1 The Text is *devdya janmane* :—The Scholiast explains *deváya* as, *deva-sanghdya*, *i.e.*. a collection of Divinities, here referring to *Ribhus* and *janmane* as *jáyamánáya*, *i.e.*, being born or having birth.

Ribhus were, formerly, men, but, by ascetic penances, they attained to the dignity of the Celestials. The *Ribhus* were the three sons of *Sudhanwan*, the son of *Angiras*, severally named *Ribhu*, *Vibhu* and *Vája*: but they were called *Ribhus*, from the name of the elder. Through their assiduous performance of good works, they acquired divinity, exercised superhuman powers and became entitled to receive praise and adoration.

2 The Text is *s'ámibhir-yajnam-ás'ata*: It has been rendered variously by different scholars. Sáyana has interpreted the expression as "*graha chamasádi nishpádanah rupai karmabhir, yajnam ashmadiyám, ás'ata vyaptavanta*," *i.e.*, they have pervaded (or accepted) our sacrifice, performed with those acts which are executed by the means of tongs, ladles and other (utensils employed in making oblations). Wilson translates it as, "Have partaken of the sacrifice performed with holy acts." Mr. Stevenson, "They pervade our sacrifice by purificatory rites." Rosen, "*Ceremoniis sacrificium.*" Langlois, "*Ils ont entoure le sacrifice de ceremonies.*" The expression suggests that perhaps the *Ribhus* were the inventors of those sacrificial implements.

3. They constructed for the Nâsatyas a car going everywhere and pleasant to sit on, and a cow yielding milk.[1]

4. The *R*ibhus, endued with the power of making their prayers unfailing, fond of peace, and successful[2] (in all pious deeds), made[3] their (aged) parents young.

5. *R*ibhus, the intoxicating *Soma*-Juices are offered to you, along with Indra, attended by the Maruts, and along with the radiant A'dityas.[4]

6. The *R*ibhus have divided, into four, the new ladle, which was completely constructed by the divine Twashtri.[5]

7. May they, moved by our excellent praises, give to (the priest, who, on) our (behalf), offers libations of

---

1 The word is *taksham* : the meaning of the verb implies mechanical formation. The *Ribhus* may have been the first to attempt the bodily representation of these appendages of *Indra* and *As'wins*.—*Wilson*.

2 The Text is *Vishthi* : Sáyana explaints it as, *Vyápti-Yukldh*, *i.e.*, meeting with no opposition in all acts, on account of the never-failing potency of their prayers.

3 *Akrata*, from *kri* to make. It does not mean here 'mechanical making.'

4 According to As'waláyana, as quoted by Sáyana, the libations offered at the third daily, or evening, sacrifice, are presented to Indra, along with the *A'dityas*, together with *Ribhu*, *Vibhu*, *Vája*, with *Vrihaspati* and the *Vis'wadévas*.—*Wilson*.

5 *Twashtri*, is described in the *Puránas* as an artizan of the celestials. In the *Védás*, he is mentioned as a Divinity who works as a carpenter for the Deities. The Scholiast, also, describes the *Ribhus* as the disciples of *Twashtri*. The act, of their making one ladle four, has very likely some more references to some innovation in the objects of libation, than to the mere multiplication of the wooden vessel. The *Nitimañjari* says, that Agni, coming to the sacrifice, performed by the *Ribhus*, became as one of them. And, to give him a share in the sacrifice, they divided the ladle into four.

Soma-Juice, three sorts of precious articles, one by one, and perfect seven times seven sacrifices.[1]

8. Offerers of sacrifices, they hold[2] (immortality, although born as mortals); by their good deeds, they obtain, among the Celestials, a share of sacrifices.

SUKTA IV. (XXI.)

Rishi and metre the same; the hymn is addressed to Indra and Agni.

I INVOKE in this sacrifice, Indra and Agni, to whom we wish to present our laudatory verses; let them, who are both profuse drinkers of the *Soma*-Juice, drink *Soma.*

2. Laud, men, Indra and Agni in sacrifices; decorate them with various ornaments and hymn them with laudatory verses.

3. We invoke Indra and Agni for singing the praises of our friend (the instituter of the rite): we invoke those drinkers of *Soma*, to drink the libation.

4. We invoke the two fierce Deities, near the rite where the libation is prepared: Indra and Agni come here.

---

1 *Tirá Sáptáni*: The Scholiast considers that *trih* may be applied to precious things, as meaning best, middling, worst, or to *sáptáni*, seven sacrifices, as classed under three heads. Thus, one class consists of the *Agnyádheyam*, seven ceremonies in which clarified butter is offered on fire; one class consists of the *Páka-Yajñas* in which dressed viands are offered to the *Vis'wadévás* and others; and one comprehends *Agnisthoma* class, in which libations of *Soma*-Juice are the characteristic offering.—*Wilson.*

If, however, the Text is literally followed, the translation would be,—"Give, one by one, thrice seven sorts of precious articles."

2 The Text is *Adharayanta*, literally, 'held' or 'enjoyed.' The Scholiast explains it fully: they were mortals, but they obtained immortality, by performing many good deeds. The *Ribhus* acquired the prestige of drinking *Soma* in the company of the Deities.

5. May those two powerful Indra and Agni, the guardians of the assembly, make the Rákshasás innocuous, and may the devourers (of men) be destitute of progeny.

6. By this unfailing sacrifice, be you rendered vigilant, Indra and Agni, in the station which affords knowledge (of the fruits of deeds), and grant us happiness.

SUKTA V. (XXII.)

THE *Rishi* and metre the same; the hymn contains twenty-one stanzas which are addressed to various Deities; or four, to the As'wins and four, to Sávitri; the next two, to Agni; the eleventh, to the goddesses collectively; the twelfth to the wives of Indra, Varuna and Agni; the two next, to heaven and earth; the fifteenth, to earth alone; the last six, to Vishnu.

(O PRIEST,) awaken the As'wins, associated for the morning (libation); let them, both, come here to drink of the *Soma*-Juice.

2. We invoke the two Divine As'wins, having the most excellent car, the best of charioteers, and residing in the celestial region.

3. As'wins, stir up[1] the sacrifice, with your whip, that is wet with the foam (of your horses) and lashing loudly.

4. As'wins, the residence, of the offerer of libation, where you are going to in your car, is not far from you.

---

1 *Mimikshatam*, mix intimately the juice of the *Soma*. It is not clear how this is to be done with the whip, allusion to which only intimates, it is said, that the As'wins should come quickly. *Tayá*, by that, may, also, mean, with that—come with that your whip; or *Kasá*, commonly a whip, may mean speech; in which case *Madhumati* and *Sunritivati*, explained wet and loud, will signify sweet and veracious—come with such speech, As'wins, and taste the libation.—*Wilson*.

5. I invoke the golden-handed Sâvitri,[1] to protect me: he will let us know of the station of the sacrificers.

6. Hymn Sâvitri, who is the drier up of water,[2] for our protection: we wish to celebrate his sacrifice.

7. We invoke Sâvitri, the enlightener of men and the distributer of various home-insuring wealth.

8. Sit down, friends, Sâvitri is soon to be lauded by us: shines there the giver of riches.

9. Agni, bring, here, the loving wives of the Celestials and Twastri, to drink the *Soma*-Juice.

10. Agni, bring the wives of the Celestials here, for our protection. O youthful (Agni), bring Hotrâ, Bhárati, Varutri and the adorable Dhishanâ.[3]

11. May the goddesses, whose wings are unclipt,[4] the protectresses of mankind, be propitiated with us, by giving us protection and great felicity.

12. I invoke Indráṇi, Varuṇaṇi and Agneyi, for our welfare, and to drink the *Soma*-Juice.

13. May the great heaven and earth sprinkle this sacrifice (with their dews) and fill us with nutriment.

14. The intelligent taste, through their pious deeds, the waters of these two, resembling clarified butter

---

1 Sávitri is a synonym of the Sun. There is a *Vaidik* legend about his being golden-handed. At a sacrifice of the celestials, Súrya undertook the office of *Ritwij*, but placed himself in the station of *Brahmâ*. The *Adhyáryu* priests, seeing him in that position, gave him the oblation, termed *Prasitra*, which cut off that hand of *Súrya* which had improperly accepted it. Thereupon, he was given a golden hand by them. It is, really, a figurative expression, descriptive of solar effulgence.

2 Here the word *Napat* is taken in its literal, sense, *i.e.*, who does not cherish but dries up water by his heat.

3 Hotrá is called the wife of Agni; Bhárati, one of the A'dityas and Dhishaná is *Vag-Dévî* or the Goddess of Speech.

4 The wives of the Celestials, being in the form of birds, no one had cut their wings.

and (abiding) in the permanent region of the *Gandharvas.*[1]

15. O earth, be thou extensive, free from thorns, and our abiding place; give us profuse happiness.

16. May the Deities protect us (from that portion) of the earth whence Vishṇu, (aided) by the seven metres, stepped.[2]

17. Vishṇu traversed this (world): three times he planted his foot,[3] and the universe was enveloped by his foot covered with dust.

18. Vishṇu, the preserver, the uninjurable, stepped three steps, upholding righteousness.

19. Behold the deeds of Vishṇu, by virtue of which the sacrificer performs all rites: he is the worthy friend of Indra.

20. The wise, always, behold the great station of Vishṇu as the eye sees, ranging everywhere in the sky.

---

1 *Antariksha*, or firmament between heaven and earth, is the region of the Gandharvas, Yakshas and Apsarás.

2 Sáyana explains *Saptadhamabhi* as, "Seven metres." Muir explains it as, "Through the seven regions." According to the *Taittiriyas*, as cited by the Scholiast, "The Celestials, headed by Vishnu, subdued the invincible earth, using the seven metres of the Védás as their instruments.

3 Commentators disagree about the meaning of the sentence *tredhá nidadhe padam*, *i.e.*, thrice he planted his step. According to Sákapuni it was on earth, in the firmament, in heaven; according to Aurnavábha, on *Samárohana* or the eastern mountain, on *Vishnupada*, the meridian sky, and *Gayas'iras*, the western mountain; thus identifying Vishnu with the Sun; and his three paces, with the rise, culmination and setting of the luminary. Allusion is made to the three paces of Vishnu in the *Vajasaneyi Samhitá* of the *Yajur Veda*, and the Scholiast there explains them to imply the presence of Vishnu in the three regions of earth, air and heaven, in the forms, respectively, of Agni, Váyu and Súrya, Fire, Wind and the Sun.

21. The intelligent, ever vigilant and always singing his praises, illumine the great station of Vishṇu.

SUKTA VI. (XXIII.)

THE *Rishi* is Medhátithi, the son of Kanwa; the metre of the first eighteen stanzas is *Gáyatrí*; that in the nineteenth stanza, *Ushnik*; and in the rest, *Anuṣhṭubh*. The hymn contains twenty-four stanzas, of which the first is addressed to Váyu; then three, to Mitra and Varuna; three, to Indra and the Maruts; three, to the Vis'wadévás; three to Pushán; seven and a half to the Waters; and the last verse and a half, to Agni.

THESE *Soma*-Juices, strong and full of blessings, have been poured out: come, Váyu, and drink them off as presented.

2. We invoke both the Deities,—Indra and Váyu, residing in the firmament, to drink off this *Soma*-Juice.

3. The intelligent invoke, for their protection, Indra and Váyu, who are fleet like the mind, have a thousand eyes[1] and are protectors of sacrifices.

4. We invoke Mitra and Varuṇa, who are present at the sacrificial ground and of pure strength, to drink the *Soma*-Juice.

5. I invoke Mitra and Varuṇa, who, with true speech, multiply pious deeds and protect the light of the sacrifice.

6. May Varuṇa protect us fully; may Mitra defend us with all defences; may they make us immensely rich.

---

1 The expression *Sahasráksha*, which is generally applied to Indra, and never to Váyu, is applied here to both for grammatical construction.

7. We invoke Indra, together with the Maruts, to drink the *Soma*-Juice: may he, with his companions, be satisfied.

8. Divine Maruts, of whom Indra is the king and Pushân,[1] the benefactor,—all hear my invocations.

9. Liberal Maruts, associated with powerful Indra, destroy Vritra; let not the evil one reign supreme over us.

10. We invoke all the Divine Maruts, who are fierce and have the (many-coloured) earth for their mother,[2] to drink the *Soma*-Juice.

11. Leaders, when you receive an auspicious offering, then the proud shout of the Maruts comes like that of the conquerors.

12. May the Maruts, born from the effulgent lightning,[3] protect us and render us happy.

13. Resplendent and quick-coursing Pushân, bring from heaven the (*Soma*-)Juice together with the variegated sacred grass as (a man brings back) a lost animal.

14. The resplendent Pushân has found the effulgent *Soma*-Juice concealed, placed in a cave,[4] strewed amongst the sacred grass.

15. Indeed, he brought to me in succession the six[5] (seasons) connected with the drops (of the *Soma*-

---

1 The *Maruts* are styled *Pusharátayah*, of whom *Pushan* is the donor.—*Wilson.*

2 The Text literally means,—"Who have *Pris'ni* for their mother." According to Sáyana, *Pris'ni* is the many-coloured earth.

3 *Haskarad-Vidyutah*: the Commentator explains it as "Variously shining."

4 According to the Scholiast, *guha sadrise durgame dyuoloke*, *i.e.*, in heaven, difficult of access like a cave.

5 The Text has only *shat*, six: the Commentator explains it as "Six Seasons," adding *Vasantadin Ritun*—the Seasons, Spring and the rest."

Juice) as (a husbandman) repeatedly ploughs (the earth) for barley.

16. Friendly Waters, that are mothers to us who are desirous of sacrificing, flow by the paths (of sacrifice) qualifying the milk with sweetness.

17. May those Waters, which are near the Sun or are associated with the Sun, gladden our sacrifice.

18. I invoke the Divine Waters, which our kine drink: oblations should be offered to the Divine Flowing (Waters).

19. Ambrosia is in the Waters; medicinal herbs are in the Waters: Saintly Priests, be prompt in their praise.

20. *Soma* has said to me, (that) all medicines, Agni—the benefactor of the Universe, and all sorts of healing herbs are in the Waters.

21. Water, make perfect the medicine that prevents all diseases for my body, that I may long behold the Sun.

22. Water, wash away whatever sin is in me, what wrong I have done, what imprecation I have pronounced or what untruth I have spoken.

23. I have, this day, entered into the Waters: we have been associated with their essence. Agni, abiding in the Waters, come and fill me with vigour.

24. Agni, bestow on me vigour, progeny and life, so that the Celestials may know the (sacrifice) of this my (employer) and Indra, with the *R*ishis, may know it.

ANUVAKA VI.

SUKTA I. (XXIV.)

THE *Rishis* is S'unaḥs'épa,[1] the son of Ajígartta; the metre is *Trishtubh*, except in stanzas three, four and five in which it is *Gáyatri*. The first verse is addressed to Prajápati; the second, to Agni; the three next, to Savitri; or the last of the three, to Bhaga; the rest, to Varuna.

OF what Divinity, of what class amongst the immortals shall we invoke the sweet name?[2] Who will give us

---

1 The story of S'unaḥs'épa has been for some time known to Sanskrit students by the version of it presented in the *Rámáyana*. He is there called the son of the *Rishi Richaka* and is sold for a hundred coins by his father to Ambarisha, king of Ayodhyâ, as a victim for a human sacrifice; on the road he comes to the Lake Pushkara, where he sees Vis'wamitra and implores his succour, and learns from him a prayer, by the repetition of which at the stake, Indra is induced to come and set him free. It is obvious that this story has been derived from the Véda, for Vis'wamitra teaches him two *Gáthás*. Manu, also, alludes to the story (10, 105) where, it is said, Ajígartta incurred no guilt by giving up his son to be sacrificed, as it was to preserve himself and family from perishing with hunger. Kullukabhatta names the son S'unaḥs'épa, and refers for his authority to the *Bahwricha Bráhmana*. The story is told, in full detail, in the *Aitaréya Bráhmana*, but the Rájá is named Haris'chandra; he has no sons and worships Varuna, in order to obtain a son, promising to sacrifice to him his first-born; he has a son, in consequence, named Rohita; but when Varuna claims his victim, the king delays the sacrifice, under various pretexts, from time to time, until Rohita attains adolescence, when his father communicates to him the fate for which he was destined; Rohita refuses submission and spends several years in the forests, away from home: he, at last, meets there with Ajígartta, a *Rishi* in great distress, and persuades him to part with his second son, S'unaḥs'épa, to be substituted for Rohita as an offering to Varuna: the bargain is concluded, and S'unaḥs'épa is about to be sacrificed, when by the advice of Vis'wámitra, one of the officiating priests, he appeals to the gods, and is, ultimately, liberated.—*Wilson*.

2 "Of whom" (*Kásyá*) may, also, be rendered "of Brahmá," or "Prajápati," one of whose names, in the Véda, is *ka*.—*Wilson*.

to the great Aditi that I may, again, behold my father and mother.

2. Let us invoke the sweet name of Agni, the foremost amongst the Divinities, that he may give us to the great Aditi and that I may, again, behold my father and mother.

3. Ever protecting Sâvitri, we solicit thy protection, who art the lord of riches.

4. That wealth which has been kept in thy hands, which is commendable and free from envy or reproach.

5. O Sâvitri, who art the possessor of wealth, through thy protection we are busy with attaining the summit of affluence.

6. Varuṇa, these birds, that are flying, have not thy physical strength, or thy prowess, or thy anger; neither these waters nor the wind, which are flowing unceasingly, surpass thy speed.

7. The royal Varuṇa of pure strength, (residing) in the baseless firmament, sustains on high a heap of light, the rays (whereof) come downwards while their base is above; may they keep the vital airs concentrated in us.

8. The royal Varuṇa has, indeed, made wide the path of the Sun,[1] (by which) to travel on his daily course;—a path to course on in pathless (firmament): may he chastise the enemy who afflicts our heart.

9. Thine, O king, are a hundred and thousand medicaments: may thy favour be extensive and deep; keep, at a distance from us, Nirriti,[2] with his face turned

---

1 According to the Commentator, the Sun's course north and south of the equator is here alluded to: he does not explain what Varuna has to do with it.—*Wilson*.

2 The Deity of Sin.

back, and free us from whatever sin we may have committed.

10. These Constellations,[1] placed on high and visible by night, where do they go to in the day? The holy acts of Varuṇa are undisturbed: (by his command) the Moon shines by night.

11. Lauding thee with a hymn, I beg thee for that[2] (life) which the sacrificer solicits with oblations. Varuṇa, undisdainful, confer a thought upon us; lauded of many, do not take away my longevity.

12. This, they repeat to me, by night and by day: the understanding of my heart, also manifests it: may he, whom the fettered S'unḥas'épa has invoked,—may that royal Varuṇa, liberate us.

13. S'unḥasépa, caught and bound to the three-footed tree,[3] has invoked the son of Aditi; may the royal Varuṇa, wise and irresistible, set him free; may he let loose his bonds.

14. Varuṇa, we pacify thy wrath with bow, sacrifices and oblations: O Asura,[4] O Prachétaḥ, O king,

---

1 The Constellations, *Rikshaḥ,* may be either, it is said, the seven *R*ishis Ursa Major, or the Constellations generally.

*R*iksha, in the sense of bright, has become the name of the bear, so called either from his bright eyes or from his brilliant tawny fur....The same name, in the sense of the bright ones, had been applied, by the Vedic poets, to the stars in general, and more particularly to that Constellation which in northern parts of India was the most prominent.—Max Muller's *Science of Language,* Vol. II., P. 395.

2 The Text is only *that*: the Commentator adds *life.*

3 It means here, the sacrificial post.

4 Sáyana explains it as "averter of misfortune." The early Aryans used to designate the Deities they worshipped as *Asurás* or *Dévás.* Afterwards when they were divided into two bands, one class (*Irans*) called their Deities *Ahurs*; and the other (Aryans), *Dévás.* The latter used to vilify the Deities of the former by calling them *Asurás.*

be present in our sacrifice and mitigate the sins we have committed.

15. Varuṇa, loosen the upper band[1] by the higher part, loosen the middle band by the middle, loosen the lower band by the lower part. O Son of Aditi, without violating thy worship, we shall become freed from sin.

SUKTA II. (XXV.)

The hymn is addressed by S'unhas'épa to Varuna: the metre is *Gáyatrí.*

As people commit mistakes, so do we, Divine Varuṇa, daily disfigure thy worship with errors.

2. Being disregardful and bent upon destroying,[2] do not make us the objects of death; being thyself wrought up with rage, do not make us the objects of thy rage.

3. For our happiness, we propitiate thy mind, Varuṇa, with our praises, as a charioteer, his weary horse.

4. My meditations, shorn of anger, revert to the desire of highly precious life,[3] as birds hover round their nest.

5. When, for our happiness, shall we bring here Varuṇa—the powerful, leader of men, and the beholder of many?

---

1 These bands, according to Sáyana, are the legatures fastening the head, feet and the waist.

2 Sáyana explains the word *Hatnavé* as *pápakananas'ílasya*, *i.e.*, "Who by nature destroys sins." But as Varuna is described here as "being enraged and bent upon destroying," it is better to adopt the literal word meaning.

3 The Text is *Vasya ishtaye*. Sáyana explains it as *Vasumatáh*, precious, and supplies *jeevanasya*, life, after it.

6. Being pleased with the sacrificer, offering clarified butter, (Mitra and Varuṇa) are partaking of the common oblation, and do not disregard it.

7. He, who knows the course of birds, flying in the sky;—he, abiding in the ocean, knows the course of ships.[1]

8. He, accepting the rite, knows the twelve months, yielding (their respective) productions; who, also, knows what is supplementarily produced.[2]

9. He, who knows the path of the vast, the beautiful and the excellent wind; and who knows those who live above.

10. Varuṇa, the accepter of holy rites, the performer of excellent deeds, has sat down, amongst the Divine Progeny,[3] to exercise supreme dominion (over them).

11. Through him the wise man sees all the marvels that have been and will be worked.

---

1 This is the duty of Varuna, as described in the Védás; for he is the Deity of Water.

2 *Vedâya upajâyate*, who knows what is *upa* additionally or subordinately produced. The expression is obscure, but in connection with the preceding, *Védamâsodwâdasa*, who knows the twelve months, we cannot doubt the correctness of the Scholiast's conclusion, that the thirteenth, the supplementary or intercalary month of the Hindu luni-solar year, is alluded to; "that thirteenth or additional month which is produced of itself, in connection with the year." The passage is important, as indicating the concurrent use of the lunar and solar years at this period, and the method of adjusting the one to the other.—*Wilson*.

3 Dr. Roer translates the passage "among his subjects." Here the sovereignty of Varuna is distinctly specified. He has been described, in many places, as the Lord Paramount of the Deities and as being freed from sin and imperfection. It is clear that he was the earliest Deity, receiving adoration from the Aryans even when they lived with the Iranis, but was ultimately superseded by Indra.

12. May that greatly wise[1] son of Aditi, direct us every day in a righteous path and prolong our lives.

13. Wearing golden armour,[2] Varuṇa clothes his well-nourished (body) whence the rays are spread around.

14. Whom enemies dare not offend; the oppressors of mankind (cannot oppress him); the iniquitous (venture not to displease) that Divine (Being).

15. Who has made profuse food for mankind, and, especially, for our belly.

16. My meditations ever turn back to him, who is seen by many, as the kine return to the pastures.

17. Since my sweet oblation has been prepared, do you, like the offerer, eat the valued (oblation); we shall, then, have a pleasant conversation.

18. I have seen him, who is worthy of being seen by all. I have seen his car upon the earth: he has accepted my laudation.

19. Hear this my invocation, Varuṇa; make us happy to-day; desirous of protection I laud thee.

20. O intelligent Varuṇa, thou shinest over heaven and earth, and all the world; do thou hear and reply (to my prayer, seeking) prosperity.

21. Loosen our upper bands, the central and the lower, so that we may live.

---

1 The word in the Text is *Sukratu*. Sáyana explains it as *Shovonaprajña*, *i.e.*, "greatly wise." It may, also, mean "The performer of good deeds."

2 Sáyana explains *drápin hiranyam* as *Suvarnamayam Kavachám*, or mail "made of gold." It has been translated by some as *golden raiment*.

SUKTA III. (XXVI.)

The Author is supposed to be S'unhasépa; the hymn is addressed to Agni: the metre is *Gáyatrí*.

O THOU, worthy of being honoured with a sacrifice, O lord of food, cover thy investing radiance;[1] complete this our sacrifice.

2. Ever youthful, adorable Agni, (becoming) our ministrant priest, (lauded) with brilliant strains, (invested) with radiance, (do thou sit here).

3. O adorable (Agni), thou art [donor] (*i.e.*, thou dost give us all desirable objects); as a father, to a son; as a kinsman, to a kinsman; as a friend, to a friend.

4. May Varuṇa, Mitra and Aryyamaṇ,[2] destroyers of enemies, sit down upon our sacred grass, as they did at the sacrifice of Manu[3].

5. O sacrificer, born before us,[4] be pleased with this our sacrifice and with our friendship, and listen to this thy laudation.

6. Whatever daily and plentiful oblation we offer to any other Deity, is assuredly offered to thee.

7. May (Agni), the lord of men, the sacrificing priest, the gracious, the adorable, be loved of us; may we, possessed of holy fires, be loved of thee.

8. As the effulgent (priests), possessed of holy fires, have taken charge of our oblation, so we, with holy fires, pray to thee.

---

1 The Text has only *Vastráni*, "clothes." Sáyana explains it as *achhádakáni têjánsi*, "investing radiance."

2 A monthly form of the Sun, said to preside over the Twilight.

3 The Scholiast explains it as "the sacrifice of Manu, the Prajápati."

4 *Purvya Hotri*, *i.e.*, "The *Hotri*, born before us." Sáyana refers to Agni.

9. O immortal Agni, let us, both—mortals (and yourself), praise mutually.

10. Agni, son of strength,[1] accept, this our sacrifice and laudation, with all fires, and grant us food.

SUKTA IV. (XXVII.)

THE *Rishi*, the Deity and metre are the same as before, except in the last stanza, where the metre is *Trishtubh* and the Vis'wadévás are addressed.

I (PROCEED) to address thee, the lord paramount of sacrifices, with encomiastic verses, (for thou dost disperse our enemies) like a horse (who brushes off flies with) his tail.[2]

2. May he, the son of strength, who moves everywhere quickly, be propitiated with us and shower down (wished-for objects).

3. Do thou Agni, who goest everywhere, ever protect us, whether near or at a distance from men wishing to do us mischief.

4. Agni, announce, to the Celestials, this our offering and these altogether new *Gáyatri* verses.

5. Reach us to the most excellent food, (that is in heaven), to the middling food (that is in the mid-air); grant us the wealth, that is near (*i.e.*, on the earth).

6. Thou, Chitrabhánu,[3] art the distributor of wealth, as the waves of a river are parted by interjacent

---

1 This epithet is applicable to Agni, for the strength required for rubbing the sticks together so as to generate fire.

2 The literal meaning is,—"We praise thee like a horse with a tail.' The Commentator supplies the rest.

3 A name of Agni: literally, he who has wonderful or various lustre.

(islets); thou pourest immediate (rewards upon the giver (of oblations).

7. The mortal, whom thou, Agni, protectest in battle, whom thou despatchest to battle, will, always, get food.

8. O subduer of foes, no one will be able to defeat this thy worshipper, for he has well-known strength.

9. May he, adored of all, take us with horses through the battle; may he, (propitiated) by the intelligent priests, be the bestower (of profuse riches).

10. O thou, who art awakened[1] by praises, enter into the oblation, for the completion of the sacrifice that benefits all mankind. (The worshipper) offers this agreeable laudation to the terrific (Agni).

11. May the vast, illimitable, smoke-bannered, effulgent Agni, be pleased with our rites and bestow on us food.

12. May Agni, the lord of men, the invoker and messenger of the Celestials, the effulgent, hear us with our hymns as a rich man (listens to encomiastic verses).

13. Salutation unto the great Deities; salutation unto the lesser, salutation unto the young, salutation unto the old; we adore the Deities, as we are able; may I not omit the laudation of the elder Divinities.

---

1 The word is *jarâbodha*, *i.e.*, *bodha* (awakened) by *jara* (praise).

SUKTA V. (XXVIII.)

The Rishi is S'unhasépa; the metre of the first six stanzas is *Anushtubh*; of the three last, *Gâyatrî*. The first four stanzas are addressed to Indra; the two next, to the domestic mortar; the next two, to the mortar and pesttle; and the ninth is of a miscellaneous appropriation either to Haris'chandra, a Prajápati; to the *Adhis'avana* or the effused libation; to the *Soma*-Juice; or to the skin (*charma*) on which it is poured.

INDRA, in the sacrifice in which the broad-based stone[1] is raised to extract the *Soma*-Juice, consider as thy own and drink the effusions of the mortar.

2. Indra, (in the rite) in which the two platters,[2] for containing the juice, as (broad) as a woman's hips, are used, consider as thy own and drink the effusions of the mortar.

3. Indra, (in the rite) in which the housewife practises egress from, and ingress into, (the sacrificial chamber),[3] consider as thy own and drink the effusions of the mortar.

4. Where they find the churning-staff (with a chord),[4] like reins to control (a horse), Indra, consider as thy own and drink the effusions of the mortar.

---

1 The stone-pestle, used for extracting Juice from *Soma*-Plants.

2 The word is *adhishavanyá*, two shallow plates for receiving and pouring out *Soma*-Juice.

3 The Scholiast explains the terms of the Text, *Apachyava* and *Upachyava*, going in and out of the hall (*s'álá*); but it should, perhaps, rather be moving up and down, with reference to the action of the pestle.—*Wilson*.

4 In churning the stick is moved by a rope passed round the handle of it, and round a post planted in the ground as a pivot.

5. Although, O Mortar,[1] thou art present in every house, (yet) give forth (in this rite) a lusty sound, like the drum of a victorious army.

6. Lord of the forest,[2] as the wind blows before thee, so do thou, O Mortar, dress this *Soma*-Juice to be drunk by Indra.

7. Implements of sacrifice, bestowers of food, loud-sounding, sport again and again, like horses of Indra champing the grain.

8. Do you two forest lords, of agreeable form, prepare with beautiful instruments of libations, our sweet (*Soma*-)Juices for Indra.

9. Bring the remains of the *Soma*-Juice from the expressing instruments and place them on a cart, sprinkle it upon the sacred (*Kus'a*-grass) and place (the remainder upon the cow-hide.)[3]

---

1 The mortar is usually a heavy wooden vessel, found in every farmer's cottage: according to Sáyana, it is the Divinities presiding over the mortar and pestle, not the implements themselves, that are addressed.—*Wilson*.

2 A large tree, but here meaning the mortar.

3 Sáyana says that this verse is addressed to *Haris'chandra*, either the ministering priest, or a Divinity so named. His function is not clearly mentioned. As it appears from the Text he is to place the remains of the libation, from the instrument, upon a cart (*Sakatasya-upari*) as supplied by the Commentator. It should be cast upon the *Pavitra*, which, as explained in the comment on the *Yajur-Véda*, means two or three blades of *Kus'a*-grass serving as a fitter. It should then be placed on a cow-hide. According to Mr. Stevenson, the *Soma*-Juice, after being expressed, is filtered through a strainer made of goat's hair and is received in a sort of ewer.

SUKTA VI. (XXIX.)

THE Rishi is Sunhas'épa : the Deity is Indra : the metre *Pankti.*

TRUTHFUL Indra, the drinker of *Soma*-Juice, even if we be unworthy, do thou, Indra, of profuse riches, enrich us with thousands of excellent cows and horses.

2. O powerful lord of food, O thou, having a handsome prominent nose, ever enduring is thy favour; therefore, Indra, of profuse riches, enrich us with thousands of excellent cows and horses.

3. Put to sleep (the two female messengers of Yama); looking at each other, let them sleep, never waking:[1] Indra, of profuse riches, enrich us with thousands of excellent cows and horses.

4. May our enemies sleep, and our friends, O hero, be awake. Indra, of profuse riches, enrich us with thousands of excellent cows and horses.

5. Indra, kill this ass (our enemy), lauding thee with such discordant speech.[2] Do thou Indra, of profuse riches, enrich us with thousands of excellent cows and horses.

6. Let the (adverse) wind, of crooked course, descend at a distance from the forest. Indra, of pro-

---

1 The Text is very elliptical and obscure: it is literally, "Put to sleep the two reciprocally looking; let them sleep, not being awakened. That two females are intended is inferable from the epithets being in the dual number and feminine gender; and the Scholiast calls them, upon what authority is not stated, two female messengers of Yama: *Yamadutyan Mithúdrisá,* he explains as "looking, after the manner of twins, at each other.—*Wilson.*

2 *Nuvantan-papayámuya* praising with this speech that is of the nature of abuse. *Nindá rupayá Váchá* is the addition of the Scholiast, who adds, therefore he is called an ass, as braying or uttering harsh sounds intolerable to hear.—*Wilson.*

fuse riches, enrich us with thousands of excellent cows and horses.

7. Kill all those who revile us; kill every one who injures us. Indra, of profuse riches, enrich us with thousands of excellent cows and horses.

SUKTA VII. (XXX.)

THE Rishi is Sunhas'épa; of the twenty-two stanzas the hymn contains, sixteen are addressed to Indra; three, to the Aswins; and three, to Ushás or personified Dawn; the metre is *Gâyatri* except in verse fifteen where it is *Trishtúbh*

LET us, who are desirous of food, please this your Indra, who is highly powerful, and of a hundred sacrifices, with drops (of *Soma*-Juice), as a well (is filled with water).

2. May he come near a hundred pure, and a thousand distilled, (libations); as (water), to low places.

3. All these (libations) being collected together, for the satisfaction of powerful Indra, are contained in his belly; as water, in the ocean.

4. This libation is (prepared) for thee; thou approachest it as a pigeon, his pregnant (mate); and, on that account, do thou accept our words (*i.e.*, prayers).

5. O lord of riches, O hero, worthy of being lauded, such is thy laudatory hymn; may thy lordly power be gratifying and genuine.

6. S'atakratu, be anxious to protect us in this battle: we will talk together in other matters.

7. At the commencement of every work, in every battle, we invoke, as friends, the most powerful Indra, for our defence.

8. If he hears our invocation, let him come to us with thousand of defences and food.

9. I invoke the male being (Indra), who visits many adorers from his ancient dwelling place,[1]—thee, Indra, whom, my father formerly invoked.

10. O thou, who art adored of all, invoked by many, a friend and protector of dwellings, we implore thee, (to be favourable) to thy worshippers.

11. O drinker of the *Soma*-Juice, O holder of the thunderbolt, O friend, (confer upon) us—thy friends and drinkers of the *Soma*-Juice—(numberless cows), with projecting jaws.[2]

12. O drinker of the *Soma*-Juice, (O) wielder of the thunderbolt, O friend, so be it; do thou so do, that we may seek thy favour, for our well-being.

13. Indra, being propitiated with us, we may have (profuse food) and cows, robust and rich in milk, with which we may be happy.

14. O high-spirited (Indra), let some other Deity as thou art, self-pleased, (and) solicited by us, grant thy praisers (all desired-for objects), as (they whirl) the axle of the wheels (of a car).[3]

---

1 The Revd. K. M. Banerjea has translated the passage thus,—"From the site of our ancient home." This rendering does not appear inappropriate, for immediately after the *Rishi* says,—"Whom my father invoked formerly."

2 The expression in the Text is *S'ipriníndm*, genitive plural of the feminine *S'iprini*, having a nose or a jaw; it cannot, therefore, refer to the previous nouns in the genitive plural, *Somapâbnâm* and *Sakhînâm*, which are masculine; and the Scholiast, therefore, supplies *gavâm*, of cows, and adds *samûha*, a multitude, or herd.—*Wilson*.

3 The verse is, throughout, very elliptical and obscure, and is intelligible only through the liberal additions of the Scholiast. The simile is, literally, "like the axle of two cars,"—*aksham na chakryoh*, which the Commentator renders, *rathasya chakrayoh*, "of the two wheels of a car,"

15. S'atakratu, thou conferest upon them, such riches as thy praisers desire, as the axle (revolves) with the movements (of the waggon).[1]

16. Indra has ever acquired riches (from his enemies), with his champing, neighing and snorting (horses); he, liberal and performer of many deeds, has given us, as a gift, a golden chariot.[2]

17. As'wins, come here, with viands borne on many horses; O destroyer of enemies, (let our house) be filled with cattle and with gold.

18. O destroyer of enemies, your chariot, harnessed for both alike, is imperishable; it courses, As'wins, through the firmament.

19. You have placed one wheel on the top of the imperishable (rock), while the other revolves in the sky.[3]

20. Ushâ, fond of laudation, immortal, what mortal is capable of offering enjoyment worthy of thee?[4] O mighty one, whom dost thou attain?

---

and adds *prakshipanti*, "they cast or turn over." The phrase seems to have puzzled the Translators;......Stevenson has, "that blessings may come round to them with the same certainty that the wheel revolves round the axle;" Dr. Roer, "as a wheel is brought to a chariot;"...... The meaning intended, is, probably, the hope that blessings should follow praise as the pivot on which they revolve, as the revolutions of the wheels of a car turn upon the axle.—*Wilson.*

1 It is like the axle by the acts. The Scholiast defines 'the acts,' the movements of the car or waggon.

2 By Indra, pleased, a golden chariot was given to S'unhas'épa.

3 The myth has not been explained by the Commentator. Wilson says:—"It may be connected with the *Pouránik* notion of the single wheel of the chariot of the Sun."

4 *Literally*,—"What mortal enjoyeth thee?" We have adopted Sáyana's interpretation.

"What mortal can be equal for thy enjoyment."—The Revd. *K. M. Banerjea.*

21. Diffusive, variegated, effulgent Ushâ, we know not (thy form), whether from near or distance.

22. O daughter of heaven, come, with these viands, and perpetuate wealth in us.[1]

ANUVAKA VII.

SUKTA I. (XXXI.)

The Deity is Agni; the *Rishi* is Hiranyastûpa, the son of Angiras. The eigth, sixteenth, and the eighteenth stanzas are in the *Trishtubh* metre; the rest, in *Jagatí*.

THOU, Agni, was the first Angiras *Rishi*;[2] a Deity, thou wast the auspicious friend of the Deities. In thy rite the intelligent, the rite-knowing, the bright-weaponed *Maruts* were created.

2. Thou intelligent Agni, the first and chiefest Angiras, gracest the rite of the Celestials. (Thou art,) for the behoof of all the world, manifold,[3] intelligent,

---

" Who and where was there a mortal to be loved to thee."—*Max Müller*.

1 Ushâ was one of the Deities adored by the Aryans. Her name and worship is, therefore, mentioned by the various branches of the Aryans. Eos and Aurora are but the different names of Ushá.

" The heroine of the stories must be the Dawn, aptly represented as a charming maiden, and her names in the *Rig-Véda*, are Arj'uní, Brisaya, Dahaná, Ushas, Saramá, and Saranyu, and all these names re-appear among the Greeks, as Argynoris, Briseis, Daphne, Eos, Helen, and Erinys."—Rájendra Lálá Mitra's *Indo-Aryans*, Vol. II., article, *Primitive Aryans*.

2 According to Sáyana, he was the first, as being the progenitor of all the Angiras, as the coals or cinders of the sacrificial fire.

3 *Vibhu* means, " of many kinds," referring to the different fires of a sacrifice.

the offspring of two mothers,[1] and presents everywhere, in various ways, for mankind.

3. Thou, Agni, art first in the Wind,[2] be manifest to the sacrificer, working with a desire to the celebration of an agreeable rite; heaven and earth tremble (at thy power); appointed as a priest, thou dost sustain the burthen in the rite; O Lord of dwellinghouses, thou hast worshipped the venerable Celestials.

4. Thou, Agni, hast announced heaven to Manu,[3] thou hast done more good to Pururavâs, who has done good to thee.[4] When thou art liberated by the attrition of thy parents, they take thee first to the east, then to the west, of the altar.[5]

5. Thou, Agni, art the showerer (of desired-for objects), the multiplier of the prosperity (of thy worshipper); thou art lauded when the ladle is lifted up; thou, the only giver of food, dost first bestow light upon him, who fully understands the invocation and makes the oblation,[6] and then upon all men.

---

1 *Dwimátá*, either of two mothers, *i.e.*, the two sticks, or the maker of two, *i.e.*, heaven and earth.—*Wilson.*

2 Literally, it means, "first in, or on, or over, the Wind," *prathamo mátariswane.* It means "Thou dost precede the Wind." According to the Scholiast, it alludes to the Text *agnirváyurráditya*, fire, air, sun, in which Agni precedes Váyu.

3 It is said that Agni communicated to Manu, that heaven is to be acquired by pious deeds.

4 We have given the literal rendering. Wilson's rendering "Thou hast more than requited Pururavás doing homage to thee," is more explanatory. The agency of Pururavás in the generation of fire by attrition, and its employment in the form of three sacrificial fires, as told in the *Vishnu Puránam* may be here alluded to.

5 The fire first is applied to kindle the *Ahavaníya* fire, and then to the *Gárhapatya.*

6 He who knows the *áhuti*, with the *Vasat kriti*, or utterance of the word *Vashat* at the moment of pouring the butter on the fire.

6. Agni, endued with most excellent knowledge, thou leadest the man, who follows improper ways, to deeds that are fitted to reclaim him; thou, who, in the strife of heroes, (grateful to them) as widely-scattered wealth, destroyest, in the combat, the mighty by the feeble.

7. Thou sustainest, Agni, that mortal (who worships thee) for daily food in the most excellent and immortal station: thou conferest on the sage, who seeks both kinds of birth,[1] happiness and food.

8. O Agni, thou art lauded by us for giving wealth; give us a son, illustrious and celebrator of sacrifices; by the new son we shall multiply sacrifices. Preserve us perfectly, heaven and earth, along with the Celestials.

9. Immaculate Agni, wide awake among the Celestials, (living) near (thy) parents[2] and confering upon us embodied (son), awake[3] us. Be favourably disposed towards the offerer of the oblation; for thou, auspicious Agni, has sown all riches.

10. Thou, Agni, art favourably disposed towards us; thou art our father,[4] thou art the giver of the duration of life; we are thy kinsmen. Uninjurable Agni, hundreds and thousands of riches are thine, who art the defender of pious deeds and attended by good men.

---

1 The sense of the expression is not at all clear. The Commentator says, "For the acquirement of bipeds and quadrupeds."

2 Agni's parents are heaven and earth.

3 The Text is literally rendered. The meaning, however, is, as the Commentator says, "favour us."

4 The word in the Text is *pitá*, *i.e.*, father. Sáyana explains it as *Pálakaḥ*, protector.

11. The Celestials, formerly, made thee, Agni, the human general of human Nahusha;[1] they made Ilâ[2] the instructress of Manu, when the son of my father was born.

12. Agni, worthy of being lauded, protect us, who are opulent with thy protection, as also the persons (of our sons); thou art the defender of the cattle of the son of my son,[3] who is busily engaged in thy adoration.

13. Agni, thou art the protector of the sacrificer; being near at hand, for the protection of the sacrifice, thou shinest as four-eyed.[4] Thou dost accept, with the mind, the hymn of thine adorer, who offers oblation to thee (who art) harmless and a benefactor.

14. Thou, Agni, desirest that (thy worshipper), lauding (thee) profusely, may get desirable and most excellent wealth; thou art called the well-intentioned father (*i.e.*, protector) of the worshipper, who ever needs protection; thou, who art greatly wise, instructest the

---

1 It is mentioned in the *Vishnu Puránam* that, Nahusha, the grandson of Pururavás, was precipitated from the celestial region for his arrogance, but it is nowhere mentioned that Agni was his general.

2 Frequent passages, in the *Védás*, ascribe to Ilá the first institution of the rules of performing sacrifices; thus in the Text she is termed *S'ásani*, which the Scholiast explains *Dharmopadésa karttri*, "The giver of instruction in duty." The *Taittiríyas* are quoted for the Text,—"Ilâ, the daughter of Manu, was the illustrator of sacrifice;" and the *Vája-saneyis* for the passage,—"She, Ilá, said to Manu, 'Appoint me to officiate in sacrifices, principal and supplementary, for by me, shalt thou obtain all thy desires.'" M. Burnouf questions,—If Ilá ever occurs in the sense of daughter of Manu in the *Védás*, and restricts its meaning to 'earth' or to 'speech.'—*Wilson.*

3 This hymn must have been written by the *R*ishi in his old age.

4 Illuminating the four cardinal points.

Infant (worshipper) and (determinest) the points of the horizon.[1]

15. Thou, Agni, dost protect, on all sides, the man who gives presents (to the priests), like a well-stitched armour.[2] The man,—who keeps sweet viands in his house, and, with them, entertains (his guests),—performs the sacrifice of life[3] and becomes an example of heaven.

16. Agni, forgive us this our negligence, this path in which we have gone astray. Thou art attainable unto those who offer libations of the *Soma*, art their father (protector), art of a favourable disposition and the accomplisher (of rites); thou makest thyself visible to mortals.[4]

17. Pure Agni, who goest about (to receive oblations), come, proceeding to the hall of sacrifice, as did Manu, Aṅgiras, Yayâti and others of old, bring here

---

1 It refers to a legend in which the Celestials, desirous of celebrating a sacrifice, could not determine the cardinal points until Agni removed the difficulty by ascertaining the South.

2 *Varma syútam*, sewn armour. The *Kavacha* was, perhaps, a quilted jacket, such as is still, sometimes, worn; the Scholiast says, "formed with needles without leaving a fissure."—*Wilson.*

3 The expression is, rather, ambiguous—*Jiva-yájam yajate*, "sacrifices a life-sacrifice." It seems rather, to denote an offering (food and hospitality) to a living being, the *Nri-Yajña*, worship of man, of Manu. The expression, however, is not incompatible with the practice of killing a cow for the food of a guest, thence denominated, as M. Langlois remarks, *goghna* "a cow-slayer." The Scholiast sanctions either sense, explaining the phrase either *jívayajana sahitam yajñam*, "a sacrifice with sacrifice of life," or *jívanishpádyam*, "that by which life is to be supported;" he, also, explains *jívaydjam* by *jiváh*, living, priests, who are worshipped by gifts.—*Wilson.*

4 *Rishikrit*, becoming present through desire for the offered oblation.

the Divinities, make them sit on the sacred grass and offer them grateful (oblation).

18. Agni, do thou thrive through this our hymn, which we compose according to our ability and knowledge; do thou grant us, by it, riches, and endow us with right undertaking, securing (sufficient) food.

SUKTA II. (XXXII.)

THE Rishi and metre are the same; the hymn is addressed to Indra.[1]

DESCRIBE the brave deeds of Indra, which the wielder of the thunderbolt had, formerly, performed; he killed the clouds; he cast the waters down (to the earth); he cut (a way) for the torrents of the mountain.[1]

2. He killed (clove) the cloud, seeking refuge on the mountain: Twashtri sharpened his far-whirling bolt; the currents of water speedily proceeded to the ocean as cows (hasten) to their calves.

3. Acting like a bull, he quaffed the *Soma*-Juice, he drank of the libation at the threefold[2] sacrifice. Maghavan took his arrow and the thunderbolt, and, therewith, struck the first-born of the clouds.

---

1 In this and subsequent *Súktas*, we have an ample elucidation of the original purport of the legend of Indra's slaying Vritra, which the *Pouránic* writers converted into a combat between Indra, the king of the Celestials and Vritra, the king of the Asuras. In the *Védás*, this legend is, merely, an allegorical narrative of the production of rain. Vritra, also named Ahi, is nothing but the accumulation of condensed vapour. Indra, with his thunderbolt or atmospheric influence, divides the accumulated clouds, which produced rain, descending upon the earth and moistening the fields. There are many hymns addressed to the slayer of Vritra before the Aryans migrated from their early home.

2 The three sacrifices termed Jyotish, Gah and A'yu.

4. Since thou hast killed the first-born of the clouds, thou hast destroyed the delusions of the deluders and, then, creating the Sun, the Dawn, the Firmament, thou hast got no enemy (to oppose thee).[1]

5. With his highly destructive thunderbolt, Indra killed the mutilated Vṛitra, covering all with darkness; like the trunks of trees felled by the axe, Ahi lies prostrate on the earth.

6. The haughty Vritra, as if he had no combatant to match him, invited Indra to encounter, the great heroe, the destroyer of many, the vanquisher of enemies; he has not escaped the contact of the fate of (Indra's) enemies. The enemy of Indra has crushed the (banks of the rivers.[2]

7. Vritra, having no foot or hand, desired to combat with Indra, who struck him with the thunder-bolt upon his shoulder (resembling the summit) of a mountain. As one shorn of virility, desirous of acquiring equality with one possessed of it (does not succeed, so did Vritra); then Vritra, mutilated of many members, slept.

8. Delightful waters flow over him lying prostrate on earth as a river (overflows) its broken (banks). Ahi has laid himself low under the feet of the waters which Vritra had obstructed by his glorious power.

9. Vritra's mother was bending over her son when Indra struck her nether part with his arrow, so the

---

1 By scattering the clouds and dispersing the darkness, Indra may be said to be the parent of the Sun and daylight; leaving no enemy that is, nothing to obscure the atmosphere.—*Wilson*.

2 The text has only *Rujánáh pipishe*, he has ground the rivers; the commmentator, supplies the banks, which he says were broken down by the fall of *Vritra*, that is, by the innundation occassioned by the descent of the rain.

mother was above and the son underneath. Then Dánu,[1] (Vritra's mother) slept (with her son) like a cow with its calf.

10. The waters flow over the nameless body of Vritra tossed into the midst of never-stopping, never-resting currents. Indra's enemy has slept a long darkness.[2]

11. The waters, the wives of Dâsa (Vritra) stood obstructed, guarded by Ahi like the cows by Panin; the passage of water stood obstructed (by Vritra); by killing Vritra he set it open.

12. When the single resplendent Vritra returned the blow (inflicted), Indra, by thy thunder-bolt, thou becamest like a horse's tail.[3] Thou hast rescued the kine; thou hast acquired, Heroe, the *Soma*-Juice[4]; thou hast let loose the seven rivers to flow.[5]

---

1 *Dánu* may be derived either from *do* to cut or from *Danu*, the wife of Kashyapa and mother of the Dánavas.

2 In the text is *tamas*, literally darkness; the commentator explains it as long sleep like death.

3 As a horse drives away the flies by its tail.

4 Alluding, it is said, to a legend of Indra's having drunk a libation prepared by *Trisiras*, also killed by Indra and to avenge which *Vritra* was created by *Twashtri*—Wilson.

5 According to one *Paurânik* legend, the *Ganges* divided on its descent into seven streams, termed the *Nalini*, *Pavani*, and *Hládini*, going to the east; the *Chakshu*, *Sitá* and *Sindhu* to the west, and the *Bhagiratha* or the Ganges proper, to the south. In one place in the Mahábhárata, the seven rivers are termed *Vaswankasárá*, *Nalini*, *Pavani*, *Gangá*, *Sitá*, *Sindhu*, *Jambunadi*; in another *Gangá*, *Yamuná*, *Plakshagá*, *Rathasthá*, *Saryu*, *Gomati* and *Gandaki*. In a text quoted and commented on by *Yáksha* we have ten rivers, named, *Gangá*, *Yamuná*, *Saraswati*, *Satudri*, *Parushni*, *Aikni*, *Marudvridha*, *Vitastá* *Arjikiyá* and *Sushomá*; of these, the *Parushni* is identified with the *Iravati*, the *Arjiki* with the *Vipásá* and the *Sushomá* with the *Sindhu*—

13. Neither the lightning, nor the thunder, nor the rain which he showered, nor the thunder-bolt harmed Indra when he and Ahi fought; and Maghavat triumphed also over other attacks.

14. When fear[1] entered, Indra, into thy heart when about to kill Ahi, what other killer of him didst thou expect, that, afraid, thou didst traverse ninety and nine streams like a (swift) hawk ?

15. Then Indra, the holder of the thunder-bolt, became the king of the moveable and the immoveable, of (hornless) quiet animals and horned cattle; he lives as the king of men; he comprehended all things (within him) as the circumference comprehends the spokes of a wheel.

Nir 3, 26. The original enumeration of seven appears to be that which has given rise to the specifications of the *Puránás.*—Wilson.

7 This fear was the uncertainty whether he should destroy *Vritra* or not. In the *Puránás* however he is described as fearing his enemy's power.

THIRD ADHYA'YA.

ANUVA'KA VII.—*(Continued.)*

SUKTA III. (XXXIII.)

THE *Rishi* is Hiranyastupa; Indra is the Deity and the metre is *Trishtubh*.

COME, let us go to Indra,[1] (to recover our stolen cattle), for he, shorn of malice, increases our most excellent understanding; thereupon he will confer on us perfect knowledge of their wealth of kine.

2. Like a hawk to its nest, I fly to that Indra who is invoked by worshippers in battle, adoring, with examplary hymns, him who is invincible and the giver of wealth.

3. The commander of the entire army has bound his quiver (on his back); the lord[2] drives the cattle to him whom he pleases. Indra, endued with most excellent understanding, giving us profuse wealth, take not advantage of us like a dealer.[3]

4. Indeed, Indra, thou hadst killed alone the wealthy robber[4] with thy hard thunder-bolt, (although the powerful Maruts) existed near thee. Coming with

---

1 The Commentator says: "The celestials are supposed to say this to one another when their cows have been stolen.

2 The word in the text is *Arya*, which means master, lord.

3 Lit. do not be to us a *Pani*, a trafficker, from *pana*, price. Indra is requested not to make a hard bargain with his worshippers.

4 *Vritra*, the *Dasyu*, literally a robber, but apparently used in contrast to *Arja* as if intending the uncivilized tribes of India. He is called wealthy because, according to the *Vajasaneyis*, he comprehends within him all gods, all knowledge, all oblations—Wilson.

the desire of meeting with manifold destructiveness from thy bow, the *Sanakas*, the neglecters of sacrifice, died.

5. Indra, those neglecters of sacrifice, contending with the sacrificers, fled with averted faces. O lord of horses, O thou, who dost never retreat from the battle-field, O terrific (Indra), thou didst blow the violators of religious rites off the celestial region, earth and sky.

6. They desired to fight with the army of faultless (Indra); men of praiseworthy characters[2] encouraged him. Like the emasculated fighting with men, they, scattered before him, and conscious (of their worthlessness, fled by precipitous paths.

7. Thou hast slain them in battle, Indra, weeping or laughing at the farthest end of the sky; thou hast consumed the robber (having dragged him) from the celestial region and hast protected the hymns (of the worshipper) pouring libations of *Soma*-Juice and lauding thee.

8. Bedecked with gold and jewels they covered the surface of the earth. They could not conquer Indra: he dispersed them with the rising sun.[3]

---

1 The followers of *Vritra* are called by this name, the meaning of which, as explained by the Scholiast *Snán-Káyanti* they who eulogize benefactors. They are called *ayajwands*, non-sacrificers, for the followers of *Vritra* were hostile to all Vedic rituals.

2 These men were, according to the Scholiast, *Angirasas* engaged in offering libations to *Indra* for nine months, in order to give him courage.

3 The followers of *Vritra* are described as the shades of the night which are dispersed by the rising of the Sun.

9. Indra, as thou enjoyest both the celestial region and earth, investing the universe with thy greatness, thou hast blown away the robbers with the hymns which are repeated on behalf of those who do not understand their meaning.[1]

10. When the waters descended not upon the ends of the earth and overspread not that giver of affluence with its productions then Indra, the showerer, grasped his bolt and with its brightness milked out the waters from the darkness (cloud).

11. The waters flowed to provide the food of the navigable (rivers). Then Indra, with highly powerful and fatal weapon, killed, within few days, (Vritra) whose thoughts were always with him.[2]

12. Indra pierced (*i.e.*, set free the waters) obstructed by (Vritra) while sleeping in the caverns of the earth and killed the horned dryer up (of the world)[3]

---

1 This passage is rather obscure, owing to the vague purport of the preposition *abhi*; *amanyamánán abhi manyamánair brahmabhih*, with prayers to be understood over those not under-standing; that is, accord- to the Scholiast, those *Yajamánás* or instituters of sacrifices, who merely repeat the *mantras* without understanding their meaning, are nevertheless to be protected by, or are to reap the benefit of those *mantras;* and with *mantras* or prayers of this description *Indra* is to be animated, or empowered to blow away or scatter the followers of *Vritra*, clouds and darkness. Rosen renders the expression, *carminibus respicientibus eos qui tuorum hymnorum sensum non perspiciunt*; M. Langlois has (*excite*) *contre ces mecreans par nos chants respectuex*—Wilson.

2 Sâyana has made the expression an adjective of Vritra. But Ramánâth Saraswati has made it an adjective of Indra explaining "With all the skill of his understanding Indra slew Vritra."

3 *Sriningam Sushnam*, the first, literally, having horns, the Scholiast explains, furnished with weapons like the horns of bulls and

Thou, Maghavan, with equal swiftness and strength didst slay, with thy thunder-bolt, the enemy defying thee to battle.

13. The active weapon of Indra fell upon his enemies; with his sharp and excellent (weapon) he destroyed their cities; he then reached Vritra with his thunder-bolt and killing him exhilarated his mind.

14. Thou, Indra, hast protected Kutsa whose praises thou dost solicit: thou hast defended the excellent Dasâdyu engaged in battle; the dust of thy horse's hoofs ascended the celestial region; the son of Switra, rose up (from waters) to be foremost among men.11

15. Thou hast protected, Maghavan, the excellent son of Switra endued with forgiveness and immersed in water, for getting lands; do thou inflict sharp pains on those of our hostile minds who have long been fighting with us.

---

buffaloes, *Sushnam*, literally drying, drying up, is applied to *Vritra* or or the cloud, as withholding the moisture necessary for fertility— Wilson.

11 Kutsa is said to be a Rishi, founder of a *Gotra*, a religious family or school, and is elsewhere spoken of as the particular friend of Indra or even as his son; he is the reputed author of several hymns: we have a Purukutsa in the *Purânâs*, but he was a Raja, the son of Mándhátri. Dasádyu is also called a Rishi; but he appears to have been a warrior; no mention of him is found in the *Purânâs*. The same may be said of Swaitreya or Switrya, the son of a female termed Switra. Switrya is described in the next stanza as having hidden himself in a pool of water through fear of his enemies—Wilson.

SUKTA IV. (XXXIV.)

THE *Rishi* the same; the hymn is addressed to Aswins; the metre is *Trishtubh*, except in the ninth and twelfth stanzas in which it is *Jagati*.

INTELLIGENT Aswins, be present with us thrice[1] to-day. Vast is your vehicle as well as your munificence; your union is regulated like that of the shining (day) and dewy (night); be kindly subject to intelligent (priests.)

2. There are three adamantine wheels in your chariot, conveying sweet articles of food; all (celestials) have known (it) when (starting) with Venâ the beloved of Soma;[2] there are three columns placed (above it) for support;[3] and in it do you travel thrice by night and thrice by day.

3. Thrice in a day do you rectify the faults (of your worshippers); sprinkle thrice to-day the oblation with sweetness; and grant us Aswins, strength-giving food, thrice, evening and morning.

4. Visit, Aswins, thrice our house, and the person who is engaged in doing good unto us; come thrice to the person who deserves your protection and instruct us in three-fold knowledge; grant us gratifying fruits thrice and thrice shower food on us as (Indra pours down) rain.

5. Aswins, thrice confer upon us riches; thrice approach the divine rite; thrice preserve our intellects;

---

1 This refers to the three diurnal sacrifices at dawn, mid-day or sunset or to the deities passing equally through the heavens, the firmament and the earth.

2 This refers to the marriage of Vená with Soma when the] Aswins filled their cart, with all sorts of good things. This legend is not to be found in the *Puránás*.

3 This means the posts created on the cart which the riders may lay hold of.

thrice grant us prosperity and food. The daughter of the Sun has got upon your three-wheeled car.

6. Thrice give us, Aswins, the celestial medicaments and those of earth and those of the firmament; confer on my son the prosperity of Sanyu;[1] protectors of wholesome medicinal herbs, give us pleasure about the three humours (of the body.)[2]

7. Aswins, who are to be thrice adored, repose daily in the triple (couch of) sacred grass upon the earth; O car-warrior Nâsatyas,[3] go from afar to the three-fold[4] (place of sacrifice) as the vital airs to living bodies.

8. Come, Aswins, with the seven mother-streams;[5] the three rivers are ready;[6] the three-fold oblation is prepared; rising above the three worlds, you defend the sun in the sky, who is established for both day and night.[7]

9. Where, Nâsatyas, are the three wheels of your triangular car? Where the three fastings and props (of the awning). When will the powerful ass be harnessed to your chariot that you may come to the sacrifice?

10. Come, Nâsatyas, to the sacrifice; the oblation is offered; drink the juice with mouths, that relish the sweet savour. Before dawn, Savitri has sent your

---

1 The son of Vrihaspati brought up by Aswins.

2 The wind or nerve-power, bile and phlegm.

3 Literally, in whom there is no untruth.

4 The text has only " to the three; the Scholiast adds' 'altars'

5 Gangá and other rivers are the parents of all the streams.

6 These are three sorts of jars or pitchers.

7 The rising and setting of the Sun indicate the arrival of both day and night.

wonderful car, shining with clarified butter (to bring you) to the rite.

11. Come Nâsatyas, with thirty-three[1] deities here to drink of the sweet (*Soma*-Juice); prolong our lives, remove our faults, restrain our enemies and live always with us.

12. Borne in your car traversing the three worlds, bring us, Aswins, wealth attended with male progeny; I call upon you, both listening to me, for protection; be to us for vigour in battle.

SUKTA V. (XXXV.)

THE *Rishi* the same; the first and ninth verses are in the *Jagati* metre, the rest in the *Trishtubh*. The deity of the whole hymn is Savitri, but in the first stanza, Agni, Mitra, Varuna and Night are mentioned as subordinate deities.

I INVOKE Agni first, for protection: I invoke Mitra and Varuna for protection; I invoke Night who is the root of rest to the world; I invoke the divine Savitri for protection.

2. Traversing, again and again, the dark firmament, arousing mortal and immortal, the divine Savitri travels in his golden chariot seeing the world.

3. The divine Savitri travels by an upward and downward path;[2] worthy of adoration, he travels with two white steeds; he comes here from a distance, destroying all sins.

4. The adorable Savitri, of many rays, having power to (remove) darkness from the world, has got

---

1 This *Sloka* is the original authority for the *Paurânik* enumeration of thirty three *Kotis* of deities.

2 Ascending from sun-rise to the meridian, and then declining.

upon his chariot, standing near, decorated with many kinds of golden ornaments and furnished with golden yokes.

5 His white-footed horses, *S'yâva,* harnessed to his chariot with a golden yoke, have shown light to mankind. Men and all the worlds are present before the divine Savitri.

6. There are three regions; two are near the sun and one leads to the dwelling of Yama.[1] The immortal (luminaries) depend upon Savitri as a car upon the pin of the axle; let him who knows (the greatness of Savitri) say it.

7. The deep-quivering, life-giving and well-directed solar ray has lighted up the three regions. Where now is the Sun? who knows to what sphere his rays have extended?[2]

8. He has lighted up the eight cardinal points, the three regions of living beings, the seven rivers; may the golden-eyed Savitri come here, conferring, upon the offerer of the oblation, desirable objects.

9. The golden-handed Savitri, the beholder of various objects, travels between the two regions of heaven and earth, removes deseases, approaches the sun[3] and covers the sky alternately with darkness and light.

---

1 Heaven and earth are the regions which lie in the immediate path of the Sun: the firmament is the road that leads to the realm of Yama, the ruler of the dead.

2 *Suparna*, the well-winged, is, in the *Nirghanta*, a synonym of *rasmi*, a ray; one of its epithets, *asura*, is here explained life-giving, *asu*, vital breath, and *ra*, who gives.—Wilson.

3 The Commentator explains it by saying that although *Savitri* and *Surya* are the same as regards their divinity, yet they are two different forms, and therefore one may go to the other.

10. May the golden-handed, life giving, well-guiding, exhilarating and affluent Savitri come here; for the deity, adored every evening, remains driving away *Rákshasás* and *Yatudhânas*.

11. Thy paths, Savitri, are prepared of old, free from dust and well made in the firmament; (coming) by these paths, easily traversable, preserve us today. Deity, speak to us.

ANUVA'KA VIII.

SUKTA I. (XXXVI.)

THE *Rishi* is Kanwa, the son of Gohara; the deity is Agni. The metre of the old verses is *Brihati* having twelve syllables in the third *Páda* or quarter of the stanza; the metre of the even verses is termed *Satobrihati*, having the first and third *Pádas* equal.

WE implore, with sacred hymns, the powerful Agni, whom other (*Rishis*) also laud for the behoof of you, who are many people, adoring the deities.

2. Men have recourse to Agni, the multiplier of strength; with oblations we adore thee; do thou, liberal giver of food, be well disposed to us here this day, and be our protector.

3. We select thee, Agni, the messenger and invoker of the deities, who art endued with all knowledge. Thy flames, who art mighty and eternal, spread around and thy rays touch the celestial region.

4. The deities Varuna, Mitra and Aryaman kindle thee, (their) ancient messenger. The man, who offers thee oblation, conquers all wealth by thy help.

5. Thou, Agni, dost give delight, art the invoker and messenger of the deities and the domestic guide

of human beings. All actions, which the celestials perform, are aggregated in thee.

6. Youthful and lucky Agni, whatever oblation is presented to thee, do thou, well disposed towards us, carry it to the powerful deities, either to-day or at any other time.

7. Likewise devout people adore thee who art bright with thine own radiance. Men, desirous of defeating their enemies, kindle him (Agni) with (seven) ministrant priests.

8. The destroying (deities along with thee) have killed Vṛitra; they have made earth, the celestial region and the firmament the spacious habitation (of living creatures); may Agni, possessed of weath, when invoked, be a benefactor to Kanwa like a horse that neighs in a conflict for cattle.[1]

9. Sit on the sacred grass, (for) thou art profusely possessed of accomplishments; shine forth, for thou art devoted to the deities; adorable and excellent Agni, emit the moving and graceful smoke.

10. Bearer of oblations, (thou art he) the most adorable whom the deities detained for the sake of Manu; whom, giver of wealth, Kanwa, the host of pious guests,[2] has detained; whom Indra detained and whom some other worshipper has detained.

11. Kanwa, attended by venerable guests, has made Agni more brilliant than the sun: his moving rays pre-eminently shine; him do these our hymns, him do we extol.

---

1 *Krandad-as'wa gavishtishu*, like a horse making a noise in wishes for cattle. The Scholiast adds *Sangrámeshu*, in battles, having for their object the wish to win cattle,—*govishayechhâyukteshu*. The relation of the simile to Agni is somewhat obscure.—Wilson.

2 *Medhyatithi*, attended by venerable (*medhya*) guests (*atithi*).

12. Agni, giver of food, complete our treasures, for (the friendship) of the deities is obtainable through thee. Thou art the well-known lord of food, thou art great, make us happy.

13. Stand up erect for our protection like the divine Savitri; being erect[1] give us food, for which we invoke thee through priests, the performers of various sacrifices.

14. Erect, preserve us, by knowledge, from sin; consume all the *Rákshasás*; raise us aloft that we may range (in the world); convey our wealth (of oblations) to the deities that we may live.

15. Youthful and most resplendent Agni, protect us from *Râkshasâs*, and from the malevolent (man) who makes no gifts; protect us from injurious (animals), and from those who seek to kill us.

16. O thou of burning rays, do thou completely destroy those who make no gifts as (potter's ware) with a club; let not one, who is inimical to us, nor the man who attacks us with sharp weapons, prevail against us.

17. Agni is solicited for power-giving (riches); he has granted prosperity to Kanwa, he has protected our friends, as well as the (sage who was) the host of the holy, and (every other) worshipper (who sought him) for riches.

18. We invoke, from afar, along with Agni, Turvasa Yadu, and Ugrâdeva; let Agni, the arrester of the robber, bring here Navavâstwa, Brihadratha and Turviti.

---

1 *Agni*, as erect, is here said to be identified with the *Yupa*, or post, to which the victims, at a sacrifice of animals, are bound; and according to *Aswálayana*, this and the next verse are to be recited on such occasions at the time of setting up the post—Wilson.

19. Manu detained thee, Agni, (to give) light to the various races of mankind. Born for the sacrifice and gratified with oblation, thou, whom men salute, hast blazed for Kanwa.

20. The flames of Agni are luminous, powerful, fearful and never to be trusted. Consume entirely the *Râkshasâs*, *Yatudhânas* and all our other adversaries.

SUKTA II. (XXXVII.)

THE Rishi is Kanwa; the deities are the Maruts; the metre is *Gâyatri*.

O YE, Kanwas,[1] hymn, for us, the strength of Maruts, sportive, without horses,[2] but shining in their cars.

2. Who, borne by spotted deer, were born self-radiant, with weapons, war-cries[3] and decorations.

3. I hear the cracking of the whips in their hands wonderfully inspiring (courage) in the fight.

4. Address, the god-given[4] prayer, to those who are your strength, the destroyer of enemies, the powerful, possessed of brilliant reputation.

---

1 *Kanwas* may mean either the members of *Kanwa's* family or intelligent priests.

2 The word is *anarvánam*: the Commentator explains it as *bhrátrivya rahitam* without a brother's son; the meaning is perfectly unintelligible. But the word *Bhrátrivya* may mean "an enemy" and hence the expression may mean "without enemy." Rosen and Langlois accept this meaning. Wilson explains *arvan* as horse and says "being without horses would not be inapplicable to the *Maruts*, whose chariot is drawn by deer."

3 *Vásibhih*, with sounds or speeches *i. e.* according to the Scholiast, with cries terrifying the enemy's army; *Vasi* is a synonym of *Vach*, speech, voice, in the *Nirghanta*—Wilson.

4 *Devattam-brahma*, the praise or prayer which recommends the oblation, obtained from the favour or instruction of the gods—Wilson

5. Laud the imperishable, sportive and resistless power of the Maruts, who were born amongst kine[1] and whose strength has been nourished by the milk.

6. Who is the oldest among you, O ye leading agitators of the celestial region and the nether world, who shake like the top (of a tree) all around?

7. Fearing your terrific and violent approach, the householder has planted a firm (pillar); for even the many-ridged mountain is moved by you.

8. At whose impetuous approach, the earth trembles like an enfeebled king through fear (of his enemies).

9. Fixed is their birthplace (the sky), yet the birds (are able) to issue from (the sphere of) their parent; for your strength is everywhere (divided) between the two (regions).

10. They are the generators of speech: they spread out the waters in their courses: they make the lowing (cattle) to enter (the water) up to their knees (to drink).

11. They drive before them in their course, the well-known, long, vast, uninjurable, rain-retaining cloud.

12. Maruts, since you have the strength, send men to their respective works, drive the clouds.[2]

13. Whenever the Maruts pass, they fill the way with roar; every one hears their (clamour).

14. Come speedily, with your quick-coursing

---

1 The Text has *Goshu-Márutam*, the tribe of *Maruts* among the cows; another Text is cited, which says the *Maruts* were born of milk for *Pris'ni Pris'niyai vai payaso marutah*.—*Wilson*.

2 Max Müller renders it thus:—"You have caused men to fall, you have caused mountains to fall." The Text is *janan acuchyavitan girracuchyavitan*.

(vehicles); the offerings of the Kanwas are prepared; be pleased with them.

15. The libation is prepared for your gratification; we are your (servants), that we may live the full term of our life.

SUKTA III. (XXXVIII.)

The *Rishi*, Deities and metre are the same.

MARUTS, who are fond of laudation, and for whom the sacred grass is trimmed, when will you take us by both hands as does a father his son?

2. Where are you now? When will you come? Pass from the celestial region, not from the terrene sphere. Where are the sacrificers crying like cattle?

3. Where, Maruts, are your new riches? Where your beautiful (articles)? Where all your auspicious (gifts).[1]

4. O sons of Pris'ni,[2] even if you become mortal, your panegyrist would become immortal.

5. Never may your worshipper become indifferent to adore you, as a deer (is never indifferent) to pasture, so that he may not tread the path of Yama.[3]

---

1 The expressions,—*sumná*, *suvita*, and *soubhagá*, indicate, severally, children and kine, jewels and gold, and horses, elephants and the like.

2 The Text has *Pris'ni-Mátarah*; but *Pris'ni* is here explained by the Scholiast by *Dhenu*, a milchcow.

3 Max Müller translates the 4th and 5th Stanzas as follow:— "If you, sons of Pris'ni, were mortals and your worshipper an immortal, then never should your praiser be unwelcome, like a deer in pasture grass, nor should he go on the path of Yama;" and gives his reasons

6. Let not the most powerful and indestructible Nirriti[1] destroy us; let him fall with our thirst.

7. Truly the resplendent and powerful (Maruts), cherished by Rudra,[2] send down the rain without wind upon the desert.

8. Like a cow, having big udders bellowing (for its calf), the lightning roars, and hence the rain is set free by the Maruts.

9. They spread darkness over the day by a water-bearing cloud[3] and thence inundate the earth.

10. When the Maruts roar, every earthly habitation (shakes), and men tremble as well.

11. Maruts, with strong hands, come along the rivers, having variegated banks, with unobstructed course.[4]

---

for so doing. "I feel justified in so doing by other passages where the same or a similar idea is expressed, *viz.*, that if the god were the poet and the poet the god, then the poet would be more liberal to the god than the god is to him."

1 A Deity of the *Rákshas's* race.

2 *Rudriyásah; Rudrasya-imé* those who are of or belonging to *Rudra*; explained *Rudrena-pálitáh*, cherished or protected by *Rudra*.

3 The Text is *Parjanya* which Sáyana has explained as cloud. "Parjanya is a God who presides over the lightning, the thunder, the rain, and the procreation of plants and living creatures."

In his *Rig Véda*, Vol. I., p. 75, Max Müller remarks thus on the word:—"It is interesting to watch the personifying process, which is very palpable in this word, and by which Parjanya becomes at last a friend and companion of Indra."—Dr. *Buhler*.

4 Max Müller gives quite a different explanation of this Stanza:—"Marut, on your strong-hoofed steeds, go on easy roads after those bright ones (the clouds)—which are still locked up." The *Védártha-Yatna*, renders it thus:—"Go, ye Maruts, along the banks of variegated rivers on strong-footed horses of unbroken speed." We do not, however, see the reasons for Max Müller's differing with the Scholiast.

12. May the felloes of your wheels be firm; may your cars and their horses be steady, and your fingers well-skilled (to hold the reins).[1]

13. (O ye priests) describe, in our presence, with words describing the true form of deities, Brahmanaspati,[2] Agni and the beautiful Mitra.

14. Make hymns by your mouths, spread it like a cloud spreading[3] rain; chant the laudatory hymn composed in *Gáyatri* metre.

15. Glorify the host of Maruts, brilliant, worthy of laudation, entitled to adoration: may they be exalted by this our worship.

SUKTA IV. (XXXIX.)

The *Rishi* and Deities are the same; the metre is *Vrikati* in the odd verses, and *Satovrikati* in the even.

O ye Maruts, when, shaking all stable objects, you direct your great vigour like a light downwards from afar, by whose sacrifice, by whose praise, (are you attracted)? to what (place of sacrifice), to whom, do you repair?

2. May your weapons be strong for driving away enemies and firm in resisting them; may your strength be worthy of praise and not (that) of a treacherous mortal.

---

1 The Text has *Susamskrita abhishavas.* Max Müller translates it as, "May your reins be well-fashioned." He says:—"*Abhisa* does not mean finger in the *Rig-Véda*, though Sáyana frequently explains it so, misled by Yáksha.

2 The lord of the *Mantra* or prayer.

3 The Text is *tatanas*; the *Védárta-Yatna* explains it as, *stanadya*, rumble.

3. O ye leaders, when you break down what is stable, when you scatter what is ponderous, then you pass through the forest of earth and the defiles of the mountains.

4. Destroyers of foes, there is no enemy of yours either in the celestial region or on this terrestrial globe; O sons of Rudra, may your strength collectively humble (your enemies).

5. They make the mountains tremble, they set apart the lords of the forest. Go, divine Maruts, whereever you like, with all your progeny, like those intoxicated.

6. You have harnessed the spotted deer to your chariot; the red deer yoked between them, (helps to) drag the car:[1] the earth[2] has heard about your coming and men are alarmed.

7. Rudrâs, we take recourse to your help, for the

---

1 The spotted deer, *Prishatî*, are always specified as the steeds of the Maruts. We then have in the Text, *prashtir-vahati rohita ; prashtih* is said to be a sort of yoke, in the middle of three horses or othe animals, harnessed in a car; but the word stands alone, without any grammatical concord, and it does not appear what is to be done with the yoke. *Rohita*, the Scholiast says, is another kind of deer, the red deer, who, *vahati*, bears or drags the car, *ratham náyati*. The sense may be something like that which is given in the translation but the construction of the original is obscure, apparently rude and ungrammatical.—*Wilson*.

Max Müller dos not accept this sense. He says,—"*Prastih* is explained by Sáyana's authority as a sort of yoke in the middle of three horses. If Sáyana's authority is to be invoked at all, one might appeal from Sáyana in this place, to Sáyana VIII., 7, 28, where *Prastih* is explained by him either by 'quick' or 'harnessed in front."'

2 The Text is *prithivi*; but Sáyana explains it as *antariksha*, 'firmament.' But why? The context supports the translation of the word by 'earth.'

sake of our progeny; come speedily to the timid Kaṇwa, as you formerly came, for our protection.

8. Should any enemy,[1] instigated by you or by man, attack us, withhold from him food and strength and your help.

9. Maruts, possessed of superior intellect and perfectly worthy of a sacrifice, uphold Kaṇwa, come to us, with perfect protectiveness, as the lightning brings the rain.

10. Givers of most excellent (articles), you possess perfect vigour; shakers (of the earth), you possess perfect strength; Maruts, despatch your anger, like an arrow to the wrathful enemy of the *R*ishis.

SUKTA V. (XL.)

The Deity is Brahmaṇaspati; the R*ishi* is Kaṇwa; the metre the same.

RISE up Brahmaṇaspati,[2] seeking the Deities we solicit thee. Bounteous Maruts, come near; Indra, be a partaker of the libation.[3]

2. Protector of strength,[4] man celebrates thee for the wealth[5] abandoned by the foe; Maruts, may he,

---

3 The word *abhas* occurs in the Text. Max Müller translates it as 'fiend.'

1 In a former passage, *Brahmanaspati* appeared as a form of Agni; in this hymn, he is associated with the Maruts although Indra is also separately named.

2 The Text is *Prás'rurvabáh*. Sáyaṇa explains it as either "be partaker of the libation," or "the destroyer of Vritra."

3 The word is *putra*: Sáyaṇa explains it as *pataka*, 'protector,' Wilson translates the word etymologically as 'son.'

4 According to the *Védártha Yatna*,—"When a battle is imminent."

who lauds you, obtain wealth, yielding beautiful horse and great vigour.

3. May Brahmaṇaspati, approach us; may the goddess of speech approach us; may the Deities drive away every enemy and conduct us to sacrifice, which is beneficial to man and (abounds) with respectfully presented offerings.

4. He who presents to the ministrant priest acceptable wealth, enjoys inexhaustible food. For him we worship in a sacrifice Ilâ,[1] attended by brave warriors, inflicting much injury and incapable of being injured by any one.

5. Indeed Brahmaṇaspati recites the sacred prayer in which the Divinities Indra, Varuṇa, Mitra, and Aryaman reside.[2]

6. O ye, Deities, let us recite that felicitous and faultless prayer at sacrifices: if you, leaders, wish for this prayer, then will all that is to be spoken reach unto you.

7. Who (except) Brahmaṇaspati may come near the man, who is devoted to the Deities, who clips the

---

1 Sáyana explains Ilá as *Manoh putri*, 'the daughter of Manu and the institutor of sacrifices. Allusion to Ilá is not out of place here because Brahmanaspati is the presiding Divinity of prayer or Sacrifice.

2 This and the next verse are directed to be recited at the *Agnistoma*-ceremony in connection with prayers addressed to Indra and the Maruts. Professor Roth cites it in proof of his theory, that Brahmanaspati is in an especial manner, the Divinity of prayer, which is not incompatible with his being identical with either Agni or Indra in the same capacity. He recites, it is said, aloud (*pravadati*) the prayer (*Mantra*), which ought to be so recited (*ukhyá*) by the mouth, according to the Scholiast, of the *Hotri*; in which *Mantra*, Indra and the rest abide, or are mystically present; or as explained in the Commentary on the next stanza, it is the *Mantra* or prayer that generates or brings them to the presence of the worshipper.—*Wilson*.

sacred grass: the sacrificer has gone with the priests (to the sacrificial chamber) for he possesses a house (abounding) internally with precious things.[1]

8. Let Brahmaṇaspati concentrate his strength; associated with the regal Divinities,[2] he kills (the enemy): in the time of danger, he maintains his station: armed with the thunderbolt,[3] there is none to encourage or discourage him in a great, or a small, battle.

SUKTA VI. (XLI.)

The *Rishi* **is** *Kanwa*: **the first three and the last three stanzas are addressed to Varuna, Mitra and Aryaman: the middle three to the A'dityas: the metre is** *Gáyatri*.

THE man whom the wise Varuṇa, Mitra and Aryaman protect, speedily subdues (his enemies).

2. He whom they heap (with riches), as if (collected) by his own hands; the man whom they defend from the malignant; every such man, safe from injury, prospers.

3. The kings (Varuṇa, etc.,) first destroy their (enemy's) forts, and then the enemies of those (who worship them) and put aside their evil deeds.

4. A'dityas, to you going to the sacrifice, the path is easy and free from thorns: no bad food is here prepared for you.

---

1 Sáyana gives two interpretations of the expression, *antarbavat* 'abounding internally with precious things,' or 'containing sons and grandsons, etc.'

2 Sáyana explains *Rajabhih* as *Varunadivih*.

3 This attribute would identify him with Indra, in which character he appears throughout this hymn.

5. A'dityas, leaders, may the sacrifice, which you come to by a straight path, lead to your gratification.

6. That mortal, (whom you favour), exempt from harm, gets all valuable wealth and offspring like himself.

7. How, my friends, shall we recite laudatory hymns (worthy) of the great glory of Mitra, Varuṇa and Aryaman?

8. I do not speak against him to you, who injures or reviles the man devoted to the Deities; I rather propitiate you with proffered riches.

9. For he (the worshipper) loves not, but fears to speak ill (of any one), as a gamester fears (his adversary) holding the four[1] (dice), until they are thrown.

SUKTA VII. (XLII.)

Rishi and metre as before: the Deity is Púshan.[2]

PUSHAN, convey us over the road, remove the wicked (obstructer of the way). Son of the Cloud, Deity, go before us.

---

1 The Text has only, *chaturaschid dadamánád vibhíyad-á-nidhátoh*, he may fear from one holding four until the fall. The meaning is supplied by the Scholiast, with the assistance of Yáska, *Chatura akshán dhárayatah kitavát*, from a gambler holding four dice; Sáyaṇa says, four *cowri* shells,—*kapardakáh*; that is, where two men are playing together, the one who has not the throw of the dice or the shells is in anxious apprehension lest it should be against him.—*Wilson*.

2 *Púshan* is usually a synonyme of the Sun; that is, he is one of the twelve *A'dityas*. He is described by the Scholiast as the presiding Deity of the earth,—*prithivyabhimání dévaḥ*; he is also the cherisher of the world; from *push*, to nourish. According to the tenour of the hymn, he is the Deity presiding especially over roads or journeyings. His being called the son of the Cloud, is not incompatible with his character

2. If a wicked (adversary), Púshan, a robber, or one who delights in evil, points out to us (the way we ought not to go), do thou drive him from the road.

3. Drive him far away, apart from the road, the hinderer of our journey, a thief, a deceiver.

4. Trample with your feet upon the mischievous (body) of that evil-minded pilferer of both (what is present and what is absent), whoever he be.

5. Sagacious and handsome Púshan, we solicit of thee that protection wherewith thou hast encouraged the patriarchs.

6. Therefore do thou, who art possessed of all prosperity, and well equipped with golden weapons, bestow upon us riches that may be liberally distributed.

7. Lead us past our opponents; conduct us by an easy path; know, Púshan, how to protect us on this (journey).[1]

---

of earth personified as a male, as, according to other Texts of the *Véda*, the earth was born of the water,—*adbhyah prithiví;* and again, earth was the essence of the water; *tad yad apâm sára ásít tat samahanyata sá prithiví abhavat,*—that which was the essence of the waters, that was aggregated, and it became earth. *Púshá* occurs also as a feminine noun, in which case it appears to be synonymous with *Prithivi*, the earth, as in the Text: *Pushádhwana pátu*, which is explained, *iyam pushá*, may this *Pushá* protect the roads; where the gender is denoted by the feminine pronoun *íyam:* and in another Text, *íyam vai pusheyam hidam sarvam pushyati,*—this is verily *Pushá*, for she cherishes this whole world. Throughout the hymn, however, *Pushan* is masculine.—*Wilson.*

1 In this and the two next verses, we have an example of what is not unfrequent, the repetition of a phrase as a sort of burden or refrain: the expression is, *Pushan iha kratum vidah,*—*Pushan*, know here, the act or business; that is, on this occasion or journey, know how to fulfil your function of giving us protection. Rosen renders it, *Pushan hic sacrificum animadverte*; *kratu* meaning an act of sacrifice, as well as act or action in general.—*Wilson.*

8. Lead us where there is abundant fodder; let there be no extreme heat by the way; Púshan, know how to protect us on this (journey).

9. Be favourable to us, fill us (with abundance), give us (all good things), sharpen us (with vigour), fill our bellies; Púshan, know how to protect us on this (journey).

10. We do not censure Púshan, but praise him with hymns; we solicit the good-looking (Púshan) for riches.

SUKTA VIII. (XLIII.)

THE *Rishi* is the same; the Deity is Rudra;[1] the third stanza is addressed to Mitra and Varuna also, and the last three verses to Soma; the metre of the last verse is *Anushtub*, of the rest, *Gáyatrí*.

WHEN may we repeat a most grateful hymn to the wise, the most bountiful and mighty Rudra, who is (cherished) in our hearts?

2. By which earth may (be induced to) grant the gifts of Rudra[2] to our cattle, our people, our cows, and our progeny.

---

1 According to the Scholiast, *Rudra* means, he who makes to weep, who causes all to weep at the end of time; thus identifying him with the destroying principle, or *S'iva*; but there is nothing in the hymn to bear out such an identification; on the contrary, he appears as a beneficent Deity, presiding especially over medicinal plants.—*Wilson.*

2 *Aditi* is here said to mean the earth, who, it is wished, may so act (*karat*), that *Rudriya* may be obtained. The meaning of *Rudriya*, according to the Scholiast, is, *Rudra sambandhi bhéshajam*,—medicament in relation to or presided over by *Rudra*, conformably to the Text, *yá te Rudra s'ivá tanuh, s'ivá vis'wá ha, bhésháji s'ivá, Rudrasya bhéshajiti*,—whatever are thy auspicious forms, O *Rudra*, they are all auspicious; auspicious are medicaments, the medicaments of *Rudra*.—*Wilson.*

3. By which Mitra, and Varuṇa, and Rudra, and all the gods, being gratified, may show us (favour).

4. We ask the felicity of S'anyu,[1] from Rudra, the encourager of hymns, the protector of sacrifices, possessed of medicaments that confer delight.[2]

5. Who is so brilliant as S'anyu, who gratifies like gold, the best of the gods, the provider of habitations ?

6. Who bestows easily-obtained happiness on our steeds, our rams, our ewes, our men, our women, and our cows ?

7. Soma, grant us prosperity more than (sufficient for) a hundred men, and much strength-engendering food.

8. Let not the adversaries of Soma, let not our enemies, harm us : cherish us, Indra, with (abundant) food.

9. Soma, who art immortal, and abidest in an excellent dwelling, have regard for thy subjects, when at their head in the hall of sacrifice thou observest them (engaged in) decorating thee.[3]

---

1 *S'anyu* is said to be the son of *Vrikaspati ;* nothing more is related of him.—*Wilson.*

2 *Jalâshabheshajam*, he who has medicaments conferring delight ; from *ja*, one born, and *lâsha*, happiness ; an unusual word except in a compound form, as *abhilâsha*, which is of current use ; or it may mean, sprung from water (*jala*), all vegetables depending upon water for their growth.—*Wilson.*

3 Apparently there is some confusion of objects in this place, *Soma*, the Moon, being confounded with *Soma*, libation.—*Wilson.*

ANUVA'KA IX.

SUKTA I. (XLIV.)

PRASKANWA, the son of Kanwa, is the *Rishi*; *Agni* is the Deity, but the two first verses are addressed also to the As'wins and to Ushas (the dawn); the metre is *Brihati* in the odd verses, *Satobrihati* in the even.

AGNI, who art immortal, and cognizant of all begotten things, bring from the dawn to the donor (of the oblation), wealth of many sorts with an excellent habitation; bring hither to-day the gods awaking with the morning.

2. For thou, Agni, art the accepted messenger of the gods, the bearer of oblations, the vehicle of sacrifices:[1] associated with Ushas and the As'wins, bestow upon us abundant and invigorating food.

3. We select to-day Agni, the messenger, the giver of dwellings, the beloved of many, the smoke-bannered, the light-shedding, the protector of the worship of the worshipper at the break of day.

4. I praise Agni at the break of day, the best and youngest (of the gods), the guest (of man), the universally-invoked, who is friendly to the man that offers (oblations), who knows all that are born, that he may go (to bring) the other divinities.

5. Agni, immortal sustainer of the universe, bearer of oblations, deserving of adoration, I will praise thee, who art exempt from death, the preserver, the sacrificer.

---

1 *Rathiradhwaránám*. Rosen renders *rathih*, *auriga*, but Sáyana, explains it, *ratha-sthaniya*, in the place of a chariot; confirmed by other Texts; as, *esha hi déva-rathah*, he (Agni) is verily the chariot of the gods, and, *ratha ha vá esha bhutebhyo dévebhyo havyam vahati*, truly he is the chariot that bears the oblation to the spirits and the gods.—*Wilson*.

6. Juvenile, Agni, whose flames delight, who art universally invoked, and art praised (by us) on behalf of the worshipper, understand (our wishes), and, granting Praskaṇwa to live a lengthened life, do honour to the divine man.[1]

7. All people kindle thee, Agni, the sacrificer, the omniscient; do thou, Agni, who art invoked by many, quickly bring hither the sapient Deities.

8. Object of holy rites,[2] (bring hither) on the dawn following the night, Savitri, Ushas, the As'wins, Bhaga,[3] and Agni: the Kaṇwas pouring out libations, kindle the wafter of the burnt offering.

9. Thou, Agni, art the protector of sacrifices of the the people, and the messenger (of the gods); bring hither to-day the gods awaking at dawn, and contemplating the Sun, to drink the *Soma*-Juice.

10. Resplendent Agni visible to all, thou hast blazed after many preceding dawns, thou art the protector (of the people) in villages, thou art the associate of man placed on the east (of the altar).[4]

11. We place thee, Agni, as Manu placed thee, who art the implement of sacrifice, the invoker, the ministering priest, very wise, the destroyer (of foes), immortal, the messenger (of the gods).

12. When, cherisher of friends, thou art present as the *Purohita* at a sacrifice, and dischargest the mission to the gods, then thy flames roar like the resounding billows of the ocean.

---

1 *Namasya daivyam janam*; that is, the *Rishi* of the hymn, Praskaṇwa.—*Wilson*.

2 *Swadhwara*; from *su*, good, and *adhwara*, sacrifice; equivalent, according to the Scholiast, to the *A'havaniya* fire.—*Wilson*.

3 *Bhaga* is one of the *A'dityas*.—*Wilson*.

4 *Purohita*, which may also mean, the domestic priest.—*Wilson*.

13. Agni, with sharp ears, hear me: let Mitra, and Aryaman, and other) early-stirring Deities, with all the accompanying oblation-bearing Gods, sit down at the sacrifice upon the sacred grass.

14. Let the munificent Maruts, who have tongues of fire, and are encouragers of sacrifice, hear our praise; let the rite-fulfilling Varuṇa, with the As'wins, and with Ushas, drink the *Soma*-Juice.

SÚKTA II. (XLV.)

THE Deity and *Rishi* are the same, except in the last stanza and the half of the preceding, which include any Deified Being; the metre is *Anushtubh*.

AGNI, do thou, in this our rite, worship the Vasus, the Rudras, the A'dityas, or any other (living) being sprung from Manu, sacrificing well and sprinkling water.[1]

2. Verily the discriminating Gods are givers of rewards to the offerer (of oblations): lord of red coursers, propitiated by our praises, bring hither the three and thirty Divinities.[2]

---

1 *Janam; Manu jatam*, a man born of *Manu*. *Jan*[a], according to the Scholiast, here signifies a Divine Being in connection with the Divinities enumerated, another man, *devata-rupam*, of a divine nature or form.—*Wilson*.

2 We have had these alluded to on a former occasion (p. 75, n.); but, according to the *Aitareya Brahmana*, 2, 18, there are two classes of thirty-three Divinities each, the one consisting of those formerly specified, who are termed also *Somapas*, or drinkers of the *Soma*-Juice, and the other of eleven *Prayâjas* (the same with the *A'pris*, p. 231), eleven *Anuyâjas*, and eleven *Upayâjas*, who are to be propitiated by oblations of clarified butter, not by libations of *Soma*. They are evidently little else than personifications of sacrifices.—*Wilson*.

3. Agni, accomplisher of solemn acts, cognisant of all who are born, hear the invocation of Praskaṇwa, as thou hast heard those of Priyamédha, of Atri, Virúpa, of Angiras.[1]

4. The performers of great ceremonies, the offerers of acceptable sacrifices, have invoked for (their protection), Agni, shining amidst the solemnities, with pure resplendence.

5. Invoked by oblations, giver of rewards, listen to these praises with which the sons of Kaṇwa invoke thee for protection.

6. Agni, granter of abundant sustenance, who art beloved of many, the sons of men invoke thee, radiant-haired, to bear the oblation (to the Gods).

7. The wise men have placed thee, Agni, in (their) sacrifices as the invoker, the ministrant priest, the donor of vast wealth, the quick-hearing, the far-renowned.

8. The wise (priests), with effused libations of *Soma*-Juice, have summoned thee, vast and brilliant Agni, to partake of the (sacrificial food), as they hold the oblation on the part of the individual who presents it.

9. Strength-generated,[2] giver of rewards, provider of dwellings, place here to-day upon the sacred grass the morning-moving Deities, or (other) Deified Being, to drink the *Soma*-Juice.[3]

---

1 The Commentator, on the authority of the *Nirukta*, 3, 17, calls these all Rishis. *Atri* and *Angiras* are always enumerated among the *Prajápatis*; *Priyamedhas* may be the same as *Priyavrata*, the son of *Swáyambhua Manu*; and we have a *Virupa* among the early descendants of *Vaivas'watá Manu*, who, as the father of *Ilá*, is the *Manu* of the *Veda*.—*Vishnu Purá na*.—*Wilson*.

2 Produced by friction, which requires strength to perform effectually.—*Wilson*.

3 In this and the next stanza, we have again an allusion to some divine or deified person, *daivyam janam*, or to some other divinity

10. Worship with conjoint invocations, Agni, the present Deified Being; bounteous Divinities, this is the *Soma*-Juice; drink it, for it was yesterday expressed.[1]

SUKTA III. (XLVI.)

THE *Rishi* as before, the Deities are the Aswins; the metre is *Gâyatri*.

DEAR USHAS, not seen till now, removes darkness from the sky; As'wins, I laud you profusely.

2. The two Deities are of comely looks, have the Ocean for their mother,[2] distribute wealth by the mind and grant habitations by the pious rites (*i.e.*, when any sacrifice is celebrated).

3. When your chariot is drawn by horses to the heavens lauded (in various places) your praises are sung by us.

4. O guides, the Sun,—the evaporator of waters, the nourisher, the protector and beholder of sacrifice, nourishes (the Deities) with our oblation.

5. Násatyas, accepting our laudations, partake of the exhilarating *Soma*-Juice that animates your understanding.

---

without particularizing him; it may be intended for *Ka* or *Prajápati*, who, with Agni, here actually addressed, would make up the thirty-three Divinities, with the *Vasus*, *Rudras*, and *A'dityas*.

1 *Tiro-ahnyam* is said to be the appellation of the *Soma*-Juice so prepared; from *Tiras*, oblique or indirect, and *Ahnyam*, diurnal; that juice which is expressed on the preceding day and offered on the succeeding.

2 *Sindhu-matarau*. The Sun and the Moon, as the Scholiast states, are said to be born of the Sea. The As'wins are said to be the Sun and the Moon. And hence they are described here as the Seaborn.

6. As'wins, give us that invigorating food which may satisfy us, having removed the darkness (of want.)[1]

7. Come, as a boat, to carry us over an ocean of laudations: harness, As'wins, your car.

8. Your vessel, vaster than the sky, stops on the seashore; your chariot (waits on the land); the drops (of *Soma*-Juice) have been mixed up for your worship.

9. Kaṇwas, (ask of the As'wins),—(How) do the rays (of the Sun proceed) from the sky? (How) does the Dawn (rise) in the region of the waters? Where do you desire to manifest your own persons.[2]

10. (The Sun's) ray created light in the Dawn; the Sun (after rising) became like gold; the Fire (entering the Sun) shone with darkened flames.

11. A good path was made for the Sun to go beyond the boundary (of night); the radiance of the luminary[3] became profusely visible.

12. The singer of laudatory verses, again and again embellishes the work of protection of the As'wins, drinking *Soma*-Juice for exhilaration.

---

1 The word in the Text is *Tamastiraḥ*; literally, disperse the darkness. Sáyana, however, means by it "the darkness of Poverty."

2 The whole of this stanza is very elliptical and obscure and largely indebted to the Scholiast; literally it would run, Rays from the sky, *Kanwas*, cause of dwelling in the place of the rivers; where do you wish to place own form? Sáyana fills up by supposing that the *Kanwas* are directed to inquire of the *As'wins* the particulars specified in the translation. Without some such addition, however conjectural it may be, it were impossible to extract any meaning out of the passage.—*Wilson.*

3 The word in the Text in one place is *Ritasya*, and in another *divaḥ*. Sáyana explains both the words as *Súrya*, the Sun. *Védárthayatna* explains it: "Lo, the good road of the true religion for crossing over (misery) has manifested itself."

13. Causers of felicity, co-dwellers with your sacrificer, as with Manu, come here to drink of the *Soma*-Juice, and (accept) our praise.

14. May Ushas follow the lustre of your approach,[1] circumambient As'wins, and may you be pleased with the oblations offered by night.

15. As'wins, do ye both drink (the oblation) and confer happiness on us through your perfect protection.

---

1 The early Aryans used to adore the mixed light and darkness as As'wins, appearing in the sky before dawn. Mr. R. C. Dutt has given an exhaustive note in the Note appended to the First *Rik* of the Third *Súkta*. According to Yáska, the mixed light and darkness appearing in the sky, after midnight and before dawn, is represented by the As'wins. Max Müller means by the two As'wins the two periods of conjunction (See *Origin and Growth of Religion* (1882) p. 219. Goldstucker holds that the *Aswins* were deified men like the *Ribhus*. He writes in a *Note* on *Muir's Sanskrit Texts*:—"The transition from darkness to light, when the intermingling of both produces that inseparable duality expressed by the twin nature of these deities."

FOURTH ADHYA'YA.

ANUVA'KA IX.—*(Continued.)*

SUKTA IV. (XLVII.)

THE *Rishi* is Praskanwa; the Deities are the As'wins: the metre of the odd verses is *Brihati*; and of the even, *Satobrihati*.

AS'WINS, multipliers of sacrifice, this most sweet *Soma*-Juice is prepared for you, drink it of yesterday's expressing and grant riches to the offerer of oblation.

2. As'wins, come in your three-columned, triangular car, beautifully embellished with gold:[1] the Kaṇwas repeat your praise at the sacrifice; graciously hear their invocation.

3. A'swins, multipliers of sacrifice, drink this most sweet *Soma*-Juice. O ye bearers of wealth, carrying wealth in (your) chariot, approach to-day the offerer of oblation.

4. Omniscient As'wins, stationed on the sacred grass heaped in three chambers, sprinkle the sacrifice with sweet juice; the illustrious Kaṇwas, with effused libations, invoke you.

5. Such desired aids as you protected Kaṇwa with, do you, cherishers of pious deeds, preserve us; multipliers of sacrifice, drink the *Soma*-Juice.

6. Handsome As'wins, as you brought, in your

---

1 *Tribandhuréṇá-trivrita-rathéna*, "with a car with three posts, and triangular," is the explanation we had before. The Scholiast here proposes a somewhat different interpretation, and would render the terms "having three undulating fastenings of timber, and passing unobstructedly through the three worlds."—*Wilson*.

chariot, bearers of wealth, abundance to Sudása,[1] so bring to us riches coveted by many, whether from the firmament or the sky beyond.

7. Násatyas, whether you are near or afar, come to us in your well-made car, with the rays of the Sun.

8. Let your seven (horses), the grace of the sacrifice, bring you to be present at our sacrifice; guides (of men), conferring food upon the pious and liberal sacrificer, sit down on the sacred grass.

9. Come, Násatyas, in your sun-clad[2] chariot, in which you have ever carried riches to the offerer of oblation, to drink of the sweet *Soma*-Juice.

10. We invoke, with chanted and recited verses, the very affluent As'wins towards us for our protection. Have you not ever drunk the *Soma*-Juice in the favourite house of the Kanwas?

SUKTA V. (XLVIII.)

The *Rishi* is the same, but the hymn is addressed to Ushas, the personified Dawn, or Aurora: the metre is the same as in the previous hymn.

USHA', daughter of the Divinity[3] of heaven, dawn upon us with riches. Vibhávari (diffuser of light), dawn upon us with abundant food; O goddess, being bountiful, dawn upon us with wealth of cattle.

---

1 Sudása is the son of Pijavana. He is called a *Rája* (king). In the *Puránás* we meet with two princes of the name of Sudása,—one in the solar line, and the other in the lunar line.

2 Literally, sun-skinned—*Súryatwachá*; that is, either surrounded, or invested, by the Sun, or like him in brightness.—*Wilson*

3 The Text has *Divas duhitá*. Sáyana explains it *dyudévatayas*—divinity of heaven. Wilson renders it as "daughter of heaven."

2. Possessed of horses, possessed of kine, givers of every sort of wealth,[1] (the Divinities of morning) are possessed of much that is necessary for the habitations (of men). Ushas, speak to me kind and beneficial words: give us the riches of the wealthy.

3. The Divine Ushas dwelt[2] (of yore): may she dawn to-day, the despatcheress of cars which are harnessed at her coming, as those who seek riches (send ships) to sea.[3]

4. Ushas, at thy approach, wise men turn their minds to benefactions. The wise Kaṇwa proclaims the name of those (liberal) men.

5. Ushas, nourishing (all), comes every day like a matron, the directress (of all domestic works), bringing all living creatures[4] to decripitude; she makes every biped engage in action and make the birds fly away (from their nests).

---

1 The three epithets are in the feminine plural, without a substantantive: *aswavatih, gomatih, vis'wasuvidah*; the Scholiast supplies, therefore, *ushodévotáh*, the divinities of dawn, as if there were many.—*Wilson.*

2 *i.e.*, Used to make dawn formerly, as she is doing to-day.

3 The Text is *Samudre na sravasyavah*, like those desirous of wealth for sea; the Commentary supplies "Send ships." In the beginning of the stanza we have *uvásha ushas*, which the Scholiast explains *puráni vásam akarot*, she has made a dwelling formerly; *i.e.*, *prabhátam kritavdti*, she produced the dawn.—*Wilson.*

4 The Text has *Jarayanti vrijanam*. Sáyana explains the first word as *Jarám prápayanti i.e.*, bringing into decripitude; and the second word, as *gamanas'ilam jangam*, *i.e.*, living or moving creatures. Wilson translates the expression as, "Conducting all transient (creatures) to decay." Benfey and Bollenson, understands the word *Jarayanti* as meaning "arouse." Muir renders the passage as, "she hastens on arousing footed creatures." We have literally followed the Scholiast.

6. She sends the diligent (to works); she despatches the solicitors (to their patrons)[1]; and shedder of dews[2] knows not delay; bestower of food at thy rising, the soaring birds do not wait (in their nests).

7. This auspicious Ushas has harnessed (her vehicles) from afar, above the rising of the Sun; and she comes gloriously upon man with a hundred chariots.[3]

8. All living beings adore her, that she may be visible; bringer of good, she lights up the world; the affluent daughter of heaven drives away the malevolent and disperses the absorbers[4] (of moisture.)

9. Shine around, Ushas, with cheering lustre; bring us profuse good luck every day and disperse darkness.

10. Bringer of good, the breath and life of all (creatures) rest in thee, for thou removest darkness; diffuser of light, come to us in thy spacious car; possessor of wondrous wealth, hear our invocation.

11. Ushas, accept the food of many sorts which exists among the human race; bring to the innocent rite the pious sacrificers who laud thee.

12. Ushas, bring from the firmament all the Deities, to drink the *Soma*-Juice; do thou give us excellent and invigorating food, together with cattle and horses.

13. May that Ushas, whose rays destroy the enemies,[5] and are seen (full of) auspiciousness, grant

---

1 The Text is *arthinah visrijati*, *i.e.*, "lets loose or despatches the solicitors." The Commentator says, "that the solicitors, having risen up early in the morning, go to the houses of their respective benefactors."

2 Muir translates the word *Odati* as "lively."

3 *i.e.*, many rays of light.

4 *Sridhah*; *Soshayitrin*; the driers up; possibly the clouds are meant.

5 The Text has *Rus'antah*, Sâyana explains it as *S'atrún hinsántah*, "destroying the enemies," Wilson translates it as "bright."

us riches, adorable unto all, easily attainable and beautiful.

14. Adorable Ushas, whom the ancient sages invoked for protection and food, do thou, (radiant) with pure light, (pleased) by our offerings, accept our laudations.

15. Ushas, since thou hast to-day set open the two gates of heaven with light,[1] grant us a spacious and secure habitation: bestow upon us, goddess, cattle and food.

16. Ushas, associate us with profuse and multiform wealth, and with abundant cattle, with all foe-destroying fame, and, giver of sustenance, with food.

SUKTA VI. (XLIX.)

THE *Rishi* and Deity are the same; the metre is *Anushtubh*.

USHAS, come by auspicious ways from above the bright (region of the) firmament; let the purple kine[2] bring thee to the habitation of the offerer of the *Soma*-Juice.

2. Ushas, in the beautiful[3] and spacious chariot which thou ridest, come to-day, daughter of heaven, to the pious offerer of the oblation.

3. White-complexioned Ushas, upon thy approach, bipeds and quadrupeds (are in motion), and the winged birds flock round from the boundaries of the sky.

---

1 The east and west points of the horizon.

2 Purple cows—the vehicles of the morning.

3 The Text has *Supés'sam*. Sáyana explains it as either *S'obhanarupayuktam*, "beautiful"; or *S'obhanahiranyayuktam*, "embellished with brilliant gold."

4. Thou, Ushas, destroying darkness, illuminest the shining universe with thy rays: the Kanwas, seeking wealth, laud thee, as thou art, with hymns.

SUKTA VII. (L.)

The *Rishi* is Praskanwa, the Deity is Súrya, the Sun. The first nine stanzas are in the *Gáyatri* metre, the last four in the *Anushubh*.

HIS coursers[1] bear on high the effulgent, all-knowing Sun, that he may be seen by all (the worlds).

2. At the approacch of the all-illuminating Sun, the Constellations[2] depart with the night, like thieves.

3. His illuminating rays behold men in succession, like blazing fires.

4. Thou, Súrya, travellest[3] (in a great way, incapable of being traversed by any); thou art visible unto

---

1 The Text has, *Ketavaḥ*. Sáyana explains it as either the rays of the Sun or its horses.

2 *Nakshatráni*, the Stars in general, or the Lunar Asterisms, which, according to different Texts, are considered to be the abodes of the Gods, or the visible forms of pious persons after death; as, *dévagrihá vai nakshatráni*, the Constellations are verily the dwellings of the Gods; and again, *yo vá iha yajate amum lokam nakshate*, either, he who performs worship here, obtains the next world, or, *sukritám vá etáni jyotinshi yan nakshatrani*, those Constellations are the luminaries of those who practise religious acts, that is, according to Sáyana, those who by attending to religious duties in this world attain *Swarga*, are beheld in the form of Constellations,—*iha loke karmánushtháya ye swargam prápnuvanti te nakshatrarúpena drisyante.*—*Wilson.*

3 Sáyana says, that, according to the *Smriti*, the Sun moves 2,202 *yojanas* in half a twinkle of the eye.—*Wilson.*

all; thou art the source of light;[1] thou shinest throughout the entire firmament.

5. Thou risest in the presence of the Maruts;[2] thou risest in the presence of mankind, and to be seen by the entire region of heaven.

6. With that light with which, thou, the purifier and defender from evil,[3] lookest upon this creature-bearing world.

7. Thou traversest the vast ethereal space, creating days and nights and seeing all creatures.

8. Divine and all-manifesting Súrya, thy seven coursers[4] bear thee, bright-haired, in thy car.

9. The Sun has yoked the seven mares[5] drawing his chariot (safely), and comes with them self-harnessed.

---

1 *Jyotishkrit*, giving light to all things, even to the Moon and the Planets, by night; for they, it is said, are of a watery substance, from which the rays of the Sun are reflected, in like manner as the rays of the Sun, falling upon a mirror placed in the door-way of a chamber, are reflected into the interior, and give it light. Sáyana also explains the whole passage metaphysically, identifying the Sun with the Supreme Spirit, who enables all beings to pass over the ocean of existence, who is beheld by all desirous of final emancipation, who is the author of true or spiritual light, and who renders everything luminous through the light of the mind.—*Wilson.*

2 The Text has, *dévanâm vis'aḥ*. Sáyana explains it as, "in the presence of the Deities, the *Maruts*." Muir translates it as, "The race of Gods." The latter is a literal rendering of the Text.

3 The Text has, *Varuna*. Sáyana explains it as, "evil-preventing Sun."

4 The name of the Sun's horses is *Harita*. It may also mean the seven rays. The seven horses are the seven days of the week.

5 The Text has, *naptyaḥ*. Sáyana explains it as, "with them the car does not fall." Muir translates it as, "daughters of the car."

10. Beholding the up-springing light above the darkness, we approach the Divine Sun among the Deities, the most excellent light.[1]

11. •Radiant with benevolent light, rising to-day and mounting into the highest heaven, do thou, O Sun, remove the sickness of my heart[2] and the yellowness (of my body).

12. Let us transfer the yellowness (of my body) to the parrots, to the starlings, or to the *Haritála* (tree).[3]

13. This A'ditya has risen with all (his) energy, destroying my enemy, for I cannot resist that foe.[4]

---

1 Sáyana also explains it as, the "Spiritual Sun." The darkness indicates the sin, and the approach to the Sun means the re-union with the Supreme Spirit.

2 *Hrid-roga* may also mean heart-burn or indigestion; *harimánam*, greenness or yellowness, is external change of the colour of the skin in jaundice or bilious affections. This verse and the two following constitute a *tricha* or triplet, the repetition of which, with due formalities, is considered to be curative of disease. Súrya, thus hymned by Praskanwa, cured him, it is said, of a cutaneous malady or leprosy under which he was labouring; accordingly Saunaka terms the couplets a *Mantra*, dedicated to the Sun, removing sin, healing disease, an antidote to poison, and the means of obtaining present happiness and final liberation. The especial worship of the Sun in India at the time of the first incursions of the Mohammedans, attributed to that luminary's having cured Samba, the son of Krishna, of leprosy, is fully related by M. Reinaud in his interesting *Mémoire sur l' Inde*, and was then, no doubt, of ancient date, originating with the primitive notions of the attributes of Súrya here adverted to. The hymn is throughout of an archaic character.—*Wilson*.

3 The Text has, *Haridrava*. Sáyana explains it as *Haritáladruma* (tree). But there is no such tree. *Haridruvá* is truly a yellow vegetable power.

4 This enemy is either sickness or disease.

ANUVA'KA X.

SUKTA I. (LI.)

THE *Rishi* is Savya,[1] the son of Angiras: the Deity is Indra; the last two verses are in the *Trishtubh* metre, the rest in *Jaguti.*

GLADDEN with laudations that ram,[2] (Indra), who is invoked by many, who is eulogised by hymns and is an ocean of wealth; whose good deeds, like the rays of light, bring about the well-being of mankind; adore the powerful and wise Indra, for the enjoyment (of riches).

2. The protecting and fostering *R*ibhus[3] hastened to the presence of Indra, of graceful motion, irradiating the firmament, imbued with vigour, the humiliator of his enemies, and the performer of a hundred sacrifices; and by them, encouraging words were uttered.[4]

3. Thou hast set open the cloud[5] for the Angirasas, thou hast shown the way to Atri, who vexes his adversaries by a hundred doors;[6] thou hast granted wealth, with food, to Vimada:[7] thou art wielding thy

---

1 Angiras performed penances for having a son like unto Indra, and accordingly the latter was born as his son Savya.

2 This refers to the legend that Indra came in the form of a ram to a sacrifice performed by Medhátithi. *Mesha* may mean "victors of enemies," says Wilson.

3 The *Ribhus*, as Sáyana holds, mean here the Maruts. When an encounter took place between Indra and V*r*itra, it was the Maruts, who, being present there, encouraged the former.

4 Their encouraging words were,—"Strike; *Bhagaván*, be valiant."

5 Sáyana has given two meanings of the word *gotra*, "a cloud," or "a herd of cattle." So the expression means either that "Indra showered rain by setting open the clouds," or "brought out the herd of cattle hidden by Pani."

6. *i.e.*, by various means or contrivances.

7 A *Maharshi.*

thunderbolt in defence of a worshipper engaged in battle.

4. Thou hast opened the receptacle of the waters; thou hast detained, in the mountain, the treasures of Vṛitra[1] and other Dánavás; when thou hadst killed Vṛitra the destroyer, thou madest the Sun ascend the sky to be seen (by all).

5. Thou, Indra, by thy devices, hast humbled the deceivers who presented oblations to their own mouths:[2] being favourably disposed towards men, thou hast destroyed the cities of Pipru, and hast well-defended *R*ijis'wan in robber-destroying (contests).[3]

6. Thou hast defended Kutsa in fatal fights with S'ushṇa; (for protecting Divodása) hospitable to his guests), thou hast destroyed S'ambara; thou hast trodden, with thy foot, upon the great Arbuda; thou wast born for the destruction of the oppressors.[4]

7. Forsooth, entire vigour has been placed in thee; thy mind delights to drink the *Soma*-Juice; it is known to us that the thunderbolt is deposited in thy hands; cut off the entire energy of the enemy.

---

1 Vritra—the head of the *Asuras*, who is described here as *Ahi*, is explained *hantrí*, "the slayer."

2 According to the *Kaus'itakis*, the *Asuras*, contemning, Agni, offered oblations to themselves, and the *Vájasaneyis* relate that when there was rivalry between the Gods and *Asuras*, the latter arrogantly said, " Let us not offer sácrifice to any one.—*Wilson*.

3 Pipru is called an *Asura*; *R*ijs'wan a worshipper whom they oppressed; *dasyu-hatyeshu*, in battles killing the *Dasyus*, robbers or barbarians.—*Wilson*.

4 S'ushṇa, S'ambara, and Arbuda are designated as *Asuras*; Kutsa is the name of a *Rishi*; *Atithigwa* is said to mean hospitable, and to be also termed Divodása; but it does not appear whether he is the same Divodása of the *Puranas*.—*Wilson*.

8. Know the *A'ryas* and they who are *Dasyus*:[1] restraining those who perform no religious rites, compel them to submit to the performer of sacrifices with *Varhis* (*Kus'a*-grass): be thou, who art powerful, the encourager of the sacrificer; I wish to laud all thy deeds in the sacrifice that gives thee satisfaction.

9. Indra abides, compelling the neglecters of holy rites to submit to those who perform them; and those who do not chant his praises, to them who are present (with them). Vamra, while praising him, growing and spreading through heaven, carried off the accumulated (materials of the sacrifice).[2]

10. When Us'anas[3] sharpened thy strength with his own, thy might, by its purified fierceness, terrified both heaven and earth. O thou having a mind favourably disposed towards man, let the will-harnessed steeds, fleet like the wind, convey thee, filled (with vigour), to (partake of the sacrificial) food.

11. When Indra is lauded along with charming Us'anas, he ascends (his car), drawn by more and more obliquely-going horses; fierce, he extracts the waters from the passing (cloud) in a torrent and has destroyed the extensive cities of S'ushṇa.

12. Thou mountest thy chariot willingly, Indra, for

---

1 The *Aryas* were those who used to perform religious rites and the *Dasyus* were inimical to them. The latter were probably the uncivilized tribes of India who had not been, till then, subdued by the *Aryas*.

2 The Text is here obscure.—*Vamra vijaghána sandihah*; *Vamra* destroyed the collections. The Scholiast says, that a *Rishi*, named *Vamra*, took advantage of Indra's absence from a sacrifice to carry away the accumulated heap of offerings, the marrow or essence of the earth.—*Wilson*.

3 *Ushanas* was the preceptor of the *Asuras*.

the sake of drinking the libations. Such in which, thou findest delight, have been prepared (at the sacrifice of S'áryáta;[1] be pleased with them, as thou art gratified by the effused *Soma*-Juices (at the sacrifices) of others, and thou shalt obtain imperishable fame in heaven.

13. Indra, thou hast given the youthful Vṛichayá[2] to the aged king Kakshívat, lauding thee and offering libations: thou, S'atakratu, wast Mená, the daughter of Vṛishaṇas'wa;[3] those thy deeds are to be recited at the time of offering libations to thee.

14. Indra has been served, so that he may help the performer of good deeds in their poverty. The laudation of the Pajras,[4] is (as stable) as the post of a doorway. Indra, the giver of riches, who desires horses, cattle, chariots and wealth, (for the sacrificers) is present.

---

1 S'aryáta was a *Rájarshi* according to the Scholiast, of the race of Bhrigu. The *Aitaréya Brahmana* calls him a prince of the race of Manu. The term is a patronymic, implying son or descendant of S'aryáti, who was the fourth son of the Manu Vaivaswata: the *Rishi* Chyavana married his daughter and a solemn sacrifice was held on the occasion, at which Indra and As'wins were present. Chyavana appropriated to himself the share of the oblation intended for the As'wins, at which Indra was very angry, and to appease him, a fresh offering was prepared. The Scholiast quotes this story from the *Kaus'ítaki*. It is detailed in the *Bhagavata* and *Padma Puranas*.—*Wilson.*

2 Kakíshwat performed many sacrifices. Indra, pleased truly, gave him a youthful wife of this name.

3 The *Bráhmana* is cited for a strange story of Indra's having himself become Mená, the daughter of Vrishanas'wa, and having afterwards fallen in love with her. The Mena of the *Purános* was the wife of Himávat, the king of mountains.—*Wilson.*

4 Pajras are said to be the same as the Aṅgirasas.

15. This adoration is offered to the showerer of rain, the self-resplendent, the possessor of true vigour, the mighty: may we, Indra, be helped, in this conflict, by many heroes, and, in a handsome house, given by thee, may we live with a learned (progeny).

SUKTA II. (LII.)

THE *Rishi* and Deity are the same; the metre of the 13th and 15th verses is *Trishtubh*; and of the rest, *Jagati*.

ADORE full well that ram who makes heaven known, in whose laudation a hundred worshippers are simultaneously engaged. Implore Indra with many prayers to ascend the chariot, which hastens like a fleet courser to the sacrifice for my protection.

2. When Indra, fond of sacrificial food, had killed Vṛitra, the obstructer of rivers, by pouring down the waters, he stood, amidst the torrents, firm like a mountain and, possessed of a thousand means of protecting (his followers), increased in strength.

3. He,—who covers the covering enemies,[1] who is spread like water in the firmament, the root of happiness (unto all), who has increased (in strength) by (drinking) the *Soma*-Juice,—him I invoke, Indra, possessed of increasing wealth, along with the intelligent priests, with a mind disposed to pious adoration, for he is the bestower of abundant food.

4. That Indra,—whom in heaven, the libations, sprinkled on the sacred grass, replenish, as the kindred rivers hastening to fill the ocean,—that Indra, whom the Maruts, the driers up of moisture, who are unobstructed,

---

1 *i.e*, who is victorious over his enemies.

and of undistorted forms, attended as auxiliaries at the death of Vṛitra.

5. His allies, exhilarated (by libations), preceded him, warring with (Vṛitra) holding the rain within himself, as rivers rush down declivities. Indra, animated by the sacrificial food, pierced Vala as did Trita break through the coverings (of the well).[1]

---

1 The Text has only, *paridhir iva tritah ;* and *tritah* may mean triple or threefold; making the phrase, "as through triple coverings," or defences; whence Rosen has, *custodes veluti a tribus partibus constitutos ;* M. Langlois is more correct, in considering *Tritah* as a proper name; but it may be doubted if he has authority for rendering it by *Soma,—ou libation qui porte le nom de Trita ;* or for the additional circumstances he narrates. The legend told by the Scholiast and confirmed by other passages of the Text, as well as by the version of the story found in the *Nitimañjarí*, is wholly different. Ekata, Dwita, and Trita were three men produced in water by Agni, for the purpose of removing or rubbing off the reliques of an oblation of clarified butter, the proper function of the sacred grass, to the three blades of which placed on the altar, the legend may owe its origin; but this does not appear from the narrative. The Scholiast, following the *Taittiríyas*, says that Agni threw the cinders of the burnt-offerings into water, whence successively arose Ekata, Dwita, and *Trita*, who, it elsewhere appears, were therefore called A'ptyas, or sons of water (*Súkta* CV. v. 9). Trita having on a subsequent occasion gone to draw water from a well, fell into it, and the *Asuras* heaped coverings over the mouth of it, to prevent his getting out; but he broke through them with ease. It is to this exploit that Indra's breaking through the defences of the *Asura*, Vala, is compared. The story is somewhat differently related in the *Nítimañjarí*. Three brothers, it is said, Ekata, Dwita, and Trita, were travelling in a desert, and being distressed by thirst, came to a well, from which the youngest, Trita, drew water and gave it to his brothers; in requital, they threw him into the well, in order to appropriate his property, and having covered the top with a cart-wheel, left him in the well; in this extremity, he prayed to all the gods to extricate him, and by their favour he made his escape. *Paridhi*, the term of the Text, means a circumference, a circular covering or lid. Mr. Colebrooke has briefly, but with his usual accuracy, cited this story in his account of the Rig-*Véda* (*As. Researches*,

6. When, Indra, thou hadst smitten, with thy thunderbolt, the cheek of the wide-extended Vṛitra, who, having obstructed the waters, reposed in the region above the firmament, thy lustre, destructive of enemies, extended and thy strength became effulgent.

7. The hymns, Indra, that glorify thee, attain unto thee, as rivulets (flow into) a lake. Twashṭṛi has increased thy becoming strength; he has sharpened thy bolt with (his) overpowering might.

---

viii., p. 388). Dr. Roth conceives Trita to be the same as Traitana, a name that occurs in a Text of the *Rig*, and, converting the latter into a deification, he imagines him to be the original of Thraetona, the *Zend* form of Feridun, one of the heroes of the *Sháh-Námá*, and of ancient Persian tradition.—*Zeitschrift der D. Morgenländischen Gesellschaft*, vol. ii., p. 216. Professor Lassen seems disposed to adopt this identification.—*Indische Alterthumskunde, Additions*. The identity of Trita and Traitana, however, remains to be established, and the very stanza quoted by Dr. Roth as authority for the latter name, is explained in the *Nitimañjari* in a very different sense from that which he has given. It is said, that the slaves of Dírghatamas, when he was old and blind, became insubordinate and attempted to destroy him, first by throwing him into the fire, whence he was saved by the *As'wins*, then into water, whence he was extricated by the same divinities; upon which Traitana, one of the slaves, wounded him on the head, breast, and arms, and then inflicted like injuries on himself, of which he perished. After these events, the sage recited in praise of the *Ás'wins* the hymn in which the verse occurs:—*Na má garannadyo mátritamá dásá yadím susamubdham abádhuk siro yad asya Traitano vitakshat swayam dása uro ansávapi gdha*,—"Let not the maternal waters swallow me, since the slaves assailed this decrepit old man; in like manner as the slave Traitana wounded his head, so has he struck it of himself, and likewise his breast and shoulders." If this interpretation be correct, there can be little relation between Trita and Traitana, and between the latter and Feridun. The former term has, however, found admission as a numeral, and apparently also as a proper name, into the *Zend* books. See M. Burnouf's "*Etudes sur les Textes Zends*," *Journal Asiatique*, April, 1845; see also the word Trita, in the Glossary of Benfey's edition of the *Sáma-Véda*.—*Wilson*.

8. Indra of accomplished deeds, desirous of going to man with thy horses, thou hast slain Vṛitra, hast showered rain, hast taken in thy hands thy thunderbolt of iron, and hast placed the sun in the sky to be seen by us.

9. Through fear (of Vṛitra, thy worshippers) composed the suitable hymn of the *Vṛihat* (*Sáma*), self-illuminating, strengthening and forming the staircase to heaven; on which his allies (the Maruts), fighting for men, (guardians) of heaven and protectors of mankind, excited Indra (to destroy him).

10. The strong heaven was rent asunder with fear at the clamour of that Ahi, when thou, Indra, wast delighted by (drinking) the effused (*Soma*-Juice), and thy thunderbolt vigorously struck off the head of Vṛitra, the obstructer of heaven and earth.

11. Had the earth, Indra, been tenfold (in its extent) and men multiplied every day, then, Maghaván, thy prowess would have been properly renowned; the exploits, achieved by thy might, are vast like the sky.

12. Indra, bent upon destroying the enemies living, in thy strength, above the wide-expanded firmament, thou hast made the earth for our preservation. Thou art the representative of the strength (of the strong.) Thou hast encompassed the firmament and the sky as far as to the heavens.

13. Thou art the measure of the extended earth;[1] thou art the protector of the (*Swarga*),[2] frequented by

---

1 *Pratimánam bhuvah*, the counter-measure of the earth; that is, according to the Scholiast, of similar magnitude and like inconceivable power.—*Wilson*.

2 *Rishwavirasya brihatah pati*, lord or protector of the great (region), in which are the pleasant (*rishwa*) gods (*vira*).—*Wilson*.

the celestials: verily, with thy greatness, thou fillest all the firmament; forsooth, there is none other such as thou.

14. Thou, Indra, of whom heaven and earth have not attained the amplitude; of whose energy the waters, flowing above the heavens, have not reached the limit; of whom, when fighting with animation, created by the *Soma*, against the withholder of the rains, (his adversaries have not equalled the prowess); thou alone hast made every thing else, (than thyself), dependent (upon thee).

15. The Maruts worshipped thee in this (battle); all the celestials in this engagement imitated thee in exultation, when thou hadst struck the face of Vritra with thy angular and fatal (bolt).[1]

SUKTA III. (LIII.)

THE *Rishi* and the Deity are the same; the metre of the 10th and 11th stanzas is *Trishtubh*; of the rest, *Jagatí*.

WE offer laudatory words to the mighty (Indra); we offer fitting praise to Indra in the house of the sacrificer engaged in the service. He (the Deity) has quickly acquired riches, as (a thief) hastily carries (off the property) of the sleeping. Praise, ill-expressed, is not prized among the givers of wealth.

2. Thou, Indra, art the giver of horses, of kine, of barley, the lord and protector of wealth, the instrument of habitation, the foremost in liberality, the most

---

1 The Text has only *bhrishtimatá badhéna*,—with the killer (or weapon) that has angles. According to the *Aitaréya Bráhmana*, the *Vajra*, or thunderbolt of Indra, has eight angles, or perhaps blades; *ashtas'rir vai vajra*.—*Wilson*.

ancient Deity; thou disappointest not desires (addressed to thee); thou art a friend to our friends; such an Indra we praise.

3. Wise and resplendent Indra, the achiever of mighty deeds; the riches, that are spread around, are known to be thine; having collected them, victor (over thy enemies) bring them to us, disappoint not the expectation of the worshipper who trusts in thee.

4. Propitiated by these (resplendent) offerings, by these libations, drive away poverty with gifts of wealth consisting of cattle and horses, and be delighted; may we, subduing our enemy, and relieved from foes by (pleased) by our libations, enjoy together abundant Indra, food.

5. Indra, may we become possessed of riches, and of food; and with energies agreeable to many, and shining around, may we prosper through thy divine power, the source of prowess, of cattle, and of horses.

6. O protector of the pious, they, who were thy allies (the Maruts), gladdened thee, while thou wast engaged in slaying Vṛitra; those oblations and libations gladdened thee, when thou, unimpeded by foes, didst destroy the ten thousand obstacles[1] opposed to him who praised thee and offered thee oblations.

7. Humiliator (of adversaries), thou goest from battle to battle, and destroyest, by thy might, city after city: with thy foe-prostrating associate (the thunderbolt,)[2]

---

1 *Das'a sahasráni vṛitráni;* the last is interpreted by A'varakáni, covers, concealments, obstructions —*Wilson.*

2 The Text has *Namyá sakhyá*: Sáyana has interpreted it, as rendered into English by Prof. Wilson, as, "foe-prostrating associate." *Védártha-Yatna* and Ramanáth Saraswatí have explained it as, "with the help of thy friend the *Rishi* Nami."

thou, Indra, didst slay afar off the deceiver named Namuchi.[1]

8. Thou hast slain Krañja and Parṇaya with thy bright gleaming spear,[2] in the cause of Atithigwa: unaided, thou didst demolish the hundred cities of Vangṛida, when besieged by *R*ijis'wan.[3]

9. Thou, renowned Indra, overthrowest, by thy not-to-be-overtaken chariot-wheel, the twenty kings of men, who had come against Sus'ravas, unaided, and their sixty thousand and ninety and nine followers.[4]

10. Thou, Indra, hast preserved Sus'ravas by thy protection, Túrvayáṇa by thy help: thou hast made Kutsa, Atithigwa, and A'yu[5] subject to the mighty, though youthful Sus'ravas.

11. Protected by the celestials, we remain, Indra, at the close of the sacrifice, thy most fortunate friends: we laud thee, for we enjoy through thee excellent offspring, and a long and prosperous life.

---

1 Namuchi is described both here and in the *Puránás* as an *Asura*.

2 The Text has *varttani*: Sáyana has explained it as, "*s'atru-prérana kus'alayá saktyá*, *i.e.*, a *sakti* capable of sending away the enemies." Langlois has translated "*varttani*" as "*Vigueur Puissante*;" and Wilson, as, "gleaming spear."

3 The first two are the names of *Asuras*; *Atithigwa* we have had before; *Vangrida* is called an *Asura*; and Rijis'wan, a *Rájá*; we have no further particulars, nor do they appear in the *Purdnas*.—*Wilson*.

4 The legend is not *Pouránik*.

5 In the *Puránas*, A'yus is mentioned as the son of Purúravás; but here is A'yu, without the final sibilant.

SUKTA LIV. (LIV.)

The *Rishi* and the Deity are the same; the metre of the 6th, 8th, 9th, and 11th stanzas is *Trishtubh*: of the other seven, *Jagati*.

Do not throw us, Maghaván, into this iniquity, into these sinful conflicts, for the limit of thy strength cannot be measured. Thou art shouting in the heavens and making the waters of the rivers roar: why shall not the earth be filled with terror?

2. Adore the wise and powerful Indra; adoring the listening Indra, laud him, who adorns both heaven and earth by his irresistible might, who is the sender of showers, and by his bounty gratifies our desires.

3. Offer pleasant laudations to the great and illustrious Indra, who is the victor of enemies and is firm-minded by his own strength. He, of great renown, who is obeyed by his horses, the showerer of bounties and impetuous, drives away the *Asurás*[1] and enemies.

---

1 The word *Asura* occurs in the Text. Sáyana has given three different meanings of the word, *viz.*, (1) *s'atrunám nirastá*, the destroyer of *Asura*-enemies; (2) *asuḥ práno valam ráti dadati*, the mighty or powerful; (3) *asavaḥ pránaḥ téna chápaḥ lakshyante*, the giver of rain. Wilson has translated it as, "the giver of rain." In the first stage of their religious life, the Aryans used to adore their Divinities by two names, the *Dévas* and the *Asuras*. Afterwards when they were divided into two branches, the Iranis used to name their Deities as *Ahurás*; and the word *Dévas* was, with them, an appellative of sinful persons. On the other hand, the Aryans used to call their Deities *Devas*; and the sinful *Dánavas* as *Asuras*. Still in many places of the *Rig-Véda* we find the Deities addressed as *Asuras*. In the middle and last parts of the *Rig-Veda*, the word *Asura* is sometimes applied to the Divinities and sometimes to the *Dánavas*. It is very difficult to ascertain the real cause of such a difference. It may be that both the branches of the Aryans, after their separation, used to apply the word *Asura* to their Divinities. Perhaps the greater portion of the *Rig-Veda* was written at this time. And afterwards as differences of opinion increased, the Iranis began to use the word *Deva* as a term signifying sinful creatures; and the Aryans, the word *Asura*, as a synonym for the *Dánavas*.

4. Thou hast shaken the summit of the spacious heavens; thou hast thyself killed S'amvara by thy foe-destroying might; thou hast hurled with exulting and determined mind the sharp and bright-eyed thunderbolt against the assembled *Asurás.*

5. Thou, loud-shouting, hast poured the rain upon the wind and on the head of the maturing and absorbing (Sun). Who is above thee in the work that thou, endowed with a mind, unaltered and bent upon destroying enemies, hast done to-day?

6. Thou hast protected Naryya, Turvasa, Yadu, and Turvíti, of the race of Varrya; thou hast protected their chariots and horses[1] in a battle undertaken for necessary wealth; thou hast destroyed the ninety-nine cities (of S'amvara).[2]

7. That eminent person, the cherisher of the pious, advances his own prosperity, who, while offering oblations to Indra, sings his praise; or who, along with the offerings he presents, recites hymns (in honour of him); for him the bounteous Indra causes the clouds to rain from heaven.

8. Peerless is his power; peerless is his wisdom; may these drinkers of the *Soma*-Juice become equal to him by the pious act, for they, Indra, who present oblations, to thee augment thy vast strength and thy manly vigour.

9. These copious *Soma*-Juices, expressed with stones and contained in ladles, are prepared for thee; they are the beverage of Indra: quaff them; satiate thine

---

1 *Ratham; etasam;* the latter is a synonym of *As'wa,* in the *Nirganta,* but the words may also mean two *Rishis.*

2 The Commentary supplies this appellation.

appetite with them; and then fix thy mind on the wealth that is to be given (to us).

10. The darkness obstructed the current of the waters; the cloud was within the belly of Vṛitra; but Indra precipitated all the waters which the obstructor had concealed, in succession, down to the hollows (of the earth).

11. Bestow upon us, Indra, increasing reputation; (bestow upon us) great, augmenting and foe-subduing strength; protect us by making us rich; cherish the wise; and confer upon us wealth with excellent progeny and food.

SUKTA V. (LV.)

THE *Rishi* and the Deity as before; the metre, *Jagatí*.

THE power of Indra was vaster than heaven: earth could not equal Indra in bulk; formidable and most mighty, he has been ever the afflicter (of the enemies of) those men (who worship him); he whets his thunderbolt for sharpness, as a bull (his horns).

2. The firmament-abiding Indra grasps the wide-spread waters with his comprehensive faculties,[1] as the ocean (receives the rivers): he rushes (impetuous) as a bull, to drink of the *Soma*-Juice; he, the warrior, ever covets praise for his prowess.

3. Thou, Indra, hast not (set open) the cloud for (thine own) enjoyment; thou rulest over the great lords of riches: that Divinity has been, by his own strength,

1 *Gribhnáti varímabhis*,—he grasps with his powers of comprehending or collecting, *samvaranaih*; or it may be, by his vastness, *urutwaih-vá*.—*Wilson*.

greatly known to us; that fierce (Indra) has been, on account of his exploits, placed by all the Celestials before them.

4. He is hymned by adoring (sages) in the forest; he stands beautifully by announcing his own strength amongst men; when protected by Indra, a wealthy sacrificer, the offerer of oblation, recites laudatory verses, Indra, the showerer of desires, engages him who is desirous of performing a sacrifice in that rite.

5. Indra, the warrior, engages in many great conflicts for (the behoof of) man, with his all-purifying prowess; when he hurls his fatal thunderbolt, every one immediately has faith in the resplendent Indra (as being highly powerful).

6. Desiring for fame, destroying the well-built houses of the *Asurás* with his power, expanding like the earth and setting the (heavenly) luminaries free from concealment, he, the performer of good deeds, enables the waters to flow for the behoof of his worshippers.

7. Drinker of the *Soma*-Juice, may thy mind be disposed to grant our desires; hearer of praises, let thy horses be present (at our sacrifice); thy charioteers are experts in restraining (thy steeds); therefore, (thy enemies) cherishing malevolent feelings against thee and carrying arms cannot injure thee.

8. Thou holdest in thy hands unexhausted wealth; thou, renowned (Indra), hast irresistible strength in thy body; thy limbs are invested with (glorious) exploits, as wells[1] (are surrounded by those who come for water); in thy members, Indra are many exploits.

---

1 Like wells, is the whole of the simile, in the usual elliptical style of the Text; the amplification is from the Commentary.—*Wilson.*

SUKTA VI. (LVI.)

The Deity, the *Rishi* and the metre are the same as in the preceding.

VORACIOUS (Indra) has risen up, as a horse (approaches) a màre, to partake of the copious libations (contained) in the (sacrificial) ladles; having stayed his well-horsed, golden and splendid chariot, he plies himself, capable of heroic (actions, with the beverage).

2. His adorers, bearing oblations, are thronging round (him), as (merchants) covetous of gain crowd the ocean (in vessels) on a voyage: ascend quickly, with a hymn to the powerful Indra, the protector of the solemn sacrifice, as women (climb) a mountain.[1]

3. He is quick in action and mighty; his faultless and destructive prowess shines in manly (conflict) like the peak of a mountain (afar), with which, clothed in iron[2] (armour), he, the suppressor of the malignant, when exhilarated (by the *Soma*-Juice), cast the wily S'ushṇa into prison and into bonds.

4. Divine strength waits, like the sun upon the dawn, upon that Indra, who is made more powerful for protection by thee, (his worshipper), who with resolute vigour resists the gloom, and inflicts severe castigation upon his enemies, making them cry aloud (with pain).

5. When thou, destroying Indra, didst distribute the (Vṛitra) hidden life-sustaining, undecaying waters through the different quarters of the heaven, then, animated (by the *Soma*-Juice), thou didst engage in

---

1 The Scholiast here also ekes out the scantiness of the Text,—as women climb a hill to gather flowers.—*Wilson.*

2 *A'yasah,* consisting of iron; that is, according to the Scholiast, whose body is defended by armour of iron, showing the use of coats of mail at this period, and intimating also, a representation of the person of Indra as an image or idol.—*Wilson.*

battle, and with exulting (prowess) slewest Vṛitra, and didst send down an ocean of waters.

6. Thou, mighty Indra, sendest down from heaven, by thy power, upon the realms of earth, the (world)-sustaining rain: exhilarated (by the *Soma*-Juice), thou hast expelled the waters (from the clouds), and hast crushed Vṛitra by a solid rock.[1]

SUKTA VII. (LVII.)

THE Deity, the *Rishi* and the metre are the same.

I OFFER, the most desirable laudation to the most bountiful, the great, the opulent, the highly powerful and stately Indra, whose irresistible impetuosity is like (the rush) of waters down a precipice, and by whom widely-diffused wealth is laid open (to his worshippers) to sustain (their) strength.

2. Indra, this entire universe was engaged in thy sacrifice; the oblations of the sacrificer (flowed) like water (falling) to a depth; the beautiful, golden, fatal thunderbolt of Indra did not sleep upon the mountain.[2]

3. Beautiful Ushas, now present the oblation in this rite to the formidable, praise-deserving Indra, whose all-sustaining, celebrated and characteristic radiance has impelled him hither and thither, (in quest) of (sacrificial) food, as (a charioteer drives) his horses (in various directions).

---

1 *Sámayá páshyá;* the latter may be either, with a stone or a spear; but the adjective *samá*, whole, entire, seems to require the former.—*Wilson.*

2 Or against the side of *Vritra*; that is, it did not stop until it had performed its office.—*Wilson.*

4. Much-lauded and most opulent Indra, we are they, who, relying (on thy favour), approach thee; accepter of praise, no other than thou recieves our commendations; do thou be pleased (with our address), as the earth (cherishes her creatures).

5. Great is thy prowess, Indra: we are thine: satisfy, Maghavan, the desires of this thy worshipper; the vast heaven has acknowledged thy might; this earth has been bowed down through thy vigour.

6. Thou, the wielder of the thunderbolt, hast shattered with thy bolt, the broad and massive cloud into fragments, and hast sent down the waters that were confined in it, to flow (at will): verily thou alone possessest all power.

ANUVA'KA XI.

SUKTA I. (LVIII.)

The Deity is Agni; the *Rishi*, Nodhas, the son of Gotama; the metre of the first five verses is *Jagati*; of the last four, *Trishtubh*.

THE immortal Agni, generated by great strength,[1] quickly issues forth,[2] when he became the invoker of the Celestials and the messenger (of the sacrificer): he, going by suitable paths, created the firmament;[3] he worships (the Deities) in the sacrifice with oblations.

---

1 The Scholiast says that fire is generated by rubbing two sticks with great force.

2 The Text has *ni tundate*. Sáyana explains it as either *nitarám vyathayati*—"gives pain," or *nirgachhâti*—"issues forth."

3 The firmament existed but in darkness, until fire, identified with light, rendered it visible, so that Agni may be said to have made or created it.—*vima ne*, or *nirmamé*.—*Wilson*.

2. Undecaying Agni, combining his food[1] (with his flame) and devouring it quickly, ascends the dry wood; (the blaze) situate on the back (of Agni), spreading hither and thither for consuming, shines like a horse and roars like a roaring (cloud) in the height of heaven.

3. The immortal and effulgent Agni, the bearer of oblations, placed in front of all by the *Rudras* and *Vasus*, the invoker (of the Celestials), who is present at a sacrifice, and conquers the wealth (of the enemies), lauded by his worshippers, and admired like a chariot amongst mankind, accepts[2] the oblations that are successively presented.

4. Urged on by the wind, and roaring loudly, Agni easily sits upon the trees with his burning tongue and diffusive energy; when, undecaying and fiercely-blazing Agni, thou rushest rapidly like a bull amongst the forest trees, thy path is blackened.

5. The flame-weaponed and breeze-excited Agni, assailing the unexhaled moisture (of the trees), with all his strength, in a volume of fire, rushes triumphant (against all things) in the forest, like a bull, and all, whether stationary or moveable, are afraid of him as he flies along.

6. The Bhṛigus amongst men, for the sake of being born as Celestials, cherished thee like a costly treasure, Agni, who sacrificest for men, who art the invoker (of the Celestials), the (welcome) guest at sacrifices, and who art to be esteemed like a loving friend.

---

1 The Text has '*adma*,' food, or what may be eaten; but the Scholiast explains it, *trina gulmádikam*, straw and twigs; in contrast to *atasa*, which presently occurs, and which he explains by *káshtha*, wood or timber.—*Wilson*.

2 It may also mean "makes repeatedly over to the houses of worshippers desirable wealth." Sáyana has given both the explanations.

7. I worship with oblations that Agni whom the seven invoking priests invite as the invoker of the Celestials; who is most worthy of adoration at sacrifices, and who is the giver of all riches: I solicit of him riches.

8. Son of strength, favourably-shining Agni, grant to thy adorers, on this occasion, uninterrupted happiness: offspring of food, preserve him who praises thee from sin with guards of iron.

9. Agni of various rays, be a house to him who lauds thee. Wealthy Agni,[1] be a source of happiness to the wealthy (sacrificers); protect, Agni, thy worshippers from sin; may Agni, who is rich with righteous deeds, come (to us) speedily in the morning.

SUKTA II. (LIX.)

THE *Rishi* is Nodhas; the Deiti, Agni, in the form of *Vais'wânara*;[2] the metre is *Tristubh*.

WHATEVER other fires there may be, they are but ramifications, Agni, of thee; all the immortals rejoice in thee: thou, Vais'wânara, art the navel of men and upholdest them like a deep-planted column.[3]

2. Agni, the head of heaven, the navel of earth, became the ruler over earth and heaven: all the

---

1 This a very unusual appellative of Agni, and is a common synonym of Indra, although, in its proper sense of a possessor of riches, it may be applied to either.—*Wilson*.

2 *Vais'wânara*; from *vis'wa*, all, and *nara*, a man; a fire common to all mankind; or, as here indicated, the fire or natural heat of the stomach, which is a principal element of digestion.—*Wilson*.

3 That is, as a pillar or post fixed firmly in the ground supports the main beam or roof of a house.—*Wilson*.

Celestials created thee, Vais'wánara, in the shape of light, for the *A'ryya*.[1]

3. Treasures were deposited in the Agni, Vais'wánara, like the permanent rays (of light) in the Sun: thou art the sovereign of all the treasures that exist in the mountains, in the herbs, in the waters, or amongst men.

4. Heaven and earth expanded as it were for their son.[2] The experienced sacrificer recites, like a bard,[3] many ancient and copious praises addressed to the graceful-moving, truly-vigorous and all-guiding Vais'wánara.

5. Vais'wánara, who knowest all that are born, thy magnitude has exceeded that of the spacious heaven: thou art the monarch of Manu-descended men; thou hast regained for the Celestials in battle, the wealth (carried off by the *Asuras*).[4]

6. I extol the greatness of that showerer of rain whom men celebrate as the slayer of Vṛitra: the Agni, Vais'wánara, killed the stealer (of the waters) and

---

1 This is the first verse of a *Tricha* to be recited at a ceremony observed on the day of the equinox. Agni is said to be the head of heaven, as the principal element, and the navel of earth, as its main source of support. The term *A'ryya* may apply either to Manu as the institutor of the first sacrifice, or to the *Yajamána*, the institutor of the present rite.—*Wilson*.

2 The Scholiast supports this affiliation by citing another Text; but that does not apply particularly to any form of Agni, but to himself: *Ubhá pitará mahayan ajáyata agnir dyává prithiví*,—Both parents, heaven and earth, expanding, Agni was born.—*Wilson*.

3 The Text has *manushya*: Sáyana explains it as, a panegyrist, or bard.

4 It is supplemented so by the Commentator.

sent them down (upon earth), and clove the (obstructing) cloud.[1]

7. Vais'wánara by his magnitude is all men,[2] and is worthy of being adored in sacrifices of nutritious viands.[3] Agni, endued with rays and truthful speech, praises, with many commendations, Purunítha, the son of S'atavani.[4]

---

1 We have Vais'wánara here evidently identified with Indra, an identification not inconsistent with *Vaidik* theogony, which resolves all the Divinities into three,—Fire, Air, and the Sun, and those three again into one, or the Sun (*Nirukta*, 7, 4); but the Scholiast says we are to understand Vais'wánara, in this verse, as the Agni of the firmament, the *Vaidyuta*, the lightning or electric fire. The firmament, or middle region, is properly that of Váyu, the Wind, or of Indra; the inferior region, or earth, is the proper sphere of Agni, and that of the upper region, or heaven, of the Sun. The Scholiast cites a passage from the *Nirukta*, 7, 21, in which it is discussed who Vais'wánara is, and two opinions are compared, one which places him in the middle region, and identifies with Indra or Váyu, or both, in which character he sends rain, an office that the terrestrial Agni cannot discharge; and another which identifies him with Súryya, or the Sun in the upper sphere. Both are, however, considered by the Scholiast to be untenable, chiefly from the etymologies of the name, which make Vais'wánara an Agni, the fire, as above stated, of the middle region, or lightning; from which, when fallen to earth, the terrestrial fire is born, and from which also the rain is indirectly generated, the burnt-offering ascending to the Sun; and it is in consequence, from the Sun that rain descends; Vais'wánara is therefore an Agni. According to *Pauránik* astronomy, Vais'wánara is the central path of the Sun; in mythology, he occurs as one of the *Dánavás*. The cloud is termed in the Text *S'ambara*, who is elsewhere called an *Asura*.—*Wilson*.

2 The Text has *Vis'wakrishti*, literally rendered, all men: it means Agni has acquired sovereignty over all men.

3 *Bharadwájeshu*; in sacrifices which present food in the shape of nutritious (*pushtikara*) oblations of clarified butter (*havis*); or it may mean, who is to be worshipped by the *Rishis* termed *Bharadwájas*, or of the *Gotra*, or race of *Bharadwája*.—*Wilson*.

4 These are *Vaidik* names; *S'atavani* is so called as the offerer of a hundred, *i.e.*, numerous, sacrifices; his son has the patronymic *S'átavaneya*.—*Wilson*.

SUKTA III. (LX.)

The Rishi is the same; the Deity is Agni; the metre *Trishtubh*.

MA'TARIS'WAN brought as a friend to Bhrigu,[1] the celebrated Vanhi, the illuminator of sacrifices, the careful protector (of his votaries), the swift-coursing messenger (of the Celestials), the offspring of two parents,[2] highly spoken of like wealth.

2. Both (Celestials and men)[3] are the worshippers of this ruler; those who are to be desired (the Celestials) and the mortals bearing oblations (are also the worshippers); for this adorable invoker (of the Celestials), the protector of people and distributor of desired-for objects, was placed by the officiating priests (upon the altar), before the Sun was in the sky.[4]

3. May our newest celebration[5] come before that Agni, who is sweet-tongued, and is to be engendered

---

1 The Wind brought Agni to the sage Bhrigu, as a friend (*ráti*); some translate it, a son, as in the Text, *rátim bhrigúnám*,—the son of the Bhrigus. The more modern Sanskrit confirms the first sense, as, although it has lost the original simple term, it preserves it in the compound *aráti*, an enemy, one not (अ) a friend (*ráti*), an unfriend.—*Wilson*.

2 The Commentator explains it as either the off-pring of heaven and earth, or produced by two pieces of wood.

3 The Text has only *ubhayásah*, the both, which the Scholiast explains either Gods and men, or the ministering priests and their employer the *Yajamána*. The same authority would repeat the phrase, Gods and men, as the sense of the Text, *Us'ija ye cha martáh*, explaining the first by *kámayamána deváh*,—those who are to be wished for, the Gods; he also proposes as an alternative for *us'ijah*, *medhávinah*, wise, or the priests, and for mortals, the *yajamánas*.—*Wilson*.

4 The priests conduct the *Yajamána* to the place where the fire has been prepared before the break of day by the *Adhwaryu*.—*Wilson*.

5 *Navyasí sukírttih*; as if the hymn were of very recent composition.—*Wilson*.

in the heart;[1] whom the descendants of Manu, sacrificing and presenting oblations to him, beget in the time of battle.[2]

4. Agni, the desirable, the purifying, the giver of dwellings, the excellent, the invoker (of the Deities), has been placed (upon the altar) among men: may he be determined upon subduing (our foes), the protector of (our) dwellings, and the lord of treasures in the sacrificial chamber.

5. We, born of the race of Gotama, laud thee, Agni, the protector of riches, with desirable (hymns): rubbing thee, the bearer of oblations, (as a rider rubs down) a horse:[3] may he, who has acquired riches by sacred rites,[4] come hither quickly in the morning.

SUKTA IV. (LXI.)

THE Deity is Indra; the *Rishi* and the metre are the same as in the previous hymn.

I OFFER acceptable adoration and oblations, offered by the preceding sacrificers, to that powerful, quick-coursing, mighty, praiseworthy and unobstructed Indra, as food (to a hungry man).

---

1 Agni, it is said, is engendered of air; but that air is the vital air, or breath, and Agni therefore is said to be produced in the heart, or in the interior of the human body.—*Wilson.*

2 In order to make burnt-offering to secure success.—*Wilson.*

3 The Text has only rubbing, or rather sweeping, thee as a horse; that is, according to the Scholiast, brushing the place of the fire for the burnt-offering, the altar perhaps, in like manner as persons about to mount a horse rub with their hands the part where they are to sit; one inference from which is, that the early Hindus had no saddles.—*Wilson.*

4 The Text has *dhiyávasu*: Sáyana explains it as, "*karmaná budhyá bá práptadhana*," *i.e.*, obtained riches by sacred rites or purified intellect.

2. I offer (oblations, acceptable as) food (to the hungry), to that Indra: I raise (to him) exclamations that may be of efficacy in discomfiting (my enemies): others (also) adore Indra, the ancient lord, in heart, in mind, and in understanding.

3. I offer with my mouth a loud exclamation, with powerful and pure words of praise, to exalt him who is the type (of all), the giver (of goo things), the great, the wise.

4. I send hymns to him (Indra), as the constructor of a car drives it to its owner, (so that he) may thence (obtain) food;[1] I send praises, to him who is entitled to commendation; and most excellent oblations, to the wise Indra.

5. For the sake of food, I combine praise with the instrument of invocation,[2] as (a man harnesses) a horse (to a car); I begin to celebrate the heroic, munificent and food-conferring Indra, the destroyer of the cities (of the *Asuras*).

6. For that Indra, verily Twashṭṛi sharpened the well-acting, sure-aimed thunderbolt for the battle, with which fatal (weapon), the mighty and lordly (Indra), desirous of killing his enemies, pierced the vital parts of Vṛitra.

7. Quickly quaffing the libations, and devouring the grateful viands (presented) at the three (daily) sacrifices which are dedicated to the creator (of the

---

1 *Ratham na tashtéva tatsinâya*; *Sina*, according to the *Nirukta*, is a synonym of food (*Nirukta*, 5, 5); *tat* implies the owner of the car, for his food.—*Wilson*.

2 *Arkam juhvá*; the latter is defined, the instrument of invocation, the organ of speech; the former means, as usual, hymn or praise in metre.—*Wilson*.

world),[1] he, the pervader of the universe,[2] stole the ripe (treasures of the *Asuras*): the vanquisher (of his foes), the hurler of the thunderbolt, encountering, pierced the cloud.[3]

8. To that Indra the women, the wives of the Celestials,[4] addressed their hymns, on the destruction of Ahi; he encompasses the extensive heaven and earth; they two do not surpass thy vastness.

9. His magnitude verily exceeds that of the heaven, and earth, and sky; Indra, self-irradiating in his

---

1 He may be so termed, as everything in the world proceeds from rain.—*Wilson.*

2 The term of the Text is *Vishnu*, applied to Indra as the pervader of all the world,—*sarvasya jagato vyapakah.*—*Wilson.*

3 *Varáha*, one of the synonyms of *Mégha*, 'cloud,' in the *Nighantu*; or it may mean sacrifice, from *vara*, a boon, and *aha*, a day. In reference to this purport, a different explanation of the Text is given, which is somewhat obscure: *Vishnu*, it is said, means the personified sacrifice (*yajña*), in which character he stole or attracted the accumulated wealth of the *Asuras*; after which he remained concealed behind seven difficult passes, or the days of initiatory preparation for the rite. Indra having crossed the seven defiles, or gone through the seven days of initiation, pierced or penetrated to, or accomplished, the sacrifice. This explanation is supported by a citation from the *Taittiríya*, which is still more obscure: This *Varaha*, the stealer of what is beautiful, (?) cherishes beyond the seven hills the wealth of the *Asuras*; he (Indra), having taken up the tufts of the sacred grass, and pierced the seven hills, slew him.—*Varáhoyam vámamoshah saptánám girínám parastád vittam védyam asuránam vibhartti; sa darbhapinjúlam uddhritya, sapta girín bhittwa, tam ahanniti.*—*Wilson.*

4 The wives of the Gods are the personified *Gáyatrí*, and other metres of the *Védas*; according to the Scholiast, the term *gnah*, preceding *dévapatnih*, usually means females, or women, whose nature, the Scholiast says, is locomotive,—*gamanaswabhavah.*—*Wilson.*

dwelling, equal to every exploit, engaged with no unworthy foe, and skilled in conflict, calls to battle.[1]

10. Indra, by his power, cut to pieces with his thunderbolt Vṛitra, the absorber (of moisture), and set free the waters obstructed by Vṛitra and capable of protecting the universe, like cows (recovered from thieves); and, consentient (to the wishes) of the giver of the oblation, (grants him) food.

11. Through his power the rivers sport, since he has, by his thunderbolt, determined their limits; establishing his supremacy (by killing Vṛitra) and granting a (recompense) to the giver (of the oblation), he, the swift-coursing, provided a resting-place for Turvíti.[2]

12. Indra, the quick-coursing and strength-endowed lord (of all), hurl thy thunderbolt at this Vṛitra and cut off his joints, as (butchers cut up) a cow,[3] that the rains may issue from him, and the waters flow (over the earth).

13. Describe, with new hymns, the former exploits of that quick-coursing Indra, when holding his weapons in battle, he encounters and destroys his foes.

---

1 The Scholiast says, he calls *the clouds* to battle, for by the mutual collision of the clouds rain is engendered —*Wilson*.

2 The name of a *Rishi*, who, the Scholiast adds, had been immersed in water: Indra brought him to dry land —*Wilson*.

3 The Text has, "cut in pieces the limbs of Vritra, as of a cow" (*gor na*); the Commentator supplies the rest, "as worldly men, the carvers of flesh, divide here and there the limbs of animals." The expression is remarkable, although it may not be quite clear what is meant by the term used by Sáyana, *vikartarah*, cutters up, or carvers: perhaps the word should be *vikretarah*, venders of meat, butchers: at any rate it proves that no horror was attached to the notion of a joint of beef in ancient days among the Hindus —*Wilson*.

14. Through fear of him, the mountains remain still; and through fear of his appearance, heaven and earth tremble: lauding repeatedly with hymns the preserving power of that beloved Indra, Nodhas speedily acquired vigour.

15. He alone (is capable of subduing his enemies), and is the powerful lord of manifold riches: give unto him the hymns which he has desired for. Indra defended the pious sacrificer Etasa, when fighting with Súryya, the son of Swas'wa.[1]

16. Indra, harnesser of steeds, the descendants of Gotama have offered to thee encomiastic hymns to secure thy presence: confer upon them manifold riches;[2] may he, who has acquired wealth by pious deeds, come here speedily in the morning.

---

1 The legend relates that a king named Swas'wa, or the lord of good (*su*) horses (*as'wa*), being desirous of a son, worshipped Súryya, who himself was born as the son of the king; at a subsequent period, in some dispute between him and the *Riski* Etasa, Indra took part with the latter.—*Wilson.*

2 The Text has *dhiyam*: it may mean either "intellect," or "riches."

FIFTH ADHYA'YA.

ANUVA'KA XI.—*(Continued.)*

SUKTA V. (LXII.)

THE *Rishi* is Nodhas; the Deity, Indra; the metre, *Trishtubh*.

WE meditate, like Aṅgiras, an excellent hymn (to be addressed) to that powerful and praise-deserving Indra, who is to be worshipped by his sacrificers (with hymns) capable of bringing him to the ceremony: let us repeat a prayer to the celebrated leader of all.

2. Do you, priests, offer to the vast and most powerful Indra, a great hymn, fit to be chanted aloud;[1] for through him our forefathers, the Aṅgirasas, adoring him, and knowing the footmarks, recovered (the stolen) cattle.

3. When the search was set on foot by Indra and the Aṅgirasas, Saramá secured food for her young;[2] then Vṛihaspati[3] killed the devourer and rescued the kine, and the Celestials, with the cattle, proclaimed their joy aloud.

4. Powerful Indra, who art to be gratified with a laudatory and well-accented hymn by the seven

---

1 The expression is *ángushyam Sáma*, a *Sáma* fit to be recited aloud,—*ághoshya-yogyam*; such as the *Rathantaras*, and other prayers, which are usually considered portions of the *Sáma Véda*; but the Commentator understands *Sáma* in this place to mean, singing or chanting of the Richas:—*Rikshu yad gánam tasya sámetyákhyá.*—*Wilson.*

2 When Indra desired the bitch Saramá to go in search of the stolen cattle, she consented to do so only on condition that the milk of the cows should be given to her young ones, which Indra promised.—*Wilson.*

3 Vrihaspati is here used as a synonym of Indra, the protector or master (*pati*) of the great ones (*brihatám*), the gods.—*Wilson.*

priests, whether engaged for nine months, or for ten; and,[1] desirous of (safe) protection, thou hast terrified by thy voice the divisible fructifying cloud.[2]

5. Destroyer of foes, praised by the Aṅgírasas, thou hast scattered the darkness with the dawn, and with the rays of the sun: thou hast made straight the elevations of the earth; thou hast strengthened the foundations of the ethereal region.

6. The deeds of that graceful Indra are most admirable: his exploits are most glorious, in that he has replenished the four rivers[3] of sweet water, spread over the surface of the earth.

7. He who is not to be attained by violence,[4] but

---

1 Sáyana identifies the priests (*vipras*) with the Aṅgirasas, who, he says, are of two orders; those who conduct sacrifices for nine months, and those who conduct them for ten. He cites the *Nirukta* for the confirmation of this (xi, 19); but the meaning of Ya'ska's interpretation of the word *Navagwá* is doubtful, as *Navagati* may mean, 'that one whose course or condition is new,' better than 'for nine.' Another explanation which he suggests,—*Navanitagati*,—is still less intelligible, for *Navanita* usually means fresh butter. The seven priests are said to be Medhátithi and other *Rishis* of the race of Aṅgiras.—*Wilson*.

2 *Adrim phaligam valam;* the last is here explained, cloud; the first, that which is to be divided by the thunderbolt; and the second, that which yields fruit, or causes grain to grow by its rain; or the three words may be considered as substantives, *Adri* implying, as usual, a mountain; *phaliga*, a cloud, and *vala*, an *Asura;* all of whom were terrified by Indra's voice or thunder.—*Wilson*.

3 No specification of these four is given beyond their being the *Ganges* and others.—*Wilson*.

4 The term *Ayásya* has perplexed the Scholiast: it may be derived from *Yása*, effort, that which is not attainable by effort; that is, according to one interpretation, not to be overcome in battle; whence Rosen has rendered it by *invictus*. It is contrasted apparently with what follows, and which requires the insertion of *Susádhya*,—easily to be reached, or influenced by praises, and the like. Other etymologies are suggested, but they are still less satisfactory.—*Wilson*.

(is easily propitiated) by those who praise him with sacred hymns, parted twofold the eternal and united (spheres of heaven and earth); the graceful Indra cherished the heaven and earth, like the sun in the august and most excellent sky.

8. (Night and dawn,) of various complexion, repeatedly born, but ever youthful, have traversed in their revolutions alternately, from a remote period, earth and heaven; night with her dark, dawn with her luminous, limbs.

9. The son of strength, assiduous in good works, diligent in pious acts, retains his ancient friendship (for his votary). Thou, (Indra,) providest within the yet immature cows, whether black or red, the mature and glossy milk.

10. From a remote time the contiguous, unshifting, and unwearied fingers practise with (all) their energies many thousand acts of devotion (towards Indra);[1] and like the wives (of the gods), the protecting sisters[2] worship him who is without shame.

11. Beautiful Indra, who art to be praised with holy hymns, the pious who are desirous of holy rites, those who are anxious for riches, and those who are wise, repair to thee with veneration: powerful Indra,

---

1 This seems to intimate that the fingers were employed in the performance of what is at present termed *mudrá*, certain intertwinings and gesticulations accompanying prayer; the Commentary understands it as merely their employment in acts of worship or homage. That the practice is not altogether modern appears from the paintings of the *Ajánta* caves, several of the persons of which are evidently performing the finger gesticulations.—*Wilson.*

2 *Patnih swasárah* may mean only the protecting or propitiatory and moving epithets of *avanih*, fingers; *Janayo na* is the expression for 'like wives;' *i.e.*, says Sáyana, *devánám*,—of the gods.—*Wilson.*

their minds adhere to thee, as affectionate wives to a loving husband.

12. Beautiful Indra, the riches that have long since been held in thy hands have suffered neither loss nor diminution. Thou, Indra, art illustrious, addicted to good works, and resolute: enrich us, thou who art diligent in action, by thy acts.

13. Mighty Indra, Nodhas, the son of Gotama, has composed for us this new hymn, (addressed) to thee, who hast been for ever, who harnessest thy coursers (to thy car), and art the sure guide (of all). May he who has acquired wealth by pious acts, come hither quickly in the morning.

SUKTA VI. (LXIII.)

Ri*shi*, the Deity, and metre as before.

INDRA, thou art the mighty one, who, becoming manifest in (the hour of) alarm, didst sustain by thy energies heaven and earth;[1] then, through fear of thee, all creatures, and the mountains, and all other vast and solid things, trembled, like the (tremulous) rays of the sun.

2. When, Indra, thou harnessest thy variously-moving horses, thy praiser places thy thunderbolt in

---

1 The term explained by the Scholiast, *balaih*, by forces, or strength, is in the Text, *s'ushnaih*, 'the driers up,' that is, it is said, of enemies. Of the circumstance alluded to, we have no other explanation than that Indra became manifest, and sustained earth and heaven when they were filled with fear of an *Asura*. Perhaps *Vritra* is intended; but the passage is obscure.—*Wilson.*

thy hands, wherewith, accomplisher of undesired acts,[1] thou assailest thine enemies, and, glorified by many, destroyest their numerous cities.

3. Thou, Indra, the best of all beings, the assailer and humiliator (of thy foes), the chief of the *R*ibhus,[2] the friend of man, the subduer of enemies, didst aid the young and illustrious Kutsa,[3] and slewest S'ushṇa,[3] in the deadly and close-fought fight.

4. Thou verily didst animate him to (acquire) such (renown) as that which, sender of rain and wielder of the thunderbolt, thou (didst acquire) when thou slewest Vṛitra, and when, munificent Hero, who easily conquerest (thy foes), thou didst put to flight the *Dasyus*[4] in battle.

5. Do thou, Indra, who art unwilling to harm any resolute (mortal),[5] set open all the quarters (of the horizon) to the horses of us who praise thee, (when we are exposed) to the aversion (of our enemies); and,

---

1 *Aviharyatakratu*; Rosen has *desideratas res faciens,* but the Scholiast has *aprepsita karman*; that is, he does actions undesired by his foes.—*Wilson.*

2 So the Scholiast explains Ri*bhukshá*,—Ri*bhúnám adhipati*; or it may mean, he who abides in the Ri*bhus*,—*téshu kritanivása*; but he understands Ri*bhu* here to mean a wise man, a sage (*medhávin*).—*Wilson.*

3 These names have occurred before in the same relation.—*Wilson.*

4 The *Dasyus* are described as the enemies of Kutsa,—*Kutsasyopakshayatárah.* Agreeably to the apparent sense of *Dasyu*, barbarian, or one not Hindu, Kutsa would be a prince who bore an active part in the subjugation of the original tribes of India.—*Wilson.*

5 Even although hostile to him; that is, Indra is in himself indifferent to those who are opposed to him, and if he undertakes their destruction, it is not on his own behalf, but in defence of his friends and worshippers, as in the case of Kutsa, alluded to in the preceding stanza.—*Wilson.*

wielder of the thunderbolt, demolish our foes, as with a club.

6. Men invoke thee, such as thou art, in the thick-thronged and wealth-bestowing conflict. May this thy succour, powerful Indra, ever be granted in war, worthy to be enjoyed (by warriors) in battle.

7. Indra, wielder of the thunderbolt, warring on behalf of Purukutsa,[1] thou didst overturn the seven cities; thou didst cut off for Sudás the wealth of Aṁhas, as if (it had been a tuft) of sacred grass, and didst give it to him, O king, ever satiating thee (with oblations).

8. Increase, divine Indra, for us throughout the earth, abundant food, (that it may be as plentiful) as water, by which, Hero, thou bestowest upon us (existence), as thou causest water to flow on every side.

9. Praises have been offered to thee, Indra, by the sons of Gotama: (they have been) uttered with reverence (to thee), borne (hither) by thy steeds: grant us various sorts of food. May he who has acquired wealth by pious acts, come hither quickly in the morning.

SUKTA VII. (LXIV.)

THE *Rishi* is the same; the Deities are the *Maruts* collectively; the metre is *Jagatí*, except in the last verse, in which it is *Trishtubh*.

OFFER, Nodhas, earnest praise to the company of the *Maruts*, the senders of rain and ripeners of fruit,

---

1 Purukutsa is called a *Rishi*; Sudás, a king; and Aṁhás, an *Asura*; but no further information is given in the Comment.—*Wilson*.

deserving of adoration. Composed, and with folded-hands, I utter the praises conceived in my mind, which are efficacious in sacred rites, (and flow readily) as the waters.

2. They were born handsome and vigorus from the sky, the sons of Rudra,[1] the conquerors of their foes, pure from sin, and purifying (all), radiant as suns, powerful as evil spirits,[2] diffusers of rain-drops, and of fearful forms.

3. Youthful Rudras, and undecaying, destructive of those who do not worship (the gods), of unobstructed progress, and immovable as mountains, they are desirous of granting (the wishes of the worshipper), and by their strength agitate all substances, whether of heaven or of earth.

4. They decorate their persons with various ornaments; they have placed, for elegance, brilliant (garlands on their breasts; lances are borne upon their shoulders, and with them and their own strength have they been born, leaders, from the sky.

5. Enriching their worshipper, agitating the clouds, devourers of foes, they create the winds and lightnings by their power: the circumambient and agitating *Maruts* milk heavenly udders, and sprinkle the earth with the water.

---

1 *Rudrasya maryah*; literally, the mortals or men of *Rudra*; but the Scholiast observes, the *Maruts* are immortal, and the term must therefore imply sons, agreeably to another Text, *á, te Pitar Marutám sumnam etu,*—may he obtain thy favour, father of the *Maruts*; or as in stanza 12, where the *Maruts* are called, collectively, *Rudrasya Súnuh*,—the son of *Rudra*.—*Wilson*.

2 *Satwino na; Satwánah* is explained, *Parames'warasya-bhúta gana*,—the troops of demons attendant on *Paramés'wara* or *S'iva*. —*Wilson*.

6. The munificent *Maruts* scatter the nutritious waters, as priests, at sacrifices, the clarified butter; as grooms lead forth a horse, they bring forth, for its rain, the fleet-moving cloud, and milk it, thundering, and unexhausted.

7. Vast, possessed of knowledge, bright-shining, like mountains in stability, and quick in motion, you, like elephants, break down the forests when you put vigour into your ruddy (mares).

8. The most wise *Maruts* roar like lions; the all-knowing are graceful as the spotted deer, destroying (their foes), delighting (their worshippers); of deadly strength in their anger, they come with their antelopes,[1] and their arms, (to defend the sacrificer) against interruption.

9. *Maruts*, who are distinguished in troops, who are benevolent to men, who are heroes, and whose strength is deadly in your anger, you make heaven and earth resound (at your coming); your (glory) sits in the seat-furnished chariots, conspicuous as (a beautiful) form, or as the lovely lightning.

10. The *Maruts*, who are all-knowing, co-dwellers with wealth, combined with strength, loud-sounding, repellers of foes, of infinite prowess, whose weapon (of offence) is Indra, and who are leaders (of men), hold in their hands the shaft.

11. Augmenters of rain, they drive with golden wheels the clouds asunder, as elephants[2] (in a herd

---

1 *Prishatibhis*, with the spotted deer, which are the *Váhanas*, or steeds of the *Maruts*.—*Wilson*.

2 *Apathyo na*; literally, "like that which is produced or occurs on the road," leaving a wide range for explanation. Sáyana therefore proposes another meaning; "like a chariot which drives over and crushes sticks and straws on the way."—*Wilson*.

break down the trees in their way): they are honoured with sacrifices, visitants of the hall of offering, spontaneous assailers of (their foes), subverters of what are stable, immovable themselves, and wearers of shining weapons.

12. We Invoke with praise the foe-destroying, all-purifying, water-shedding, all-surveying band of *Maruts*, the offspring of Rudra: (priests) to obtain prosperity, have recourse to the dust-raising and powerful band of *Maruts*, receiving libations from sacred vessels,[1] and showering down (benefits).

13. The man whom, *Maruts*, you defend with your protection, quickly surpasses all men in strength; with his horses, he acquires food; and with his men, riches: he performs the required worship, and he prospers.

14. *Maruts*, grant to your wealthy (worshippers, a son),[2] eminent for good works, invincible in battle, illustrious, the annihilator (of his adversaries), the seizer of wealth, the deserver of praise, and all-discerning; may we cherish such a son and such a grandson for a hundred winters.

15. Grant us, *Maruts*, durable riches, attended by posterity, and mortifying to our enemies: (riches) reckoned by hundreds and thousands, and ever increasing; may they who have acquired wealth by pious acts, come hither quickly in the morning.

---

1 *Rijíshinam*, which Rosen renders *hostes vincentem*, and M. Langlois, *victorieuse;* but the Commentary offers no such signification. The *Maruts*, it is said, are worshipped at the third or evening ceremonial, according to the Text, *Rijísham abhishunwanti*,—"they (the priests) pour the *Soma*-Juice into the vessel." *Rijísham*, in its ordinary sense, is a frying-pan; but here it may mean any sacrificial vessel.—*Wilson*.

2 *Putra*, son, is supplied by the Comment; the concluding phrases authorize the addition.—*Wilson*.

ANUVA'KA XII.

SUKTA I. (LXV.)

THE Deity is Agni; the *Rishi*, Parás'ara, son of S'akti, the son of Vas'ishtha: the metre is *Dwipada-Virát*.[1]

THE intelligent Divinities, all equally pleased, followed thee, Agni, by thy footmarks, when hiding in the hollow (of the waters),[2] like a thief (who has stolen) an animal; thee, receiving oblations and carrying them to the Deities: all the Celestials, worthy of adoration, sit down near thee.

2. The Deities followed the traces of the fugitive; the search was made everywhere, and earth became like the celestial region; the waters swelled (to conceal him), who was much enlarged by laudation, and was manifested as it were in the womb in the waters, the source of sacrificial food.[3]

3. Agni is beautiful as nourishment, vast as the earth, the giver of food as a mountain, and delightful as

---

1 Each stanza is divided into half, and each two *Padas* are considered as forming a complete stanza; hence this hymn and the five following are said to be *Das'Archa*, or to have ten stanzas each, whilst in fact they have only five.—*Wilson*.

2 The Text has *Guhá chatantam*; the word *Guhá*, as explained by the Scholiast, means either the depth of the waters, or the hollow of the *As'watha*-tree, in both of which Agni hid himself for a season.

3 A fish revealed to the Gods where Agni had hidden, as, according to the *Taittiríyas*, "he, concealing himself, entered into the waters; the Gods wished for a messenger to him; a fish discovered him." Védárthayatna, however, gives a different interpretation of this *Rik*:—"Of the truthful (Agni) the Gods obey the ordinances; (to him) the earth like heaven, became the home. Him the waters nourish, who is well-born in the womb, the altar of the sacrifice, (and) well-nourished with prayers."

water; he is like a horse urged to a charge in battle, and like flowing waters;[1] who can arrest him?

4. He is the friend of the waters, like a brother to his sisters; he consumes the forest as a king slays his enemies; when excited by the wind, he traverses the woods and shears the hairs of the earth.[2]

5. He breathes amidst the waters like a sitting swan; awakened at the dawn, he restores by his operations consciousness to men; he is a creator, like *Soma*;[3] born from the waters, (where he lurked) like an animal with coiled-up limbs, he became enlarged, and his light (spread) afar.

---

1 The epithets are in the Text attached to the objects of comparison, although equally applicable to Agni; thus he is *pushtirna ranwá*—like grateful nourishment; *kshitirna prithwí*,—like the vast earth; etc. Several of the comparisons admit of various interpretations; as the first may signify the increase of desired fruits or rewards, as the consequence of sacrifices with fire; in no case does it import the *frugum maturitas* of Rosen.—*Wilson.*

2 Fruits, flowers, grasses, shrubs, etc., are described as the hairs of the earth.

3 *Somo na védhah*; in like manner as *Soma* creates or causes useful plants to grow, so Agni creates or extracts from them their nutritive faculty. The Agni here alluded to is the fire of digestion, the heat of the stomach: *Agnir annado annapatis'cha*,—Agni is the eater and sovereign of food; and in the *Vajasanéyi Yajush* we have, *etavad va idam annam annadas'cha Soma eva annam Agnir annadah*,—inasmuch as there is food and feeder, so *Soma* is the food, and the feeder is Agni. —*Wilson.*

SUKTA II. (LXVI.)

Deity, *Rishi*, and metre the same.

AGNI,—who is of variegated form like wealth, who is the surveyor of all like the Sun, who is the protector of life like the vital air (*Práṇa*), who is the doer of good like a son, who upholds the universe like a horse, who is the giver of gratification like a cow, who is pure and radiant,—consumes the forests.

2. Like a beautiful mansion,[1] he protects property; he (nourishes people) like barley; he is the conqueror of (hostile) men; he is like a *Rishi*, the praiser (of the Deities), eminent amongst (devout) persons, delighted like a steed:[2] may he bestow upon us food.

3. Agni, of unattainable effulgence, is like a vigilant sacrificer;[3] he is (an ornament to all in the sacrificial chamber), like a woman in a dwelling;[4] when he shines with wonderful lustre, he is like the white (sun); or like a golden chariot amongst men, resplendent in battle.

4. He terrifies (his adversaries) like an army sent (against an enemy), or like the bright-pointed shaft of an archer. Agni, as Yama, is all that is born; as Yama,

---

1 The Text has *ranvo*: Sáyana explains it as *ramaníyaḥ*: literally, beautiful. Wilson translates it as secure.

2 The Text has *Vájeena prítaḥ*: literally, "delighted like a steed," Sáyana supplements the ellipsis, and Wilson translates this explanatory passage as,—"as a spirited horse (goes to battle), [so] he (Agni) repairs delighted to the hall of sacrifice."

3 The Text has *Kraturna nityas*: Sáyana explains it as,—"as the performer of a sacrifice takes care that nothing vitiates the rite, so Agni defends it from interruption by *Rákshasás*.—*Wilson*.

4 The Text is elliptical: its meaning is,—" he is an ornament to all in the sacrificial chamber like a woman in a dwelling."

all that will be born:[1] he is the lover of maidens,[2] the husband of wives.[3]

5. Let us approach that blazing Agni with animal and vegetable offerings,[4] as cows hasten to their pens. He has tossed about his flames, like running streams of water; the rays commingle (with the radiance) visible in the sky.

SUKTA III. (LXVII.)

Deity, *Rishi* and metre the same.

BORN in the woods; the friend of man, Agni protects his worshipper, as a king favours a man shorn

---

1 *Yamo ha jâto, yamo janitwam*, is the phraseology of the Text, and is somewhat obscure; according to the Scholiast, *Yama* here has its etymological purport only; he who gives the desired object to the worshippers,—*yachchhati dadâti-kâmân stotribhyah*, in which sense it is a synonym of Agni,—*yam Agnir uchyaté*; or it may be applied to him as one of the twins (*yama*), from the simultaneous birth of Indra and Agni, according to Yáska. *Játa* is said to imply all existing beings; *janitwa*, those that will exist: both are identical with Agni as Yama, from the dependence of all existence, past, present, or future, upon worship with Fire.—*Wilson*.

2 Because they cease to be maidens when the offering to Fire, the essential part of the nuptial ceremony, is completed.—*Wilson*.

3 The wife bearing a chief part in oblations to Fire; or a legend is alluded to, of Soma, having obtained, it does not appear how, a maiden, gave her to the *Gandharba*, Vis'wavasu; he transferred her to Agni, who gave her to a mortal husband, and bestowed upon her wealth and offspring. The whole of this stanza is similarly commented upon in the *Nirukta*, 10, 21.—*Wilson*.

4 So the Commentator explains the terms *charâthâ* and *vasatyâ*, invocations prompted by minds purified by offerings of moveable things, that is, animals; or of immoveable things, as rice, and the like: *tat prabhavaih hridayâdibhih sâdhyâhutih*; or, *pas'u parbhava hridayadisâdhanayâhutyâ*.—*Wilson*.

of decrepitude, able as a defender, adorable as a performer of (good) works, may he, the invoker of the Deities, the bearer of oblations,[1] be the performer of excellent works.

2. Holding in his hand all (sacrificial) wealth, and hiding in the hollows (of the waters), he filled the Deities with alarm; the leaders (the Deities), the upholders of acts, then knew Agni when they recited the prayers conceived in the heart.

3. Like the unborn (Sun) he sustains the earth and the firmament, and props up the heaven with true prayers.[2] O Agni, the source of sustenance unto all, do thou protect the pasture that is grateful unto animals and repair to the cave which is unfit for grazing.[3]

4. He who knows Agni hidden in the cave; he who approaches him who is the maintainer of sacrifice,[4] those who, after performing a sacrifice, laud him, to them he, forsooth, promises affluence.

---

1 *Havyaváh*, here used generally, is, properly, the bearer of oblations to the Gods; the *Véda* recognizing besides the usual fires, three Agnis: *Havyaváh* or *Havyaváhana*, that which conveys offerings to the Gods; *Kavyaváh*, which conveys them to the *Pitris* or *Manes;* and *Saharakshas*, that which receives those offered to the *Rákshasas.*—*Wilson.*

2 According to the *Taittiriyas*, the Gods, alarmed at the obliquity of the region of the Sun, and fearing that it might fall, propped it up with the metres of the *Véda*, an act here attributed to Agni.—*Wilson.*

3 *Guhá guham gáh*; Rosen has, *de specu in specum procedas;* but *Guhá* here means, apparently, any arid or rugged tract unfit for pasture, or as the Commentary says, *sancharáyogyam sthánam*,—"a place unfit for grazing," and which Agni may, therefore, scorch up with impunity. —*Wilson.*

4 The Text has *Ritasya*, which Sáyana explains either as truth or sacrifice.

5. The wise, (first) adoring Agni, as they do a dwelling,[1] perform sacrifices—(Agni) who implants their (peculiar) virtues in herbs, and places flowers and fruits in mother-like herbs, and who is the giver of knowledge and sustenance.

SUKTA IV. (LXVIII.)

The *Rishi*, the Deity and the metre the same.

THE bearer (of the oblations), (Agni), mixing them (with other ingredients), ascends to heaven, and clothes all things, moveable and immoveable,[2] and the nights themsevles, (with light), radiant amongst the Celestials, and in himself alone comprehending the virtues of all these (substances).[3]

2. O Divine Agni, when thou art born living[4] from the dry wood, (by attrition), then all (thy worshippers) perform the sacred ceremony, and obtain verily true divinity by lauding thee, who art immortal, with hymns that reach thee.

3. Laudatory hymns are addressed to him when he comes (to the sacrifice); sacrifice[5] is performed

---

1 In building a house, worship is first offered to the edifice, and it is then put to use. So Agni is to be first adored, and then employed in any sacrificial rites.—*Wilson.*

2 *i.e.*, the entire universe.

3 Or it may be rendered, " he alone snrpasses the glories (*mahitwá*) of all these Gods ;" as Rosen has it, *excellit deus, deorum magnitudine.* —*Wilson.*

4 The Text has *Jeevan* : literally, " living :" but Sâyana explains it as *prajvalan*, " burning ;" for the living condition of the Fire is nothing but burning.

5 The Text has *Dhiti* : The Scholiast explains it as,—" that in which the *Soma*-Juice is quaffed " *i.e.*, a sacrifice.

when he comes; he is the source of sustenance unto all; all (worshippers) perform all rites[1] (for him). Do thou, Agni, knowing (his works), grant riches to him who presents to thee oblations, or who wishes (to be able to present them).

4. Thou hast abided with the descendants of Manu[2] as the invoker (of the Deities); thou art indeed the lord of their wealth; they desire (of thee) procreative energy in their bodies,[3] and, shorn of stupefaction, they live for ever with their excellent sons.[4]

5. Hastening to obey the commands of Agni, like sons (obedient to the orders) of a father, they celebrate his worship: abounding in food, Agni sets open before them treasures that are at the doors of the sacrifice, and he who delights in the sacrificial chamber has studded the sky with constellations.

SUKTA V. (LXIX.)

The *Rishi*, the Deity and the metre the same.

WHITE (Agni), like (the Sun), the lover of the dawn, is the illuminator of all, and fills united (heaven and

---

1 The Text has *Apángsi*: Sáyana explains it as, *Dars'apurna másádini karmáni*, *i.e.*, "religious rites held half-monthly and at the Full-Moon in honour of the departed Manes when oblations are offered to the Sacred Fire."

2 With mankind.

3 *i.e.*, "through thy favour they obtained sons," as explained by the Scholiast in the next line of the Commentary.

4 The Text has *samjánata swai dakshais amaras*: The Scholiast gives two interpretations of the Text. One we have given in the translation. The word *daksha* means *prána*, vital air. So the passage means,—"associated with their own vital airs, they know all things." The word *samjánata*: may mean either "live for ever" or "contemplate."

earth with light), like the lustre of the radiant (sun). Thou, as soon as manifested, hast pervaded all the world with devout acts, being (both) the father and son of the Celestials.[1]

2. The wise, the humble and discriminating Agni, is the giver of flavour to food, as the udder of cows (gives sweetness to the milk); invited (to the ceremony), he sits in the sacrificial chamber, diffusing happiness, like a benevolent man, amongst mankind.

3. He diffuses happiness in a dwelling, like a son (newly) born; he overcomes enemies in battle, like an animated charger; when I, along with other men, invoke Divinities living in one place, thou, Agni, assumest all (their) celestial natures.[2]

4. (The Rákshasás)[3] never interrupt the rites performed for thee, since thou conferrest on the sacrificers happiness (as a reward); for should (such spirits) disturb thy sacrifice, then, assisted by leaders, (Maruts), equally (competent) like thyself,[4] thou puttest the intruders to flight.

---

1 *Devánám pitá putrah san.* The passage is also explained, the protector, either of the Gods or of the priests (*ritwijám*), and their messenger, that is, at their command, like a son: but the expressions are, probably, to be used in their literal sense, with a metaphorical application. Agni, as the bearer of oblations, may be said to give paternal support to the Gods, whilst he is their son as the presenter to them of sacrificial offerings.—*Wilson.*

2 *Tad devatárúpo bhavati,*—he becomes of the form or nature of that Deity; as in the Text, *Twam Agni Varuno jáyase twam Mitro bhavasi*, etc.,—Thou art born as Varuna, thou becomest Mitra.—*Wilson.*

3 The Text has *Nakih minanti*: Sáyana explains it as, "Rákshasás do not obstruct them."

4 *Samán nair nribhih,*—with equal leaders, or men; that is, with the Maruts.

5. May Agni, who is possessed of manifold light, like the lover of the dawn,[1] the granter of habitations, and of cognizable form, know (the desires of) this, (his worshipper); (his rays), spontaneously bearing the oblation, open the doors (of the sacrificial chamber), and all spread through the visible heaven.

SUKTA VI. (LXX.)

Rishi, etc., as before.

WE solicit abundant (food). Agni, who is to be approached by meditation, and shines with pure light, pervades all holy rites, knowing well the acts that are addressed to the Deities, and (those which regulate) the birth of the human race.

2. (They offer oblations) on the mountain, or in the mansion, to that Agni, who is within the waters, within woods,[2] and within all movable and immovable things, immortal, and performing pious acts, like a benevolent (prince) among his people.

3. Agni, the lord of night,[3] grants riches to (the

---

1 The word in the Text is *jara*, which means "lover." Sáyana explains it as, *jaráyitri*, which Wilson translates as "the extinguisher." He writes:—"This phrase is here, as well as in the first verse, *usho na járah*; the latter being explained by *jaráyitri*—the causer of decay. The sun obliterates the dawn by his superior radiance."

2 He is the *garbha*, the embryo, the internal germ of heat and life, in the waters, etc., all which depend for existence upon natural or artificial warmth.—*Wilson*.

3 *Kshapá-vat*, having or possessing the night, as then especially bright and illuminating; as the Text, *ágnéyí vai rátrih*,—night is characterized by Agni: so also in one of the Mantras of the (*Agnyádheya* ceremony, we have, *Agnir-jyotih*, *Jyotiragnih-swáhá* (*Vájasaneyí Samhitá*, p. 64); or the term may be rendered also, capable of destroying (the Rakshasas)—*Wilson*

worshipper) who adores him with sacred hymns. Agni, who art omniscient, and knowest the origin of Gods and men, protect all these (beings dwelling) upon earth.

4. Agni, whom many variously-tinted (mornings) and nights increase, whom, invested with truth, all movable and immovable things augment, has been propitiated, and is kindly seated at the holy rite, as the invoker (of the Gods), and rendering all (pious) acts (productive of reward.

5. Agni, confer excellence upon our valued cattle, and may all men bring us acceptable tribute; offering in many places sacrifices to thee, men receive riches from thee, as (sons) from an aged father.

6. (May Agni), who is like one who succeeds (in his undertakings), and acquires (what he wishes for), who is like a warrior casting a dart, and resembles a fearful adversary, who is brilliant in combats, (be to us a friend).

SUKTA VII. (LXXI.)

The Deity and *Rishi* are the same, but the metre is *Trishtubh.*

THE contiguous fingers, loving the affectionate Agni, as wives love their own husbands, please him (with offered oblations), and honour him, who is entitled to honour, (with gesticulations), as the rays of light (are assiduous in the service) of the dawn, which is (at first) dark, (then) glimmering, and (finally) radiant.

2. Our forefathers, the Angirasas, by their praises (of Agni), terrified the strong and daring devourer, (Pani), by the sound; they made for us a path to

the vast heaven, and obtained accessible day, the ensign of day,[1] (A'ditya), and the cows (that had been stolen).

3. They secured him, (Agni, in the sacrificial chamber), they made his worship the source of wealth;[2] whence opulent votaries preserve his fires and practise his rites. Free from all (other) desire, assiduous in his adoration, and sustaining gods and men by their offerings, they come into his presence.[3]

4. When the diffusive vital air[4] excites Agni, he becomes bright and manifest[5] in every mansion, and the institutor of the rite, imitating Bhrigu, prevails on him to perform the function of messenger, as a prince

---

1 *Kétu*, the indicator, or causer of day being known; that is, according to the Scholiast, *A'ditya*, the Sun.—*Wilson.*

2 *Aryáh*, explained *dhanasya swáminah*; it does not appear why Rosen renders it *matrons*.—*Wilson.*

3 This and the preceding stanza are corroborative of the share borne by the Angirasas in the organization, if not in the origination, of the worship of Fire.—*Wilson.*

4 *Mátaris'wan* is a common name of Váyu, or wind; but it is here said to mean, the principal vital air (*mukhya-prána*), divided (*vibhrita*) into the five airs so denominated, as in a dialogue between them, cited by the Scholiast: "To them said the Arishta breath, 'Be not astonished; for I, having made myself five-fold, and having arrested the arrow, sustain life).' "—*Wilson.*

5 *Jenya*, from *jana*, to be born; or it may be derived from *ji*, to conquer, and be rendered 'victorious;' as, according to the *Taithiríyas*, the "Gods and Asuras were once engaged in combat; the former, being alarmed, entered into fire, therefore they call Agni all the Gods, who having made him their shield, overcame the Asuras." So in the *Aitaréya Bráhmana*, "the Gods having awoke Agni and placed him before them at the morning sacrifice, repulsed, with him in their van, the Asuras and Rakshasas at the morning rite."—*Wilson.*

who has become a friend sends an ambassador to his more powerful (conqueror).[1]

5. When (the worshipper) offers an oblation to his great and illustrious protector, the grasping (Rákshas), recognizing thee, Agni, retires, but Agni, the archer, sends after him a blazing arrow from his dreadful bow, and the God bestows light upon his own daughter, (the dawn).

6. When (the worshipper) kindles thee in his own dwelling, and presents an oblation to thee, daily desiring it, do thou, Agni, augmented in two ways, (as middling and as best), increase his means of sustenance: may he whom thou sendest with his car to battle, return with wealth.

7. All (sacrificial) viands concentrate in Agni, as the seven great rivers flow into the ocean: our food is not partaken of by our kinsmen,[2] therefore do thou, who knowest (all things), make our desires known to the Gods.

8. May that (digestive) faculty (of Agni) which regards food, be imparted to the devout and illustrious protector of priests, as the source of virile vigour;[3] and may Agni be born as (his) robust, irreproachable, youthful, and intelligent son, and instigate him (to acts of worship).

---

1 This expresses a notion still current amongst the nations of the East, that the mission of an envoy to a foreign prince, is an acknowledgment of the latter's superiority.

2 That is, we have not any to spare for others.

3 That is, the vigour derived from the digestive Agni; or, *retas* may be rendered, 'water;' when the passage will mean, "may fire and water, or heat and moisture, be spread through the earth for the generation of corn."

9. The Sun, who traverses alone the path of heaven with the speed of thought, is at once lord of all treasures: the two kings, Mitra and Varuṇa, with bounteous hands, are the guardians of the precious ambrosia of our cattle.

10. Dissolve not, Agni, our ancestral friendship, for thou art cognizant of the past as well as of the present; in like manner as light (speeds over) the sky, so decay impairs (my body); think of me before that source of destruction (prevails).[1]

SUKTA VIII. (LXXII.)

Rishi, etc., as before.

1. AGNI, holding in his hands many good things for men, appropriates the prayers addressed to the eternal creator.[2] Agni is the lord of riches, quickly bestowing (on those who plaise him) all golden (gifts).

2. All the immortals, and the unbewildered (Maruts), wishing for him was (dear) to us as a son, and was everywhere around, discovered him not; oppressed with fatigue, wandering on foot, and cognizant of his acts, they stopped at the last beautiful (hiding-)place of Agni.

3. Inasmuch, Agni, as the pure (Maruts) worshipped thee, (equally) pure, with clarified butter for three

---

1 Which is tantamount to asking Agni to grant immortality,—*Amritatwam prayachchhéti yávat*.—*Wilson*.

2 *Swátmábhimukham karoti*,—he makes them present or applicable to himself; the Creator is named *Védhas*, usually a name of *Brahmá*, and is here associated with *s'ás'wata*, the eternal; this looks as if a First Cause were recognized, distinct from Agni and the elemental Deities, although, in a figurative sense, they ate identified with it.—*Wilson*.

years, therefore they acquired names worthy (to be repeated) at sacrifices, and, being regenerated, obtained celestial bodies.[1]

4. Those who are to be worshipped, (the Gods), inquiring between the expansive heaven and earth for Agni), recited (hymns) dedicated to Rudra:[2] the troop of mortal[3] (Maruts), with (Indra), the sharer of half the oblation,[4] knowing where Agni was hiding, found him in his excellent retreat.

5. The Gods, discovering thee, sat down, and with their wives paid reverential adoration to thee upon their knees.[5] Secure on beholding their friend, of

---

1 The Text has only *S'uchayah*, 'the pure;' the Scholiast supplies Maruts, for whom, it is said, seven platters are placed at the *Agni-chayana* ceremony, and they are severally invoked by the appellations, *Idris'*, *Anyádris'*, *Tádris'*, *Pratidris'*, *Mitah*, *Samitah*, and others. In consequence of this participation with Agni of sacrificial offerings, they exchanged their perishable, for immortal, bodies, and obtained heaven. The Maruts are, therefore, like the Ribhus, deified mortals.—*Wilson.*

2 The allusion to Agni's hiding himself. occurring previously, also in verse 2, has already been explained, but we have here some further curious identifications, from which it appears that Rudra is Agni; the hymns of the Gods are addressed to Agni, and are therefore termed *Rudriyá*, for Rudra is Agni. *Rudra-agniḥ;* the legend which is cited in explanation, from the *Taittiríya* branch of the *Yajush*, relates, that during a battle between the Gods and Asuras, Agni carried off the wealth which the former had concealed; detecting the theft, the Gods pursued the thief, and forcibly recoveerdtheir treasure; Agni wept (*arodít*) at the loss, and was thence called *Rudra*.—*Wilson.*

3 The Text has only *martta*, 'the mortal;' the Scholiast supplies *Marudgana*.—*Wilson.*

4 Here also we have only the epithet *nemadhita*, 'the half-sharer,' from *nema*, a half; to which, according to the *Taittiríya* school, *Indra* is entitled at all sacrifices; the other half goes to all the Gods,—*sarve-dévâh éko arddhah, Indra éka évâparo arddhah*.—*Wilson.*

5 *Abhijnu;* or it may be applied to Agni kneeling before them. —*Wilson.*

being protected, thy friends, the Gods, abandoned the rest of their bodies in sacrifice.[1]

6. (Devout men), competent to offer sacrifices, have known the thrice seven mystic rites comprised in thee,[2] and with them, worshipped thee: do thou, therefore, with like affection, protect their cattle, and all that (belongs to them), movable or stationary.

7. Agni, who art cognizant of all things to be known, ever provide for the subsistence of men, grief-alleviating (food); so shalt thou be the diligent bearer of oblations, and messenger of the Gods, knowing the paths between (earth and heaven), by which they travel.

8. The seven pure rivers that flow from heaven (are directed, Agni, by thee: by thee the priests), skilled in sacrifices, knew the doors of the (cave where) the treasure, (their cattle), were concealed; for thee Saramá discovered the abundant milk of the kine with which man, the progeny of Manu still is nourished.[3]

---

1 So the Text, *Dévah yajñam atanwata*, "The Gods verily constituted the sacrifice;" but the expression is still obscure, and refers to some legend, probably which has not been preserved.—*Wilson*.

2 *Grihyáni padá(ni)*,—secret or mysterious steps by which heaven is to be obtained; meaning the ceremonies of the *Vedas*. These are arranged in three classes, each consisting of seven, or the *Páka yajñas*, those in which food of some kind is offered, as in the *Aupásana*, *Homa*, *Vais'wadeva*, *&c.*; the *Havir-yajñas*, those in which clarified butter is presented, as at the *Agnyádheya*, *Dars'a*, *Púrnamása*, and others; and the *Soma-yajñas*, the principal part of which is the libation of the *Soma*-Juice, as the *Agnishtoma*, *Atyagnishtoma*, etc. All these are comprised in Agni, because they cannot be celebrated without fire.—*Wilson*.

3 These circumstances are stated in the Text absolutely, without any reference to the instrument, or agent. The Scholiast supplies "Agni, by thee, etc.;" but the completion of the ellipse is consistent with prevailing notions; the sun, nourished by burnt offerings, is

9. Thou hast been fed, (Agni, with oblations), ever since the A'dityas, devising a road to immortality, instituted all (the sacred rites) that secured them from falling,[1] and mother earth, Aditi, strove with her magnitude to uphold (the world), along with her mighty sons.

10. (The offerers of oblations) have placed in this (Agni) the graceful honours (of the ceremony, and the two portions of clarified butter that are the two eyes[2]

---

enabled to send down the rain which supplies the rivers; the Angirasas recovered their cattle when carried off by Vala through the knowledge obtained by holy sacrifices; and Indra sent Saramá on the search, when propitiated by oblations with fire. Hence, Agni may be considered as the prime mover in the incidents.—*Wilson.*

1 It may be doubted if either of the former translators has given a correct version of this passage: Rosen has, *Diu cunctas luce destitutas per noctes stant;* M. Langlois has, *Qui s'élèvent assurant la marche de (l'astre) voyageur.* The Text has, *ye vis'wá swapatyáni*, interpreted by Sáyana, *sobhanáni apatana-hétu-bhutáni*,—those which were the prosperous causes of not falling; that is to say, certain sacred acts, which secured to the A'dityas their station in heaven; or, that immortality, the way to which they had made or devised. This interpretation is based upon a *Taittiríya* Text:—"The A'dityas, desirous of heaven (*su-varga*, or *swarga*), said, 'Let us go down to the earth;' they beheld there that (*Shat-trins'adrátra*) rite of thirty-six nights; they secured it, and sacrificed with it." It is to this, and a similar rite of fourteen nights, connected with the *Ayanas*, or 'comings' of the A'dityas, that allusion is made. Some reference to solar revolutions may be intended, although it is not obvious what can be meant, as no such movement is effected by thirty-six nights or days, and the Scholiast terms them *Karmáni*, 'acts or ceremonies.' *A'tastha* is also explained, they made or instituted: *A'tasthuh swapatyáni* means, according to him, *chaturdas'a-rátra shat-trimsadrátráadityánam ayanádíni karmáni kritavantah*,—they made the rites or acts which were the *Ayanas* and others of the A'dityas, (and which were for) thirty-six or fourteen nights.—*Wilson.*

2 An expression found also in another Text; or there are, as it were, two eyes of a sacrifice, which are the two portions of the clarified butter.—*Wilson.*

(of the sacrifice) ; then the immortals come from heaven, and thy bright flames, Agni, spread in all directions like rushing rivers, and the Gods perceive it (and rejoice).

SUKTA IX. (LXXIII.)

The *Rishi*, Deity, and metre are the same.

AGNI, like a patrimonial wealth, is the giver of food ; he is a director, like the instructions of one learned in scripture ; he rests in the sacrificial chamber like a welcome guest, and like an officiating priest, he brings prosperity on the house of the worshipper.

2. He who is like the divine Sun, who knows the truth (of things), preserves by his actions (his votaries), in all encounters ; like nature,[1] he is unchangeable, and, like soul,[2] is the source of happiness : he is ever to be cherished.

3. He who, like the divine (Sun), is the supporter of the universe, abides on earth like a prince, (surrounded by) faithful friends ; in his presence, men sit down like sons in the dwelling of a parent, and (in purity he resembles) an irreproachable and beloved wife.

4. Such as thou art, Agni, men preserve thee constantly kindled in their dwellings, in secure places, and offer upon thee abundant (sacrificial) food : do thou, in

---

1 *Amati*, the term of the Text, is explained *Rúpa* or *Swarúpa*,—peculiar form or nature ; as this is essentially the same in all the modifications of earth, or any other element, so Agni is one and the same in all the sacrifices performed with fire.—*Wilson*.

2 As soul is the seat and source of all happiness, so Agni, as the chief agent of sacrifice, is the main cause of felicity both here and ereafter.—*Wilson*.

whom is all existence, be the bearer of riches (for our advantage).

5. May thy opulent worshippers, Agni, obtain (abundant) food ; may the learned (who praise thee) and offer thee (oblations), acquire long life ; may we gain in battles booty from our foes, presenting their portion to the Gods for (the acquisition of) renown.

6. The cows, loving (Agni, who has come to the hall of sacrifice), sharing his splendour, have brought with full udders (their milk) to be drunk. The rivers, soliciting his good will, have flowed from a distance in the vicinity of the mountain.

7. (The Gods), who are entitled to worship, soliciting thy good will, have intrusted to thee, resplendent Agni, the (sacrificial) food, and, (for the due observance of sacred rites), they have made the night and morning of different colours, or black and purple.

8. May we, mortals, whom thou hast directed (to the performance of sacrifices) for the sake of riches, become opulent : filling heaven and earth, and the firmament (with thy radiance), thou protectest the whole world like a (sheltering) shade.[1]

9. Defended, Agni, by thee, may we destroy the horses (of our enemies) by (our) horses, their men by (our) men, their sons by (our) sons, and may our sons, learned, and inheritors of ancestral wealth, live for a hundred winters.

10. May these our praises, sapient Agni, be grateful to thee, both in mind and heart ; may we be competent to detain thy well-supporting wealth, offering upon thee their share of the (sacrificial) food to the Gods.

---

1 As anything affording shade keeps off the heat of the sun, so Agni guards the world against affliction.—*Wilson.*

ANUVA'KA XIII.

SUKTA I. (LXXIV.)

The Deity is Agni; the *Rishi*, Gotama, son of Rahúgana; the metre, *Gáyatrí*.

HASTENING to the sacrifice, let us repeat a prayer to Agni, who hears us from afar.

2. Who, existing of old, has preserved wealth for the sacrificer, when malevolent men are assembled together.

3. Let men praise Agni as soon as generated, the slayer of Vṛitra,[1] and the winner of booty in many a battle.

4. (The sacrificer), in whose house thou art the messenger of the Gods, whose offering thou conveyest for their food, and whose sacrifice thou renderest acceptable—

5. Him, Aṅgiras, son of strength, men call fortunate in his sacrifice, his Deity, his oblations.

6. Bring hither, radiant Agni, the Gods, to (receive) our praise and our oblations for their food.

7. Whenever thou goest, Agni, on a mission of the Gods, the neighing of the horses of thy (swift-) moving chariot, however audible, is not heard.

8. He who was formerly subject to a superior, having been protected, Agni, by thee, now stands in thy presence as an offerer (of oblations) without bashfulness, and supplied with food.

9. Verily, divine Agni, thou art desirous of bestowing upon the offerer (of oblations) to the Gods, ample (wealth), brilliant, and giving vigour.

---

1 *Vritra* may be here understood, an enemy in general; or, Agni may be identified with Indra.—*Wilson*.

SUKTA II. (LXXV.)

Rishi, Deity and metre as before.

ATTEND to our most earnest address, propitiatory of the Gods, accepting our oblations in thy mouth.

2. And then, most wise Agni, chief of the Angirasas, may we address (to thee) an acceptable and gratifying prayer.

3. Who, Agni, amongst men is thy kinsman? who is worthy to offer thee sacrifice? who, indeed, art thou, and where dost thou abide?

4. Worship for us, Mitra and Varuṇa; worship for us, all the Gods; (celebrate) a great sacrifice; be present in thine own dwelling.

SUKTA III. (LXXVI.)

Rishi and Deity as before; the metre is *Trishtubh*.

WHAT approximation of the mind, Agni, to thee, can be accomplished for our good; what can a hundred encomiums (effect); who, by sacrifices, has obtained thy might; with what intent may we offer thee (oblations)?[1]

2. Come, Agni, hither; invoker, (of the Gods), sit down;[2] be our preceder; for thou art irresistible: may the all-expansive heaven and earth defend thee, that thou mayest worship the Gods to their great satisfaction.

3. Utterly consume all the Rákshasás, Agni, and be the protector of our sacrifices against interruption.

1 That is, it is not possible to offer sacrifice, praise, or prayer that shall be worthy of Agni.—*Wilson.*

2 In the chamber where burnt-offerings are presented.

Bring hither the guardian of the *Soma*-Juice, (Indra),[1] with his steeds, that we may show hospitality to the giver of good.

4. I invoke (thee), who art the conveyer (of oblations), with thy flames, with a hymn productive of progeny (to the worshipper); sit down here with the Gods, and do thou, who art deserving of worship, discharge the office of *Hotri*, or of *Potri*, and awaken us, thou who art the depositary and generator of riches.

5. As at the sacrifice of the holy Manu, thou, a sage amongst sages, didst worship the Gods with oblations, so also, Agni, veracious invoker of the Gods, do thou to-day (present the oblations), with an exhilarating ladle.

SUKTA IV. (LXXVII.)

Rishi, etc., as before.

WHAT (oblations) may we offer to Agni? what praise is addressed to the luminous (Agni) that is agreeable to the Gods? that Agni who is immortal and observant of truth, who is the invoker of the Gods, the performer of sacrifices, and who, (present) amongst men, conveys oblations to the Deities.

2. Bring hither, with praises, him who is most constant in sacrifices, observant of truth, and the invoker (of the Gods), for Agni, when he repairs to

---

1 *Somapati*, which is a rather unusual appellative of Indra. The latter name is not in the Text, but the Deity is indicated by *Haribhyám*, his two steeds.—*Wilson*.

the Gods on the part of man, knows those (who are to be worshipped), and worships them with reverence.[1]

3. For he is the performer of rites, he is the destroyer and reviver (of all things),[2] and, like a friend, he is the donor of unattained wealth ; all men reverencing the Gods, and approaching the well-looking Agni repeat his name first in holy rites.

4. May Agni, who is the chief director of sacrifices, and the destroyer of enemies, accept our praise and worship with oblations, and may those who are affluent with great wealth, who are endowed with strength, and by whom the sacrificial food has been prepared, be desirous to offer adoration.

5. Thus has Agni, the celebrator of sacrifices, and by whom all things are known, been hymned by the pious descendants of Gotama ; to them has he given the bright *Soma*-Juice to drink, along with the sacrificial food, and, gratified by our devotion, he obtains nutriment (for himself).

---

1 The expression of the Text is *manasá*, 'with the mind ;' but the Scholiast reads *namasá*, 'with reverence,' asserting that the letters *n* and *m* are transposed.—*Wilson*.

2 The words are *marya* and *sádhu ;* the Commentator explains the first, the killer or extirpator of all, and the latter, the producer.—*Wilson*.

SUKTA V. (LXXVIII.)

The *Rishi* and Deity are the same; the metre is *Gáyatrí*.

KNOWER and beholder of all that exists, Gotama[1] celebrates thee, Agni, with praise: we praise thee repeatedly with commendatory (hymns).[2]

2. To thee, that (Agni) whom Gotama, desirous of riches, worships with praise, we offer adoration with commendatory (hymns).

3. We invoke thee, such as thou art, the giver of abundant food, in like manner as did Añgiras: we praise thee repeatedly which commendatory (hymns).

4. We praise thee repeatedly with commendatory (hymns), who art the destroyer of Vṛitra, and who puttest the Dasyus to flight.

5. The descendants of Rahúgaṇa have recited sweet speeches to Agni: we praise him repeatedly with commendatory (hymns).

SUKTA VI. (LXXIX.)

The *Rishi* is the same, Gotama; the hymn consists of four *Trichas*, or triads; the Deity of the first is the Agni of the middle region, the ethereal or electric fire or lightning; the Deity of the other triads is Agni in his general character; the metre of the first of them is *Trishtubh*, of the second, *Ushnih*, and of the last two, *Gáyatrí*.

THE golden-haired Agni is the agitator of the clouds when the rain is poured forth, and, moving with the

---

1 The word is *Gotamáh*, in the plural, whence Rosen renders it *Gotamidæ*; the Scholiast limits it to the sense of the singular, asserting that the plural is used honorifically only.—*Wilson*.

2 *Mantras* is supplied by the Commentator; the Text has only *dyumnaih*, 'with bright,' or those manifesting Agni's worth.—*Wilson*.

swiftness of the wind, shines with a bright radiance. The mornings know not (of the showers),[1] like honest[2] (people), who, provided with food, are intent upon their own labours.

2. Thy falling (rays), accompanied by the moving (*Maruts*), strike against (the cloud); the black shedder of rain has roared; when this is done, (the shower) comes with delightful and smiling (drops), the rain descends, the clouds thunder.

3. When this, (the lightning, Agni), nourishes the world with the milk of the rain, and conducts it by the most direct ways[3] to (the enjoyment of) water, then Mitra, Aryaman, Varuṇa, and the circumambient (troops of *Maruts*) pierce through the (investing) membrane into the womb of the cloud.

4. Agni, son of strength, lord of food and of cattle, give us abundant sustenance, thou who knowest all that exists.

5. He, the blazing Agni, who is wise, and the granter of dwellings, is to be praised by our hymns: Oh! thou whose mouth (glows) with many (flames),[4]

---

1 Agni, in his manifestation of lightning, takes part in the production of rain by piercing the clouds; the dawn is not concerned in the operation; but this is said, not to depreciate the excellence of *Ushas*, but to enhance that of Agni.—*Wilson.*

2 *Satyáh*, true, sincere; there is no substantive; but *Prajáh*, people, or progeny, is supplied by the Commentary; Rosen substitutes *mulieres*, *satyáh* being feminine, but so also is *Prajá*.—*Wilson.*

3 Or uses; as drinking, washing, bathing, and the like.—*Wilson.*

4 *Purvaníka*; from *puru*, many, and *aníka*, face or mouth; flames are understood, agreeably to a common name of Agni, *Jwálá-jihva*, flame-tongued. Rosen has evidently read the *mukha* of the Commentary, *sukha*, and explains *purvaníka*, *multis gaudiis fruens*.—*Wilson.*

shine (propitiously, so) that food-providing wealth may be ours.

6. Shining Agni, drive off (all disturbers of the rite), either by thyself or (thy servants), whether by day or by night; sharp-visaged Agni, destroy the Rákshasás, entirely.

7. Agni, who in all rites art to be praised, guard us with thy protection, (propitiated) by the recitation of the metrical hymn.[1]

8. Grant us, Agni, riches that dispel poverty, that are desirable (to all), and cannot be taken (from us) in all encounters (with our foes).

9. Grant us, Agni, for our livelihood, wealth, with sound understanding, conferring happiness, and sustaining (us through life).

10. Gotama, desirous of wealth, offers to the sharp-flaming Agni pure prayers and praises.

11. May he, Agni, who annoys us, whether nigh or afar, perish; and do thou be to us (propitious) for our advancement.

12. The thousand-eyed.[2] all-beholding Agni, drives away the Rákshasás, and, (praised by us) with holy hymns, he, (the invoker of the Gods), celebrates their praise.

---

1 *Gáyatra*; either a portion of the *Sáma* so termed, or the *Gáyatri* metre, according to the Scholiast.—*Wilson*.

2 The literal rendering of the epithet of the Text, *Sahasráksha*, which identifies Agni with Indra; but Sáyana interprets it, having countless flames.—*asankhyátajwálah*.—*Wilson*.

SUKTA VII. (LXXX.)

THE *Rishi* is Gotama, as before, but the Deity is Indra, ; the metre is *Pankti*.

MIGHTY wielder of the thunderbolt, when the priest[1] had thus exalted thee (by praise), and the exhilarating *Soma*-Juice (had been drunk), thou didst expel, by thy vigour, Ahi from the earth, manifesting thine own sovereignty.[2]

2. That exceedingly exhilarating *Soma*-Juice, which was brought by the hawk[3] (from heaven), when poured forth, has exhilarated thee, so that in thy vigour, thunderer, thou hast struck Vṛitra from the sky, manifesting thine own sovereignty.

3. Hasten, assail, subdue ; thy thunderbolt cannot fail : thy vigour, Indra, destroys men ; slay Vṛitra, win the waters, manifesting thine own sovereignty.

4. Thou hast struck Vṛitra from off the earth and from heaven ; (now) let loose the wind-bound, life-sustaining rain, manifesting thine own sovereignty.

5. Indignant Indra, encountering him, has struck with his bolt the jaw of the trembling Vṛitra, setting the waters free to flow, and manifesting his own sovereignty.

---

1 The *Brahmá,* which the Scholiast interprets *Bráhmana.*—*Wilson.*

2 The burthen of this and of all the other stanzas of this hymn is *archannanu swarájyam ;* the first term usually implies worshipping, honouring, but the Commentator gives as its equivalent, *prakatayan : swasya swâmitwam prakatayan,*—making manifest his own mastership or supremacy.—*Wilson.*

3 *Syenábhrita,* as Rosen translates it. *accipitri delatus ;* the Scholiast says it was brought from heaven by the *Gáyatri,* having the wings of a hawk.—*Wilson.*

6. Indra has struck him on the temple with his hundred-edged thunderbolt, and, exulting, wishes to provide means of sustenance for his friends, manifesting his own sovereignty.

7. Cloud-borne Indra, wielder of the thunderbolt, verily thy prowess is undisputed, since thou, with (superior) craft, hast slain that deceptive deer,[1] manifesting thine own sovereignty.

8. Thy thunderbolts were scattered widely over ninety-and-nine rivers;[2] great is thy prowess; strength is deposited in thy arms, manifesting thine own sovereignty.

9. A thousand[3] mortals worshipped him together; twenty[2] have hymned (his praise); a hundred (sages) repeatedly glorify him; so, Indra, is the oblation lifted up, manifesting thine own sovereignty.

10. Indra overcame by his strength the strength of Vṛitra: great is his manhood, wherewith, having slain Vṛitra, he let loose the waters, manifesting his own sovereignty.

11. This heaven and earth trembled, thunderer, at thy wrath, when, attended by the *Maruts*, thou slewest Vṛitra by thy prowess, manifesting thine own sovereignty.

12. Vṛitra deterred not Indra by his trembling or his clamour; the many-edged iron thunderbolt fell upon him: (Indra) manifesting his own sovereignty.

---

1 The Commentary says *Vritra* had assumed the form of a deer, but nothing further relating to this incident occurs.—*Wilson.*

2 Put for any indefinite number.—*Wilson.*

3 The sixteen priests employed at a sacrifice, the *Yajamána* and his wife, and two functionaries entitled the *Sadasya* and *S'amitri*, directors, probably, of the ceremonies of the assembly, not of the worship.—*Wilson.*

13. When thou, (Indra), didst encounter with thy bolt Vṛitra, and the thunderbolt (which he hurled), then, Indra, the strength of thee determined to slay Ahi was displayed in the heavens, manifesting thine own sovereignty.

14. At thy shout, wielder of the thunderbolt, all things, moveable or immoveable, trembled; even Twashtṛi shook with fear, Indra, at thy wrath, manifesting thine own sovereignty.

15. We know not of a certainty the all-pervading Indra: who (does know him, abiding) afar off[1] in his strength? for in him have the Gods concentrated riches, and worship, and power, manifesting his own sovereignty.

16. In like manner as of old, so in whatever act of worship Atharvan, or father Manu, or Dadhyañch[2] engaged, their oblations and their hymns were all congregated in that Indra, manifesting his own sovereignty.

---

1 The expression is very elliptical; *ko-viryá-parah*, being, literally, who—with vigour—afar: the Scholiast completes the sentence, as in the Text.—*Wilson.*

2 *Manush-pitá*, Manu, being the progenitor of all mankind. *Dadhyañch*, or Dadhíchi, is a well-known R*ishi*, the son of Atharvan, of whom mention subsequently more than once recurs.—*Wilson.*

SIXTH ADHYA'YA.

ANUVA'KA XIII.—*(Continued.)*

SUKTA VIII. (LXXXI.)

THE *Rishi*, Deity, and metre as before.

INDRA, the slayer of Vṛitra, has been augmented in strength and satisfaction by (the adoration of) men :[1] we invoke him in great conflicts as well as in little ; may he defend us in battles.

2. For thou, hero, Indra, art a host ; thou art the giver of much booty ; thou art the exalter of the humble ; thou bestowest (riches) on the worshipper who offers thee oblations, for abundant is thy wealth.

3. When battles arise, wealth devolves on the victor ; yoke thy horses, humblers of the pride (of the foe), that thou mayest destroy one and enrich another :[2] place us, Indra, in affluence.

4. Mighty through sacrifice, formidable (to foes), partaking of the sacrificial food, Indra has augment-

---

1 The Scholiast explains this,—"a Deity acquiring vigour by praise increases ;" that is, becomes more powerful and mighty. The notion is clear enough, but although 'increases' is the literal rendering of *varddhaté*, it expresses its purport but incompletely.—*Wilson*.

2 We have a legend in illustration of this passage : Gotama, the son of Rahúgana, was the *Purohita* of the Kuru and Srinjaya princes, and, in an engagement with other kings, propitiated Indra by this hymn, who, in consequence, gave the victory to the former. Rosen puts the phrase interrogatively, *Quemnam occisurus es, quemnam opulentiæ dabis* ? but the Scholiast explains *kam*, whom, by *kamchit*, any one, some one ; that is, Indra gives the victory to whomsoever he is pleased with.—*Wilson*.

ed his strength ; pleasing in appearance, having a handsome chin, and possessing (bright) coursers, he grasps the iron thunderbolt in his contiguous hands for (our) prosperity.

5. He has filled the space of earth and the firmament (with his glory) ; he has fixed the constellations in the sky : no one has been ever born, nor will be born, Indra, like to thee : thou hast sustained the universe.

6. May Indra, the protector, who returns to the giver (of oblations) the food that is fit for mortals, bestow (such food) on us : distribute thy wealth, which is abundant, so that I may obtain (a portion) of thy riches.

7. The upright performer of (pious) acts is the donor of herds of cattle to us, when receiving frequent enjoyment (from our libations) : take up, Indra, with both hands, many hundred (sorts) of treasure ; sharpen (our intellects), bring us wealth.

8. Enjoy along with us, O hero, the suffused libation for (the increase of our) strength and wealth : we know thee (to be) the possessor of vast riches, and address to thee our desires ; be, therefore, our protector.

9. These, thy creatures, Indra, cherish (the oblation) that may be partaken of by all ; thou, lord of all, knowest what are the riches of those men who make no offerings : bring their wealth to us.

SUKTA IX. (LXXXII.)

THE Deity and *Rishi* are the same; the metre is *Pankti*, except in the last stanza, where it is *Jagatí*.

APPROACH, Maghavan, and listen to our praises; be not different (from what thou hast hitherto been);[1] since thou hast inspired us with true speech, thou art solicited with it; therefore, quickly yoke thy horses.

2. (Thy worshippers) have eaten the food which thou hadst given, and have rejoiced, and have trembled through their precious (bodies); self-illuminated sages have glorified thee with commendable thoughts; therefore, Indra, quickly yoke thy horses.

3. We praise thee, Maghavan, who lookest benignly (upon all); thus praised by us, repair (in thy car), filled with treasure, to those who desire thy presence: Indra, quickly yoke thy horses.

4. May he ascend that chariot which rains (blessings), and grants cattle, and which provides the vessel filled with the mixture of *Soma*-Juice and grain:[2] quickly, Indra, yoke thy horses.

5. Performer of many (holy) acts, let thy steeds be harnessed on the right and on the left, and when

---

1 The Text is merely *má atathá iva*,—(be) not, as it were, non-such; that is, according to Sáyana, be not the contrary of that propitious Divinity which thou hast always been to us; the rest of the stanza is equally obscure: "Since thou makest us possessed of true speech (*sunritávatah*), therefore thou art asked (*át arthayása it*) *arthayase eva*;" that is, to accept our praises. In this hymn, also, we have a burthen repeated at the close of each stanza.—*Wilson.*

2 *Patram hariyojanam*, a plate or patera filled with *hariyojanam*; the appellation of a mixture of fried barley, or other grain, and *Soma*-Juice.—*Wilson.*

exhilarated by the (sacrificial) food, repair in thy chariot to thy beloved wife: quickly, Indra, yoke thy horses.

6. I harness thy long-maned steeds with (sacred) prayers: depart; take the reins in your hands: the effused and exciting juices have exhilarated thee, wielder of the thunderbolt; thus filled with nutriment, rejoice with thy spouse.

SUKTA X. (LXXXIII.)

Rishi and Deity as before; the metre is *Jagatí.*

THE man who is well protected, Indra, by thy cares, (and dwells) in a mansion where there are horses, is the first who goes to (that where there are) cows; enrich him with abundant riches, as the unconscious rivers[1] flow in all directions to the ocean.

2. In like manner, as the bright waters flow to the sacrificial ladle, so they (the Gods) look down (upon it); as the diffusive light (descends to earth), the Gods convey it, desirous of being presented to them by progressive (movements to the altar), and are impatient to enjoy it, filled with the oblation, as bridegrooms long for (their brides).[2]

---

1 *Vichétasaḥ ápah*; the epithet is explained by the Scholiast, 'the sources of excellent knowledge,'—*vis'ishtajñánaketubhútáh*; and Rosen renders it, accordingly, *sapientiam conferentes*; but it seems preferable to understand the prefix *vi* in its sense of privation, for it is not very intelligible how the waters should confer, or ever possess, intelligence.—*Wilson*.

2 In this stanza, as usual in the more elaborate metres, we encounter strained collocations and elliptical and obscure allusions,

3. Thou hast associated, Indra, words of sacred praise with both (the grain and butter of oblation), placed together in ladles, and jointly presented to thee, so that (the sacrificer), undisturbed, remains (engaged in thy worship, and is prosperous ; for to the sacrificer pouring out oblations (to thee), auspicious power is granted.

4. The Aṅgirasas first prepared (for Indra) the sacrificial food, and then, with kindled fire, (worshipped him) with a most holy rite : they, the institutors (of the ceremony), acquired all the wealth of Paṇi, comprising horses, and cows, and (other) animals.

5. Atharvaṇ first by sacrifices discovered the path (of the stolen cattle) : then the bright Sun, the cherisher of pious acts, was born.[1] Atharvaṇ regained the cattle ; Kávya (Us'anas) was associated with him.[2]

---

imperfectly transformed into something intelligible by the additions of the Scholiast ; thus, *avah pas'yanti*, 'they look down,' is rendered special by adding *dévâh*, 'the Gods,' who look down, it is said, upon the sacrificial ladle, *hotriyam*, well pleased to behold it filled with the intended libation. The Text, again, has only "as diffused light ;" the Comment adds, "descends on earth." In the next phrase we have, "the Gods lead that which is pleased by the libation, and wishes for them, either by progressive movements, or in an eastern direction (*práchair*), as bridegrooms delight." What is so led, and whither ? The ladle, *chamasa*, the altar, *védi*, as well as the bride or maiden, *kanayaká*, are filled up by the Comment. The same character of brevity and obscurity pervades the entire hymn.—*Wilson*.

1. *A'jani* ; but it may mean, as the Scholiast says, "the Sun appeared, in order to light the way to the cave where the cows were hidden.—*Wilson*.

2. With Indra, according to the Comment, which also identifies Kávya with Us'anas, and the latter with Bhrigu ; "*Kávyaḥ Kaveḥ putra Us'aná Bhriguḥ*," meaning, however, perhaps, only that Us'anas was of the family of Bhrigu.—*Vishnu Purána*, 82, n.—*Wilson*.

Let us worship the immortal (Indra), who was born to restrain (the Asuras).[1]

6. Whether the holy grass be cut (for the rite) that brings down blessings,[2] whether the priest repeats the (sacred) verse in the brilliant (sacrifice), whether the stone (that expresses the *Soma*-Juice) sound like the priest who repeats the hymn, on all these occasions Indra rejoices.

SUKTA XI. (LXXXIV.)

THE Deity and the *Rishi* are the same, but the metre is diversified. The first six stanzas are in the *Anusktubh* measure; the three next, in *Ushnih*; the three next, in *Panktí*; the three next, in *Gáyatrí*; and the next three, in the *Trishtubh*; the nineteenth verse is in the *Brikati*-, and the twentieth, in the *Sato-Brikati*-, metre.

THE *Soma*-Juice has been expressed, Indra, for thee: potent humbler (of thy foes), approach; may vigour fill thee (by the potation), as the Sun fills the firmament with his rays.

2. May his horses bear Indra, who is of irresistible prowess, to the praises and sacrifices of sages and of men.

3. Slayer of Vṛitra, ascend thy chariot, for thy horses have been yoked by prayer; may the stone

---

1 The Text has only *yamasya játam*; the Comment explains the former, *asuránám niyamanártham*.—*Wilson.*

2 *Swápatyáya*; resolving this into *Su* and *ápatya*, Rosen renders it, *egregiam prolem conferentis causa*, and M. Langlois has, *le chef de famille, jaloux d'obtenir une heureuse postérité* Sáyana understands it differently, and explains it by *Sobhanápatana ketubhútáya*,—for the sake of the descent, or coming down, of what is good.—*Wilson.*

(that bruises the *Soma*) attract, by its sound, thy mind towards us.

4. Drink, Indra, this excellent, immortal, exhilarating libation, the drops of which pellucid (beverage) flow towards thee in the chamber of sacrifice.

5. Offer worship quickly to Indra; racite hymns (in his praise); let the effused drops exhilarate him; pay adoration to his superior strength.

6. When, Indra, thou harnessest thy horses, there is no one a better charioteer than thou; no one is equal to thee in strength; no one, although well-horsed, has overtaken thee.

7. He who alone bestows wealth upon the man who offers him oblations, is the undisputed sovereign, Indra:—ho![1]

8. When will he trample with his foot upon the man who offers no oblations, as if upon a coiled-up snake;[2] when will Indra listen to our praises?—ho!

9. Indra grants formidable strength to him who worships him, having libations prepared:—ho!

10. The white cows drink of the sweet *Soma*-Juice thus poured forth, and, associated with the bounti-

---

1 This verse and the two following end with the unconnected term *Anga*, which the Scholiast interprets 'quick;' but it is more usually an interjection of calling; so Rosen has *Ohe!* M. Langlois, *Oh viens!—Wilson.*

2 The Text has *kshumpa*, explained, *ahichchhatraka;* properly, a thorny plant, but apparently intended by the Scholiast for a snake coiled up, or one sleeping in a ring, which is therefore killed without difficulty: *mand'alákarena s'ayánam kaschid-anáyásena hanti.* Rosen prefers the usual sense, *pede fruticem velut conteret.—Wilson.*

ful Indra, for the sake of beauty, rejoice: abiding (in their stalls), they are expectant of his sovereignty.[1]

11. Desirous of his contact, those brindled cows dilute the *Soma*-Juice with their milk: the milch-kine that are loved of Indra, direct his destructive thunderbolt against his foes, abiding (in their stalls), expectant of his sovereignty.

12. These intelligent kine reverence his prowess with the adoration (of their milk); they celebrate his many exploits as an example to later (adversaries); abiding (in their stalls), expectant of his sovereignty.

13. Indra, with the bones of Dadhyañch, slew ninety times nine Vṛitras.[2]

---

1 This, which constitutes the burthen of the triad, is rather obscure; the Text is, *vasviranu swarájyam*, literally, dwelling after, or according to, his own dominion. Sáyana does not make it more intelligible: "Those cows," he says, "who, by giving milk, are the means of providing habitation (*nivásakárinyah*), remain looking to the kingdom of him, or Indra;" so Rosen has, *domicilium procurantes, quæ ipsius dominium respicientes adstant.*—*Wilson.*

2 Dadhyañch, also named Dadhícha and Dadhíchi, is a well-known sage in *Pauránik* legend, of whom, it is said, that his bones formed the thunderbolt of Indra. The story seems to have varied from the original *Vaidik* fiction, as we shall have subsequent occasion to notice (*Súkta* CXVI.). In this place, the story told by the Scholiast also somewhat differs. He relates, that while Dadhyañch, the son of Atharvan, lived, the Asuras were intimidated and tranquillized by his appearance, but when he had gone to *Swarga*, they overspread the whole earth. Indra, inquiring what had become of him, and whether nothing of him had been left behind, was told that the horse's head with which he had at one time taught the Madhuvidyá to the As'wins, was somewhere in existence, but no one knew where. Search was made for it, and it was found in the lake S'aryanavat, on the skirts of Kurukshétra; and with the bones of the skull, Indra slew the Asuras, or, as otherwise explained, foiled the nine times ninety, or eight hundred and ten, stratagems or devices of the Asurás or Vritras. The Scholiast accounts for the

14. Wishing for the horse's head hidden in the mountains, he found it at S'aryanávat.

15. The (solar rays) found on this occasion the light of Twashtṛi verily concealed in the mansion of the moving Moon [1]

16. Who yokes to-day to the pole of the car (of Indra) his vigorous and radiant steeds, whose fury is unbearable, in whose mouths are arrows, who trample on the hearts (of enemies), who give happiness (to friends). (The sacrificer) who praises their (performance of their) duties obtains (long) life.[2]

---

number, by saying, that, in the beginning, the *A'surímaya*, or demoniac illusion, was practised in the three worlds, for three periods in each,—past, present, and future, whence it was ninefold; each being exerted with three *s'aktis*, or energies, made the number twenty-seven; each of these again being modified by the three *gunas*, they become eighty-one, and the scene of their display extending to each of the ten regions of space, the total reaches the nine times ninety of the Text, or eight hundred and ten This seems to be pure invention, without any rational or allegorical meaning —*Wilson*

1 The Text has only "they found;" the Scholiast, following Yáska (*Nir*. 4. 25). supplies *A'ditya rásmayah*, the rays of the Sun. Twashtri is here used for the Sun, being one of the A'dityas; or, according to the Scholiast, for Indra, to whom the hymn is addressed, and who is also one of the A'dityas. The purport of the stanza is apparently the obscure expression of an astronomical fact, known to the authors of the *Védás*, that the Moon shone only through reflecting the light of the Sun; so it is said, "the rays of the Sun are reflected back in the bright watery orb of the Moon;" and again, "the solar radiance, concealed by the night, enters into the Moon, and thus dispels darkness by night as well as by day." According to the *Nirukta*, 2. 6, it is one ray of the Sun (that named Sushumna) which lights up the Moon, and it is with respect to that, that its light is derived from the Sun. The *Purânas* have adopted the doctrine of the *Védas*.—*Vishnu Purana*, 36

2 Another interpretation may be assigned to this verse, which turns upon rendering *Kah* by Prajápati, instead of *who*, and *ga* by

17. Who goes forth, (through dread of foes, when Indra is at hand); who is harmed (by his enemies); who is terrified; who is aware that Indra is present, who that he is nigh?[1] What need is there that any one should importune Indra for his son, his elephant, his property, his person, or his people?

18. Who praises the (sacrificial) fire, (lighted for Indra), or worships him with the oblation of clarified butter, presented in the ladle, according to the constant seasons?[2] To whom do the Gods quickly bring (the wealth) that has been called for? What sacrificer, engaged in offering oblations and favoured by the Gods thoroughly knows Indra?

19. Powerful Indra, be present and be favourable to the mortal (who adores thee): there is no other giver of felicity, Maghavan, than thou; hence, Indra, I recite thy praise.

20. Granter of dwellings, let not thy treasury, let not thy benefits,[3] ever be detrimental to us. Friend of mankind, bring to us, who are acquainted with prayers, all sorts of riches.

---

words of the Véda, instead of *horses*; making, "Prajápati combines to-day with the burthen of the sacrifice the sacred words that are effective, brilliant, essential, emitted from the mouth, animating the heart, and productive of happiness: the worshipper who fulfils the object of such prayers, obtains life."—*Wilson.*

1 That is, we know it very well, and are therefore secure in his presence at this ceremony; or *Kah* may again be explained by Prajápati, with the sense of the stanza modified accordingly.—*Wilson.*

2 *Ritubhir dhruvebhiḥ*; in which *ritu* may have its ordinary sense of 'season;' or the passage may mean, 'presented by the Divinities called *Ritus*, who preside over sacrifices,' as in the Text, *Ritavo vai práyájah,*—the *Ritus* are the chief sacrifices; *i.e., prayájadevatáḥ,*—the Deities presiding over them.—*Wilson.*

3 *Utayaḥ*, benefits, assistances; but it may be read, *dhútayaḥ*, shakers, agitators; *i.e.*, the Maruts, or winds.—*Wilson.*

ANUVA'KA XIV.

SUKTA I. (LXXXV.)

THE Deities are the Maruts, the *Rishi*, Gotama: the metre of the fifth and twelfth verses is *Trishtubh*, of the rest, *Jagatí*.

THE Maruts who are going forth decorate themselves like females: thy are gliders (through the air), the sons of Rudra, and the doers of good works, by which they promote the welfare of earth and heaven: heroes, who grind (the solid rocks), they delight in sacrifices.

2. They, inaugurated by the Gods,[1] have attained majesty; the sons of Rudra have established their dwelling above the sky: glorifying him (Indra) who merits to be glorified, they have inspired him with vigour: the sons of Pris'ni have acquired dominion.

3. When the sons of earth[2] embellish themselves with ornaments, they shine resplendent in their persons with (brilliant) decorations; they keep aloof every adversary: the waters follow their path.[3]

4. They who are worthily worshipped shine with various weapons: incapable of being overthrown, they are the overthrowers (of mountains): Maruts, swift as thought, intrusted with the duty of sending rain, yoke the spotted deer to your cars.

5. When, Maruts, urging on the cloud, for the sake of (providing) food, you have yoked the deer to

---

1 *Ushitasah*, wetted, sprinkled with holy water by the Gods,—*Devair-abhishiktah*.—*Wilson*.

2 Here they are called *Gomatarah*, having for their mother the cow; that is, the earth under that type, equivalent to *Pris'ni* in the preceding stanza.—*Wilson*.

3 That is, rain follows the wind.—*Wilson*.

your chariots, the drops fall from the radiant[1] (Sun), and moisten the earth, like a hide, with water.

6. Let your quick-paced, smooth-gliding coursers bear you hither); and, moving swiftly, come with your hands (filled with good things): sit, Maruts, upon the broad seat of sacred grass, and regale yourselves with the sweet sacrificial food.

7. Confiding in their own strength, they have increased in (power); they have attained heaven by their greatness, and have made (for themselves) a spacious abode: may they, for whom Vishṇu defends (the sacrifice) that bestows all desires and confers delight, come (quickly), like birds, and sit down upon the pleasant and sacred grass.

8. Like heroes, like combatants, like men anxious for food, the swift-moving (Maruts) have engaged in battles: all beings fear the Maruts, who are the leaders (of the rain), and awful of aspect like princes.

9. Indra wields the well-made, golden, many-bladed thunderbolt, which the skilful Twashtṛi[2] has framed for him, that he may achieve great exploits in war. He has slain Vṛitra and sent forth an ocean of water.

10. By their power, they bore the well aloft, and clove asunder the mountain that obstructed their path: the munificent Maruts, blowing upon their

---

1 *Arusha* is the term of the Text,—'the radiant,' which may apply either to the Sun or to the Agni of lightning, either being in like manner the source of rain.—*Wilson*.

2 *Twashtri* here reverts to his usual office of artisan of the gods.

pipe,[1] have conferred, when exhilarated by the *Soma*-Juice, desirable (gifts upon the sacrificer).

11. They brought the crooked well to the place (where the *Muni* was), and sprinkled the water upon the thirsty Gotama:[2] the variously-radiant (Maruts) come to his succour, gratifying the desire of the sage with life-sustaining (waters).

12. Whatever blessings (are diffused) through the three worlds, and are in your gift, do you bestow upon the donor (of the oblation), who addresses you with praise; bestow them, also, Maruts, upon us, and grant us, bestowers of all good, riches, whence springs prosperity.

SÚKTA II. (LXXXVI.)

Rishi and Deities the same; the metre is *Gáyatri.*

THE man in whose mansion, resplendent Maruts, descending from the sky, you drink (the libation), is provided with most able protectors.

2. Maruts, bearers of oblations, hear the invocation of the praises of the worshipper with or (without) sacrifices.[3]

---

1 *Dhamanto vánam.* The Scholiast explains *vánám* to be a lute, a *viná* with a hundred strings,—a short of Æolian harp, perhaps; *dhamanta*, 'blowing,' would better apply to a pipe, a wind instrument.

2 In this and the next stanza, allusion is made to a legend in which it is related that the *Rishi Gotama*, being thirsty, prayed to the *Maruts* for relief, who thereupon brought a well from a distance to his hermitage. This exploit is subsequently (Sukta CXVI.) related to the *Aswins.*

3 The expression is *yajnair-vá*, 'with sacrifices or;' the 'without' is supplied by the Scholiast.

3. And may he for whom ministrant priests have sharpened[1] the sapient (troop of the Maruts), walk among pastures crowded with cattle.

4. The libation is poured out for the hero (band) at the sacrifice, on the appointed days, and the hymn is repeated, and their joy (is excited).

5. May the Maruts, victorious over all men, hear (the praises) of this (their worshipper), and may (abundant) food be obtained by him who praises them.

6. Enjoying the protection of you who behold all things, we have offered you, Maruts, (oblations) for many years.

7. Maruts, who are to be especially worshipped, may the man whose offering you accept be ever prosperous.

8. Possessors of true vigour, be cognizant of the wishes of him who praises you, and toils in your service, desirous of (your favour.)

9. Possessors of true vigour, you have displayed your might, with the lustre (of which) you have destroyed the Rákshasas.

10. Dissipate the concealing darkness; drive away every devouring (foe); show us the light we long for.

---

1 *Atakshata*, have sharpened, *i.e.*, have excited or animated, by their offerings.

SUKTA III. (LXXXVII.)

Rishi and Deities as before; metre, *Jagati*

ANNIHILATORS (of adversaries,) endowed with great strength, loud-shouting, unbending, inseparable[1] partakers of the evening oblation,[2] constantly worshipped and leaders (of the clouds), (the Maruts), by their personal[3] decorations, are conspicuous (in the sky), like certain rays of the sun.

2. When, Maruts, flying like birds along a certain path (of the sky), you collect the moving passing (clouds) in the nearest portions (of the firmament), then coming into collision with your cars, they pour forth (the waters); therefore, do you shower upon your worshipper the honey-coloured rain.[4]

---

1 Always associated in troops.—*Wilson*.

2 The term is *Rijíshinaḥ*, which is not very clearly explained; *Rijisha*, in ordinary use, means a frying-pan, but here the Scholiast seems to consider it as a synonym of *Soma*, the Maruts being thus named because they are entitled, at the third daily ceremonial, or the evening worship, to a share of the effusion of the *Rijísha*,—*Rijíshasya abhishavát*; or the term may signify, he adds, "the acquirers or receivers of the juices,"—*Prárjayitáraḥ rasánám*; from *rij*, to acquire; Rosen has, *lance sacrificiis culti*; M. Langlois, *amis de nos sacrifices*.—*Wilson*.

3 *Stribhiḥ*, covering, or clothing; from *stri*, to cover; an epithet of *anjibhih*, ornaments; *swasarírasyáchchhádakair ábharanaiḥ*.—with ornaments covering their own persons. As the word is separated from the substantive, however, by the intervening simile, "like some rays" (*kechid usrá iva*), it has been understood in a different sense by former translators: thus, Rosen has, *Ornamentis dignoscuntur, vari lucis radii velut qui stellis effunduntur*; and M. Langlois, *Les Maruts brillent sous leurs parures, comme les nuages sous les feux des étoiles*; but *stribhiḥ* cannot have any relation to *stars*.—*Wilson*.

4 *Madhuvarnam*, having the colour of honey; or, according to the Commentator, being equally pure or pellucid (*swachchha*).—*Wilson*.

3. When they assemble (the clouds) for the good work, earth trembles at their impetuous movements, like a wife (whose husband is away): sportive, capricious, armed with bright weapons, and agitating (the solid rocks), they manifest their inherent might.

4. The troop of Maruts is self-moving, deer-borne, ever young, lords of this (earth), and invested with vigour: you, who are sincere liberators from debt,[1] irreproachable, and shedders of rain, are the protectors of this our rite.

5. We declare by our birth our ancient sire, that the tongue (of praise) accompanies the manifesting (invocation of the Maruts) at the libations of the *Soma*; for, inasmuch as they stood by, encouraging Indra in the conflict, they have acquired names that are to be recited at sacrifices.

6. Combining with the solar rays, they have willingly poured down (rain) for the welfare (of mankind), and, hymned by the priests, have been pleased partakers of the (sacrificial food); addressed with praises, moving swiftly, and exempt from fear, they have become possessed of a station agreeable and suitable to the Maruts.

---

1 By making their worshippers wealthy.—*Wilson.*

SUKTA IV. (LXXXVIII.)

Rishi and Deity as before; the metre of the first and last stanzas *Prastara-pankti* of the intermediate four, *Jagati*.

COME, Maruts,[1] with your brilliant, light-moving, well-weaponed, steed-harnessed chariots; doers of good deeds, descend like birds, (and bring us) abundant food.

2. To what glorifier (of the Gods) do they repair with their ruddy, tawny, car-bearing horses for his advantage? bright as burnished (gold), and armed with the thunderbolt, they furrow the earth with their chariot-wheels.

3. Maruts, the threatening (weapon) are upon your persons, (able to win) dominion: (to you) they raise lofty sacrifices, like (tall) trees: well-born Maruts, for you do wealthy worshippers enrich the stone (that grinds the *Soma*-Plant).

4. Fortunate days have befallen you, (sons of Gotama), when thirsty, and have given lustre to the rite for which water was essential; the sons of Gotama, (offering) oblations with sacred hymns, have raised aloft the well (provided) for their dwelling.

5. This hymn is known to be the same as that which Gotama recited, Maruts, in your (praise), when

---

1 The Scholiast here proposes various etymologies of the name Marut, some of which are borrowed from Yáska, *Nir.* 11, 13. They *sound (ruvanti,* from *ru*), having attained mid-heaven (*mitam*); or, They *sound* without measure (*amitam*); or, They *shine* (from *ruch*) in the clouds *made* (*mitam*) by themselves; or, They *hasten* (*dravanti*) in the sky. All the minor Divinities, that people the mid air said in *Védás* to be styled Maruts, as in the Text, "All females whose station is the middle heaven, the all-pervading masculine Váyu, and all the troops (of Demigods), are Maruts." Sáyana also cites the *Pauránik* tradition of the birth of the forty-nine Maruts, in seven troops, as the sons of Kas'yapa—(*Vishnu Purána*).

he beheld you seated in your chariots with golden wheels, armed with iron weapons, hurrying hither and thither, and destroying your mightiest foes.

6. This is that praise, Maruts, which, suited (to your merits), glorifies every one of you. The speech of the priest has now glorified you, without difficulty, with sacred verses, since (you have placed) food in our hands.

SUKTA V. (LXXXIX.)

THE *Rishi*, as before, Gotama; but the hymn is addressed to the Vis'wadévas. The metre of the first five stanzas and of the seventh is *Jagati*; of the sixth, *Virátsthána*, and of the last three, *Trishtubh*.

MAY auspicious works, unmolested, unimpeded, and subversive (of foes), come to us from every quarter; may the gods, turning not away from us, but granting us protection, day by day, be ever with us for our advancement.

2. May the benevolent favour of the gods (be ours); may the bounty of the gods, ever approving of the upright, light upon us; may we obtain the friendship of the gods, and may the gods extend our days to longevity.

3. We invoke them with an ancient Text,[1] Bhaga, Mitra, Aditi, Daksha, Asridh, Aryaman, Varuṇa, Soma, the As'wins; and may the gracious Saraswati grant us happiness.[2]

---

1 *Purvayá nividá; nivid* is a synonym of *vách*, speech, or a text; here said to be a Text of the *Véda*.—*Wilson*.

2 Most of these, here included amongst the Vis'wadévas, have occurred before; but the Scholiast here also explains their functions:—

4. May the wind waft to us the grateful medicament;[3] may mother earth, may father heaven, (convey) it (to us);[4] may the stones that express the *Soma*-Juice, and are productive of pleasure, (bring) it (to us); As'wins, who are to be meditated upon, hear (our application).

5. We invoke that lord of living beings, that protector of things immovable, Indra, who is to be propitiated by pious rites, for our protection; as Púshan has ever been our defender for the increase of our riches, so may he (continue) the unmolested guardian of our welfare.

Bhaga and Mitra are A'dityas, and the latter is especially the lord of day, as, by the text, *maitram vá ahar*,—the day is dependent on Mitra. Aditi is the mother of the gods; Daksha is called a *Prajápati able* to make the world; or, he is the creator (*Hiranyagarbha*), diffused among breathing or living creatures as breath or life; as by the Text, *Práno vai Daksha*,—Daksha verily is breath. Asridh, from *sridh*, to dry up; undrying, unchanging; that is the class of *Maruts*. Aryaman is the sun, as by the Text, *Asau vá Aditya aryama*,—he, the sun, is Aryaman. Varuna is named from *vri*, to surround, encompassing the wicked with his bonds; he is also the lord of night, as by the Text, *Váruní ratri*,—the night is dependent on Varuna. *Soma* is twofold; the plant so called on earth, and the moon, as a Divinity in heaven. The As'wins are so termed either from having horses (*as'wavantau*), or from pervading all things, the one with moisture, the other with light, according to Yáska, who also states the question; Who were they? which is thus answered; according to some, they are heaven and earth; to others, day and night; according to others, the sun and moon; and, according to the traditionists (*Aitihásika*), they were two virtuous princes.—*Nirukta* 12, 1.—*Wilson*.

3 *Bhéshajam*; that medicament which the As'wins, as the physicians of the gods, are qualified to bestow. No other specification is given.—*Wilson*.

4 Earth is so termed, as producing all things necessary for life, and heaven as sending rain, and therefore indirectly nourishing all things.—*Wilson*.

6. May Indra, who listens to much praise, guard our welfare; may Púshan, who knows all things, guard our welfare; may Tárkshya,[1] with unblemished weapons, guard our welfare.

7. May the Maruts, whose coursers are spotted deer, who are the sons of Pris'ni, gracefully-moving, frequenters of sacrifices, (seated) on the tongue of Agni,[2] regarders (of all), and radiant as the sun, may all the gods come hither for our preservation.

8. Let us hear, gods, with our ears, what is good; objects of sacrifice, let us see with our eyes what is good; let us, engaged in our praises, enjoy, with firm limb and (sound) bodies, the term of life granted by the gods.[3]

9. Since a hundred years were appointed (for the life of man), interpose not, gods, in the midst of our passing existence, by inflicting infirmity on our bodies, so that our sons become our sires.[4]

---

1 *Tárkshya* is a patronymic, implying son of Triksha and, according to the Scholiast, Garuda. He is termed in the Text *Arishtanémi*,—he who has unharmed or irresistible (*arishta*) weapons (*némi*); or the latter may imply, as usual, the circumference of a wheel,—whose chariot-wheel is unimpeded; but *Arishtanémi* occurs in the *Váyu Purána*, as the name of a *Prajápati*, so that the passage might mean *Arishtanémi*, the son of *Triksha*, which, according to some authorities, is a name of the patriarch Kas'yapa: the same make *Tárkshya* a synonym of *Aruna*, the personified dawn. It is doubtful if we have any reference to the vehicle of *Vishnu*, *Garuda*.—*Wilson.*

2 This may be predicated of all the deities, as they receive oblations through the mouth of Agni.—*Wilson.*

3 *Devahitam*; whence it may be rendered, as the Scholiast proposes, in the singular, understanding by *Déva*, *Prajápati*, either a patriarch or Brahmá. The Commentator says the limit of human life is 116 or 120 years, but the stanza specifies a century.—*Wilson.*

4 That is, let us not become so feeble and infirm as to be, as it were, infants, and to require the paternal care of our own sons.

10. Aditi[1] is heaven; Aditi is the firmament; Aditi is mother, father, and son; Aditi is all the gods; Aditi is the five classes of men;[2] Aditi is the generation and birth.[3]

SUKTA VI. (XC.)

THE *Rishi* is the same, the deities are various, the mere *Gáyatri.*

MAY Varuna and the wise Mitra lead us, by straight paths, (to our desires) and Aryaman,[4] rejoicing with the gods.

2. For they are the distributors of wealth (over the world); and, never heedless, discharge their functions every day.

3. May they, who are immortal, bestow upon us mortals. happiness, annihilating our foes.

4. May the adorable Indra, the Maruts, Pushan, and Bhaga, so direct our paths, (that they may lead) to the attainment of good gifts.

---

1 Aditi, literally meaning the independent or the indivisible, may here signify either the earth, or the mother of the gods, according to the Scholiast. According to *Yáska*, the hymn declares the might of Aditi,—*aditer vibhutim achachate* (*Nir.* 4, 23); or, as Sáyana, "Aditi is hymned as the same with the universe.

2 As before noticed, the five orders of men are said to be the four castes and the outcastes. It is also interpreted five classes of beings, or Gods, men, *Gandharbas* (including *Apsarasas*), Serpents, and *Pitris;* Gods *Asuras*, and *Rákshasas.*

3 *Játam* is the actual birth of beings, *Janitwam,* the faculty of being born, generation. Rosen renders the terms, *natum* and *nasciturum.*

4 Aryaman is said to be the sun in his function of separating day from night.

5. Pushan, Vishnu,[1] Maruts, make our rites restorative of our cattle; make us prosperous.

6. The winds[2] bring sweet (rewards) to the sacrificer; the rivers bring sweet (waters); may the herbs yield sweetness to us.

7. May night and morn be sweet; may the region of the earth be full of sweetness; may the protecting heaven be sweet to us.

8. May Vanaspati be possessed of sweetness towards us; may the sun be imbued with sweetness; may the cattle be sweet to us.

9. May Mitra be propitious to us; may Varuna, may Aryaman, be propitious to us; may Indra and Brihaspati be propitious to us; may the wide-stepping Vishnu be propitious to us.

SUKTA VII. (XCI.)

THE *Rishi* is still Gotama, the deity is Soma; from the fifth to the sixteenth stanza the metre is *Gáyatrí*; the seventeenth, *Ushnih*, the rest, *Trishtubh*.

THOU, Soma, art thoroughly apprehended by our understanding; thou leadest us along a straight path: by thy guidance, Indra, our righteous fathers obtained wealth amongst the gods.

2. Thou, Soma, art the doer of good by holy acts; thou art powerful by thine energies, and knowest all things; thou art the showerer (of benefits) by the bounties, and (art great) by thy greatness; thou, the

---

1 Vishnu is said to mean the pervader, or pervading deity.

2 The term of the text is *Evayávan*, which is explained by the Scholiast, the troop of Maruts, from their going with horses (*evaih*).

guide of men, hast been well nourished by sacrificial offerings.

3. Thy acts are (like those) of the royal Varuna:[1] thy glory, Soma, is great and profound; thou art the purifier (of all), like the beloved Mitra; thou art the augmenter of all, like Aryaman.

4. Endowed with all the glories (that are displayed) by thee in heaven, on earth, in the mountains, in the plants, in the waters, do thou, illustrious[2] Soma, well-disposed towards us, and devoid of anger, accept our oblations.

5. Thou, Soma, art the protector, the sovereign of the pious,[3] or even the slayer of Vritra; thou art holy sacrifice.[4]

6. Thou, Soma, fond of praise, the lord of plants, art life to us: if thou wilt, we shall not die.

---

1 *Rajno te Varunasya.* The Scholiast would seem to argue that Varuna here means that which is enclosed in a cloth, or the *Soma* plant that has been purchased for a sacrifice,—*Yágárthan áhritah krito vastrenávritah Soma* Varunah, chiefly because *Soma* is the king of the Brahmans; as by the text of the *Veda, Soma asmákam Brahmanánám Rájá,*—Soma is the king of us Brahmans; and *Somarájno Brahmanáh,*—the Brahmans have Soma for king. But in that sense the moon, not the plant, is usually understood by *Soma,* and there does not appear any reason for understanding the term Varuna in any other than its usual acceptation. The title of *Rájá* we have already seen is not unfrequently assigned to him, although, as the following stanzas show, it was equally given to *Soma.*

2 Or royal (*Rájan*) *Soma.*

3 *Satpatis twam, Rájá uta. Sat* may be explained, also, according to the Scholiast, by Brahman, making the sentence, "the protector, or lord (*Pati*), or the king (*Rájá*), of the Brahmans."

4 *Soma* may be considered as identifiable with sacrifice, from the essential part it performs in it (*tadrupo bhavati sádhyatwád yajnánam*).

7. Thou bestowest, Soma, upon him who worships thee, whether old or young, wealth, that he may enjoy, and live.

8. Defend us, royal Soma, from every one seeking to harm us: the friend of one like thee can never perish.

9. Soma, be our protector with those assistances which are sources of happiness to the donor (of oblations.

10. Accepting this our sacrifice, and this our praise, approach, Soma, and be to us as the augmenter of our rite.

11. Acquainted with hymns, we elevate thee with praises; do thou, who art benignant, approach.

12. Be unto us, Soma, the bestower of wealth, the remover of disease, the cognizant of riches, the augmenter of nutriment, an excellent friend.

13. Soma, dwell happy in our hearts, like cattle in fresh pastures, like men in their own abodes.

14. The experienced sage commends the mortal who through affection, divine Soma, praises thee.

15. Protect us, Soma, from calumny, preserve us from sin; pleased with our service, be our friend.

16. Increase, Soma: may vigour come to thee from every side: be diligent in the supply of food (to us.)

17. Exulting Soma, increase with all twining plants, be to us a friend: well supplied with food, we may prosper.

18. May the milky juices flow around thee; may sacrificial offerings and vigour be concentrated in the destroyer of foes; and, being fully nourished, do thou

provide, Soma, excellent viands in heaven for our immortality.

19. Whichever of thy glories (men) worship with oblations, may our sacrifice be invested with them all: come to our mansions, Soma, who art the bestower of wealth, the transporter (over difficulties); attended by valiant heroes, the non-destroyer of progeny.

20. To him who presents (offerings), Soma gives a a milch-cow, sweet horse, and a son who is able in affairs, skilful in domestic concerns, assiduous in worship, eminent in society, and who is an honour to his father.

21. We rejoice, Soma, contemplating thee, invincible in battle, triumphant amongst hosts, the granter of heaven, the giver of rain, the preserver of strength, born amidst sacrifices, occupying a brilliant dwelling, renowned and victorious.

22. Thou, *Soma*, hast generated all these herbs, the water, and the kine; thou hast spread out the spacious firmament; thou hast scattered darkness with light.

23. Divine and potent *Soma*, bestow upon us, with thy brilliant mind, a portion of wealth: may no (adversary) annoy thee; thou art supreme over the valour of (any) two (mutual) opponents: defend us (from our enemies) in battle.[1]

---

1 There is evidently great confusion in this hymn between *Soma*, the moon, and *Soma*, the acid Asclepias. Few passages indicate the former distinctly, except, perhaps, verse 22, which alludes to the function of scattering darkness by light.

SUKTA VIII. (XCII.)

The *Rishi* is Gotama, the deity is *Ushas* (the dawn), except in the last triad, which is addressed to the *Aswins*. The metre of the first four verses is *Jagati*, of the last six, *Ushnih*, of the rest *Trishtubh*.

THESE divinities of the morning[1] have spread light (over the world); they make manifest the light in the eastern portion of the firmament, brightening all things, like warriors burnishing their weapons; the radiant and progressing mothers[2] (of the earth), they travel daily (on thair course).

2. Their purple rays have readily shot upwards; they have yoked the easily-yoked and ruddy kine (to their car); the deities of the dawn have restored, as of yore, the consciousness (of sentient creatures), and, bright-rayed, have attended upon the glorious sun.

3. The female leaders (of the morning) illuminate[3] with their inherent radiance the remotest parts (of the heaven), with a simultaneous effort, like warriors[4] (with their shining arms in the van of battle), bringing every kind of food to the performer of good works, to the bountiful, and to the worshipper who presents libations.

---

1 We have the term *Ushasah* in the plural, intending, according to the commentator, the divinities that preside over the morning; but, according to *Yáska*, the plural is used honorifically only, for the singular personification.—*Nirukta*, 12. 7.

2 Or *mátri* may mean simply maker, author; authors of light.—*bhaso nirmatryah*.—*Nirukta*, 12. 7.

3 *Archanti*; literally, worship; that is, the heavens; but the term is used for spreading over, or extending.

4 The text has only "like warriors;" the Scholiast explains the comparison,—"as they spread with bright arms along the front of the array, so the rays of the dawn spread along the sky before the coming of the sun.

4. Ushas cuts off the accumulated (glooms), as a barber (cuts off the hair);[1] she bares her bosom as a cow yields her udder (to the milker); and, as cattle hasten to their pastures, she speeds to the east, and, shedding light upon all world, dissipates the darkness.

5. Her brilliant light is first seen towards (the east); it spreads and disperses the thick darkness: she anoints her beauty as the priests anoint the sacrificial food in sacrifices: the daughter of the sky[2] awaits the glorious sun.

6. We have crossed over the boundary of darkness. Ushas restores the consciousness (of living beings); bright-shining, she smiles, lik a flatterer, to obtain favour, and, lovely in all her radiance, she has swallowed for our delight, the darkness.

7. The brilliant daughter of the sky, the exciter of pleasant voices,[3] is praised by the descendants of Gotama. Ushas, grant us food associated with progeny and dependants, and distinguished by horses and cattle.

8. May I obtain, Ushas, that ample wealth which confers fame, posterity, troops of slaves, and is characterized by horses; which thou, who aboundest in riches, and art the giver of food, displayest, (when gratified) by hymns and holy sacrifices.

---

1 *Nritur iva*, 'like a barber,' is the phrase of the text; or *Nrituh* may mean a dancing-girl, when the translation will be, "Ushas displays graces, like a dancing-girl" (*pesánsi vapate*); the former meaning either darkness or elegance, the latter, either to cut off, or to possess. There is no point of similitude expressed in Rosen's version, *Tenebras dissipat Aurora, veluti saltatrix*.

2 *Duhitá divah*, the daughter of heaven, or the sky.

3 With the appearance of dawn, the cries of various animals and birds, and the voices of men, are again heard.

9. The divine (Ushas), having lighted up the whole world, spreads, expanding with her radiance, towards the west, arousing all living creatures to their labours; she hears the speech of all endowed with thought.

10. The divine and ancient Ushas, born again and again, and bright with unchanging hues, wastes away the life of a mortal, like the wife of a hunter cutting up and dividing the birds.[1]

11. She has been seen illuminating the boundaries of the sky, and driving into disappearance the spontaneously-retiring (night);[2] wearing away the ages of the human race, she shines with light like the bride of the sun.[3]

12. The affluent and adorable Ushas has sent her rays abroad, as (a cowherd drives) the cattle (to pasture), and spreads expansive, like flowing water; she is beheld associated with the rays of the sun, unimpeding sacred ceremonies.[4]

13. Ushas, possessor of food, bring us that various wealth by which we may sustain sons and grandsons.

---

1 Like a *Swaghni;* literally, the wife of a dog-killer, but explained *Vyádhastri,* as in the text.

2 *Swasáram* is the only term in the text, explained, *Swayam sarantim,*—going of her own accord; the Scholiast adds *night,* otherwise, we might have understood it in its usual sense of 'sister;' making night the sister of morning.

3 *Járasya yoshá. Jára.* meaning the causer of the decay, or disappearance, of night is explained by, *Surya,* the sun.

4 *Aminati daivyáni vratáni,* not injuring, that is, favouring divine rites or offerings to the gods, which are to be performed by daylight, or after dawn; as by the text, *na rátram na Sáyam asti devayá ajushtam,*—sacrifice is not acceptable to the gods at night, or in the evening.

14. Luminous Ushas, possessor of cows and horses, true of speech, dawn here to-day upon this (ceremony), that is to bring us wealth.

15. Possessor of food, Ushas, yoke, indeed, to-day, your purple steeds, and bring to us all good things.

16. Aswins, destroyers of foes, turn with favourable intentions your chariot towards our abode, which contains cattle and gold.

17. Aswins, who have sent adorable light from heaven[1] to man, bring us strength.

18. May the steeds awakened at dawn bring hither, to drink the *Soma*-Juice, the divine Aswins, who are the givers of happiness, the destroyers of foes, seated in a golden chariot.

SUKTA IX. (XCIII.)

The Rishi is Gotama, the deities are Agni and *Soma* : the metre of the three first stanzas is *Anushtubh* ; of three, beginning with the ninth, *Gâyatrî* ; of the eighth, *Jagati* or *Trishtubh*, and of the rest, *Trishtubh*.

AGNI and Soma showerers (of desires), favourably hear this my invocation, graciously accept my hymns, and bestow felicity on the donor (of the oblation).

2. Agni and Soma, grant to him who addresses this prayer to you both, store of cattle with sound strength and good horses.

---

12 As before observed, the Aswins are sometimes identified with the sun and moon.

3. Agni and Soma, may he who offers you the oblation of clarified butter, enjoy sound strength, with progeny, through all his life.

4. Agni and Soma, that prowess of yours, by which you have carried off the cows that were the food of Pani, is (well) known to us; you have slain the offspring of Brisaya,[1] and you have acquired the one luminary (the sun[2]), for the benefit of the many.

5. You two, Agni and Soma, acting together, have sustained these constellations in the sky; you have liberated the rivers that had been defiled from the notorious imputation.[3]

6. Agni and Soma, the wind brought one of you from heaven, a hawk carried off the other by force from the summit of the mountain;[4] growing vast by praise,

---

1 *Brisayasya sesha;* the latter is a synonyme of *apatya*, offspring.—*Nirukta*, 3, 2. Brisaya is said to be a synonyme of *Twashtri*, here styled an *Asura*. The offspring of *Twashtri* is Vritra; and the agency of Agni and *Soma* in his death is explained by identifying them with the two vital airs, *Prána* and *Apána*, the separation of which from Vritra was the approximate cause of his death.

2 By the destruction of Vritra, the enveloping cloud, or gathered darkness, the sun was enabled to appear in the sky.

3 The imputation, or charge, of Brahmanicide, was incurred by Indra, it is said, in killing Vritra, who was a Brahman, but which guilt he transferred to river, women, and trees. This looks rather like a *Pauranik* legend. One of a more *Vaidik* character is also given; the rivers were defiled by the dead body of Vritra, which had fallen into them: their waters were consequently unfit to bear any part in sacred rites until they were purified by Agni and *Soma*, that is, by oblations to fire, and libations of *Soma*-Juice.

4 The legend relates that Váyu brought Agni from heaven at the desire of Bhrigu, when performing a sacrifice; *Soma* was brought from *Swarga*, on the top of Mount *Meru*, by *Gáyatrí*, in the shape of a hawk; these are clearly allegorical allusions to the early use of fire and the *Soma* plant in religious ceremonies.

you have made the world wide for (the performance of) sacrifice.

7. Agni and Soma, partake of the proffered oblation; be gracious to us; showerers (of desires), be pleased; prosperous and diligent protectors, be propitious, and grant to the sacrificer health and exemption from ill.

8. Agni and Soma, protect his sacrifice and defend him from ill, who, with a mind devoted to the gods, worships you with clarified butter and oblations: grant to the man engaged (in devotion) extreme felicity.

9. Agni and Soma, endowed with the like wealth, and invoked by a common invocation, share our praises, for you have (ever) been the chief of the gods.[1]

10. Agni and Soma, give ample (recompense) to him who presents to you both this clarified butter.

11. Agni and Soma, be pleased with these our oblations, and come to us together.

12. Agni and Soma, cherish our horses, and may our cows, affording (milk that yields butter for) oblations be well nourished; give to us, who are affluent, strength (to perform) religious rites, and make our sacrifice productive of wealth.

---

1 The term is simply *Devatrá*, explained *deveshu prasastah*. Another text is quoted, which states that Agni and *Soma* are they who are the two kings of the gods (*Rájánau va etau devánám yad agnishomau.*)

ANUVA'KA XV.

SUKTA I. (XCIV.)

The *Riski* is Kutsa, the son of Angiras; the deity is Agni, associated in three parts of the eighth stanza with the gods in general, and in the half of the last with different divinities. The metre of the two last stanzas is *Trishtubh*, of the rest, *Jagati*.

To him who is worthy of praise, and all-knowing, we construct, with our minds, this hymn, as (a workman) makes) a car: happy is our understanding when engaged in his adoration: let us not suffer injury, Agni, through thy friendship.[1]

2. He, for whom thou sacrificest, accomplishes (his objects), abides free from aggression, and enjoys (wealth, the source of) strength; he prospers, and poverty never approaches him: let us not suffer injury, through thy friendship.

3. May we be able to kindle thee: perfect the rite, for through thee the gods partake of the offered oblations: bring hither the A'dityas[2] for we love them: let us not suffer injury, Agni, through thy friendship.

4. We bring fuel, we offer oblations, reminding thee of the successive seasons (of worship); do thou thoroughly complete the rite, in order to prolong our lives: let us not suffer injury, Agni, through thy friendship.

5. His genial (flames), the preservers of mankind, spread around, and both bipeds and quadrupeds are

---

1 This last clause is the burden of all the stanzas except the concluding two: *Sakhye má rishámá vayam tava,*—May we not be injured in or by thy friendship; that is, according to the Scholiast, Do thou preserve us.

2 The sons of Aditi, that is, all the gods.

enlivened by his rays; shining with various lustre, and illuminating (the world by night), thou art superior to the dawn: let us not, Agni, suffer injury through thy friendship.

6. Thou art the sacrificing or the invoking priest, thou art the principal (presenter of the offering), the director (of the ceremonies), their performer, or by birth the family priest;[1] thus conversant with all the priestly functions, thou performest perfect the rite: let us not, Agni, suffer injury through thy friendship.

7. Thou art of graceful form, and alike on every side, and, although remote, shinest as if nigh: thou seest, divine Agni, beyond the darkness of night: let us not, Agni, suffer injury through thy friendship.

8. Gods,[2] let the chariot of the offerer of the libation be foremost;[3] let our denunciations overwhelm the wicked: understand and fulfil my words: let us not suffer injury, Agni, through thy friendship.

9. Overcome with your fatal (weapons) the wicked and the impious, all who are enemies whether distant

---

1 Agni is here identified with the chief of the sixteen priests engaged at solemn sacrifices. He is the *Adhwaryu,* usually called the reciter of the *Yajush,* here defined by the Scholiast as the presenter of the offerings; he is the *Hotri,* or invoking priest; he is the *Prasástri,* or the *Maitráváruna,* whose duty it is to direct the other priests what to do and when to perform their functions; he is the *Potri,* or priest so termed, and the family or hereditary *Purohita:* or *Purohita* may be the same as the Brahmá of a ceremony, being to men what Brihaspati is to the gods.

2 *Deva.* All the gods are here considered to be but portions or members of Agni

3 *Purva,* before; the Scholiast explains this by *mukhya,* principal; otherwise, it might be thought that we had here an allusion to chariot-races.

or near, and then provide an easy (path) for the sacrificer who praises thee: let us not, Agni, suffer injury through thy friendship.

10. When thou hast yoked the bright red horses, swift as the wind, to thy car, thy roar is like that of a bull, and thou enwrappest the forest trees with a banner of smoke: let us not, Agni, suffer injury through thy friendship.

11. At thy roaring, even the birds are terrified: when thy flames, consuming the grass, have spread in all directions, (the wood) is easy of access to thee and to thy chariots: let not, Agni, suffer injury through thy friendship.

12. May this, (thy adorer), enjoy the support of Mitra and of Varuna: wonderful is the fury of the Maruts: (dwellers in the region) below (the heavens,[1] encourage us: let us not suffer injury, Agni, through thy friendship.

13. Thou, brilliant (Agni), art the especial friend of the gods; thou, who art graceful in the sacrifice, art the confirmer of all riches: may we be present in thy most spacious chamber of sacrifice; let us not, Agni, suffer injury through thy friendship.

14. Pleasant is it to thee when thou art lighted in thine own abode, and, propitiated by libations, art praised (by the priests): then, much delighted, thou givest rewards and riches to the worshipper: let us not, Agni, suffer injury through thy friendseip.

15. (Fortunate is the worshipper) to whom, (assiduous) in all pious works, thou, possessor of riches, indivisible Agni, grantest exemption from sin, whom

1 Below *Swarga loka*, or in the *Antariksha*, or firmament.

thou associatest with auspicious strength, may he be (enriched) by thee with wealth that comprehends progeny.

16. Do thou, divine Agni, who knowest what is good fortune, on this occasion prolong our existence, and may Mitra, Varuna, Aditi,—ocean, earth, and heaven, preserve it to us.[1]

---

1 This verse terminates the following hymns, with one exception, as far as the hundred and first Sukta. Mitra, Varuna, and Aditi have been before noticed. By Sindhu, is to be understood the divinity presiding over, or identified with, flowing water; and it may mean either the sea, or flowing streams collectively, or the river Indus. *Prithivi* and *Dyu* are the personified earth and heaven. These are requested to *honour*, meaning to preserve or perpetuate, whatever blessing has been asked for (*tan mámahantam*); from *maha, to* venerate or worship; *tad, that,* refers here to *A'yus,* or life.